Completeness

Other Books by Philip Crosby

Cutting the Cost of Quality (1967)
The Art of Getting Youir Own Sweet Way (1972, 1981)
Quality is Free: The Art of Making Quality Certain (1979)
Quality Without Tears: The Art of Hassle-Free Management (1984)
Running Things: The Art of Making Things Happen (1986)
The Eternally Successful Organization: The Art of Corporate Wellness
(1988)
Let's Talk Quality: 96 Questions You Always Wanted to Ask Phil Crosby
(1989)
Leading: The Art of Becoming an Executive (1990)

Completeness:

Quality for the 21st Century

Philip B. Crosby

A DUTTON BOOK

DUTTON
Published by the Penguin Group
Penguin Books USA Inc., 375 Hudson Street,
New York, New York 10014, U.S.A.
Penguin Books Ltd, 27 Wrights Lane,
London W8 5TZ, England
Penguin Books Australia Ltd, Ringwood,
Victoria, Australia
Penguin Books Canada Ltd, 10 Alcorn Avenue,
Toronto, Ontario, Canada M4V 3B2
Penguin Books (N.Z.) Ltd, 182–190 Wairau Road,
Auckland 10, New Zealand

Penguin Books Ltd, Registered Offices:
Harmondsworth, Middlesex, England

First published by Dutton, an imprint of New American Library, a division of Penguin
Books USA Inc.
Distributed in Canada by McClelland & Stewart Inc.

First Printing, August, 1992
10 9 8 7 6 5 4 3 2 1

 REGISTERED TRADEMARK—MARCA REGISTRADA

LIBRARY OF CONGRESS CATALOGING IN PUBLICATION DATA:

Crosby, Philip B.
Completeness: quality for the 21st century/Philip B. Crosby.
    p. cm.
Includes index.
ISBN 0-525-93475-8
1. Total quality management. I. Title.
HD62.15.C76 1992
658.5′62—dc20   91–46275
                                                                       CIP

Printed in the United States of America
Set in Times Roman
Designed by Leonard Telesca

Dedicated to the girls of the House of Hope
who will be the ladies of the 21st century

Contents

Acknowledgments

I appreciate that the Boards of Directors of Proudfoot PLC, and Philip Crosby Associates, Inc., permitted me to "retire" this year in order to write and speak on this subject. I still serve as a consultant to PCA and share my work with them. It is, as they say, like the difference between a drunk and an alcoholic: The drunk doesn't have to go to the meetings. It makes life much easier to be out of the managerial process for the first time in forty years; I don't have to limit my writing time to airplanes, hotel rooms, weekends, and evenings. It is wonderful to be able to sit down in the morning and write for several hours without interruption. I limit my speeches to two or three a month, and am able to have a "reality" session now and then with senior executive teams who want to try out their strategies on someone who doesn't want their jobs. In the winter my wife and I are in Florida, and in the summer we are up in the mountains of North Carolina doing the same thing. We formed a little company, Career IV, to permit things to be handled legally and efficiently. My daughter, Phylis, has taken charge of Career IV, to my pleasure. She is an experienced executive and keeps me between the rails—it is great to have a "complete" boss.

I would like to thank my assistant, Debbie Eifert, for her help on this book while she was processing other material. Special thanks also to my agent, Al Lowman, for his patience.

My wife, Peggy, is always solid in her encouragement, patience, and love. She is a treasure.

I hope you will have an enjoyable and prosperous twenty-first century.

Best regards,

Philip Crosby
Winter Park, Florida
Highlands, North Carolina

Introduction

"What do we do after Total Quality Management?"
People ask me that question continually—in airports, after speeches, while I'm eating out, and during casual conversations. They forget, or perhaps didn't know, that I have never recommended they fool around with TQM in the first place. They are just a set of initials without definition or formulation that have been used by organizations in order to avoid the hard work of really managing quality. People are so busy working on techniques such as "building teams," and doing statistical process control, that they never get around to actually learning how to build prevention into their organization. They have missed the boat—fortunately, it is still tied up at another pier and there is time to change. But a lot of time has been wasted chasing fairy dust instead of being real about quality.

The problem of quality has always been management's lack of understanding of their responsibility for causing a culture of prevention in their company. That is what quality management is supposed to do. It is a matter of determining exactly what the customers (both internal and external) want; describing what has to be accomplished in order to give that to the customer; and then meeting those requirements every time. Back in 1961, I began introducing a concept I called Zero Defects for this purpose. The idea was to help everyone in and around the organization to concentrate on learning how to do their job right the first time. As we improved our understanding of how to do things we would create clearer and more effective requirements. However, we always had a standard of doing things right the first time, every time.

Since 1961, I have written several books about this process, explained its virtues in dozens of articles and hundreds of speeches. I have tried to explain that it is a matter of philosophy, not techniques. While all of this has been well accepted, many executives and quality professionals still think all this can be delegated to some agency that is going to apply ointment to the situation. The real world does not permit that. Quality has to become the fabric of the operation. Quality means conformance to carefully determined requirements. It does not mean goodness; those who go into this next century thinking it does and that it can be implemented by some vague system are just not going to survive. Let me discuss a case history from the first half of the nineteenth century.

At that time, the best known "birthing hospital" of Europe was in Vienna. Other medical facilities used the Vienna Hospital as a benchmark, students fought to gain admittance, and its professors were in demand for speeches and demonstrations. The faculty and staff were very advanced, particularly in treating the puerperal infection ("childbed fever") that attacked half of the patients. A large percentage of those patients died, and those who recovered were damaged for life.

The treatment was based on forcing the evil humors out of the patient's body. Carefully measured (by statistical evaluation) amounts of blood were withdrawn by specific techniques, some patients were wrapped in extremely hot towels to scourge the disease out of them. Doctors had heated arguments over the best way to inflict what we would call abuse on their patients. They had no way of knowing that there was a world of microscopic bacteria that caused these problems. They were using techniques to solve a problem they did not understand.

In 1844, Ignaz Philipp Semmelweis, a Hungarian, was placed in charge of the hospital. He proposed to the management that he would try to do something about childbed fever and was instructed to mind his own business. "There was nothing to do about it," they said, "it is just the way life is." However, Semmelweis had developed a theory that the doctors and students were somehow carrying the disease around with them. He had noticed that the area of the hospital run by the midwives had a lower incidence of infection. He attributed this to the fact that they never went to the autopsy room and they were more concerned about personal cleanliness than the doctors, who just wiped their hands on their jackets.

Over everyone's protests Semmelweis insisted that the entire staff wash their hands in a solution of chlorinated lime before touching patients. The doctors were furious at this undignified and illogical act of prevention. However, they had no choice and so followed instructions. In the first month the infection rate disappeared and the deaths dropped from 18.7 percent to 1 percent.

Instead of receiving appreciation Semmelweis was rejected by his professional colleagues and driven from the hospital. He gave papers on the subject for a while, but his health failed and he was admitted to a place for the insane where he died. Twenty years later, Lister, in London, was more successful in getting the professionals to realize their responsibility for not doing harm to the patients. However, it was many years before management learned to appreciate prevention over techniques for solving already existing problems. Today very few business leaders realize that they have not made this change. Quality management today is a sea of confusion where people are searching for the right set of initials, and executives make charismatic speeches on a subject that they do not really understand. It is a shame.

These business people remind me of the Lilliputians in Swift's *Gulliver's Travels,* who fought an unending war over which end of a boiled egg should be approached when it was to be opened. The Little Enders and the Big Enders were both devoted to their beliefs without ever pausing to consider the overall problem. Spending time measuring things in ever greater detail does little to prevent the problems that reduce productivity, destroy businesses, and take the purpose out of people's lives. Think how many women and children died because of the stubbornness and pride of Semmelweis's colleagues. Think of how many customers have been disappointed because management would not get involved in understanding their world.

Quality (meaning getting everyone to do what they have agreed to do) is the skeletal structure of an organization; finance is the nourishment; and relationships are the soul. All of this comes together in what I call *Completeness*. Management has learned that they cannot delegate the policies and decisions of finance, and they must learn the same about the other two. Executives spend most of their time on finance and turn the rest over to functional professionals whose main concern is to protect their own turf and pride. It is hard to find any of these who are more interested in the company as a whole than in the success of their own functions. It is as if they feel they have to get reelected all the time. In the twenty-first century, management will not have the latitude to fail regularly and still get on somehow, as is the pattern today.

As a media designated "guru," I have been instrumental in teaching thousands of managers, executives, and regular folks how to understand and accomplish quality management. After twenty-five years of running quality for companies I founded an organization, in 1979, called Philip Crosby Associates, Inc. PCA has had hundreds of clients throughout the world, in all sorts of businesses, and in each case has helped them change their culture to one of positive improvement. This change came about because each person in the organization learned to understand quality in the same way and learned an individual role in the whole plan of prevention. While not all of them did everything they could, these companies have grown a new life, have saved enormous amounts of money, and now have a sense of wellness. Moreover, they are comfortable in dealing with the global economy.

These executives, who are way ahead of their peers, still splat, however, on the bottom of the pool now and then. Certainly their dive is shorter than it would have been, and there may even be a few feet of water in the target area—but a splat is a splat. The rush to quality management has been a dramatic change for the better as people at these companies will testify. Their results should encourage others to leap aboard and many are doing that on a regular basis. These are the executive groups who have thought the problem and its solution through to the end and are willing to work hard on it. They constitute a growing part of the business community. I see a growth of understanding of the problem and a desire for a solution in many areas, particularly health care, insurance, banking, and other service areas. These companies recognize that they are in for the long pull, but that the rewards are worth it.

Not everyone is interested in working hard or the long pull, however, and now I see the concepts and efforts of quality management's construction being diluted through superficial programs and techniques. Now that everyone seems to be aware of the value of installing prevention management as a way of life, many are trying to shortcut the concepts. But wanting to find a shortcut shows that you do not really understand the subject in the first place. For instance, most of the media determinedly intertwines quality *control* and quality *management;* they are as much alike, as Mark Twain said, as "lightning and lightning bug." Quality control is based on statistical actions and techniques that contain the nonconformances of processes by applying a series of screens and sieves. In contrast, quality management is committed to running the whole operation based on prevention, so that there is nothing to sieve out. Quality control is run by technicians; quality management, by management. Those who have done this for a living recognize the difference in both results and comprehension.

It might help to review the past in order to place this vague-sounding dichotomy in perspective. Quality has always been a problem for manufacturing companies because their product went through some sort of process until completion. At the end of the process, the customer could easily see if the product met the anticipated need or not. (Service organizations had a little more latitude because the customer was involved in the process, and it was possible to make corrections as the relationship proceeded.) Quality control was developed for the purpose of containing nonconformances within a manufacturing process by statistical means. Work was measured as it went along and it was possible to tell from a few samples if that particular part of the operation was under control. Statistical process control is still an effective way of running a manufacturing process, but it is hardly a management system. Its weakness is the assumption that the process can never be totally effective at all times, and therefore errors are to be expected. This produces the concept known as Acceptable Quality Levels (AQL).

In the mid-1950s, the U.S. government wrote a policy/procedure on quality called MIL-Q-5923 that laid the foundation for the problems concerning quality that have caused so much strife. Its title was "The Control of Nonconforming Material." Everyone who obtained a government manufacturing contract was obliged to comply with this document. The requirement was to have the capability of inspecting or testing material and then taking the defective items and separating them so they did not become confused with the good stuff. This led to a complex system of Material Review Boards (MRB), by which nonconformances were evaluated as to whether they could be reworked to specifications, modified to be used, or used as is. Consequently, the thought that nothing could be made properly all the time received official endorsement. As quality-control people moved from government contract work to commercial, they carried these concepts with them. Colleges taught quality control also.

In the late 1950s, a system of quality management specification was produced (MIL-Q-9858). This laid out pages of requirements for a quality assurance system. Companies were evaluated for their compliance with these requirements and needed to have procedures that showed they were meeting them. Only about a quarter of these had to do with the final product meeting the specifications and other requirements of the purchase order. The rest were merely procedural. As a result, hardly anything the government ordered conformed to their expectations. This was solved by installing a system of waivers and deviation approvals. The paperwork all came out even, but the material was suspect. It is still that way.

When I created the concept of zero defects in 1961 it was for the purpose of getting rid of Acceptable Quality Levels (AQLS). My thought was that we should do exactly as we agreed to do rather than spending a lot of time and money keeping track of the differences. This concept was met with derision by the opinion leaders of the quality-control field, to the extent that the ASQC (American Society for Quality Control) board actually passed a resolution against it. None of this bothered me, and I kept on preaching. It wasn't until the Japanese invasion of the early 1970s, however, that the American public awoke and began demanding to receive what they had ordered. Working harder at the old-fashioned concepts would not produce this, so the pendulum began to swing toward quality management. What made the difference was management's new policy of zero defects rather than AQLs. Suddenly, "good enough" was no longer good enough. Through this change companies regained market share and cut their cost of quality dramatically.

Now the trend is for management to turn quality back to the professionals, and all the old criteria are beginning to return. The government's Baldrige award criteria read much like MIL-Q-9858; they have little to do with final quality in products or services. If a company does everything detailed in the criteria there is no reason to believe that the customers will have a better chance of receiving what they ordered. (In Europe a specification known as ISO 9000 is used to the same negative result.) Yet the great mass of executives assume that if the government puts it out then it must be right. This is like turning back the clock thirty years.

But the twenty-first century is almost upon us, and both quality control and quality management are going to be clearly inadequate for the coming decades. They will be like the old punched card IBM data systems compared with modern computers: too slow and too cumbersome. There will be no opportunity to measure after the fact, or to compare the good with the not-so-good. Customers are getting smarter. Success will be preordained before any work is done; there will only be the usable and the discarded.

This had been dawning on me for some time, but I had put off doing anything about it. It seemed to me that people would eventually work their way around to recognizing the situation. Then, I began to realize that it would not be so. It was "déjà vu all over again," as Yogi Berra says. Back in 1961, I thought everyone would leap with joy at the thought of losing the chains and bindings of our daily work. Big mistake. The reaction was that I was trying to force them into the poorhouse. "Quality costs too much" was the cry. (In reply I wrote *Quality Is Free* for those executives who wanted to understand the subject.) With the memory of all that in mind, I have been laying back on the subject of Completeness. But the time has come to develop this concept. I will concentrate on the broader opportunity of the growth of the executive role in the hope of changing the way executives think about their whole business. If it can be properly accomplished it will be apparent to them that they should not treat corporate integrity the way they deal with the United Fund drive. In this connection, I have begun to think of the twenty-first-century executive as a *Centurion*. These managers need to be identified in some way so as to recognize that they will be vastly different from twentieth-century executives because their focus must be on the new century rather than on patching up the problems of the old one. Management will become a much more serious business in the next decade and century.

Facing what I feel will be the facts of the twenty-first century has made me finally accept what I have known for twenty years—that quality management is never going to be enough. Even if it were done properly by itself, it wouldn't do the complete job. People, particularly quality professionals, are always going to look at it as an overlay, or add-on, rather than as the fabric of the organization. I have not been able to convince clients that there was more involved; as a matter of fact I rather shied away from trying to do that. I guess I felt like the preacher who gave six sermons in a row on the first commandment. When the elders asked him if he was ever going to switch subjects, he told them he would do that as soon as the congregation started obeying the commandment he was talking about. I have felt the same way about quality management, but it is time for me to change.

So I have decided to go ahead with the "other nine commandments" and get into the business of preventing messes at the bottom of swimming pools. I have been thinking about Completeness for a long time, and included some of my developing thoughts in recent books. Also, I've written a few essays and pieces on it. Even so, I have tossed out all those notes and have written this book from scratch. I have also included some conjectures in the last several chapters about what life in the twenty-first century might be like for those of us who have to run something then. I will deal with the cases involved as though they were operating at that time in the future but will refrain from too much postulation.

Completeness is involved only with management. The persons who make up the management corps of a company are the main source of trouble for that organization, just as they are responsible for most of the good things that happen. Good and bad both require about the same amount of effort; the difference is in what management takes seriously. Their priorities determine what the employees and suppliers will be doing. If the targets are sound and properly aimed in the manner of well– thought out strategies and policies, then success could be just around the corner. If they are based on fairy tales, then the organization could be eaten by the wolf. Strategies change over time, but fairy tales are with us forever. (We only have to look at the 1980s to realize that obviously smart people can convince themselves to believe the unbelievable—for example, that debt is good for you.) We are talking reformation, not revolution.

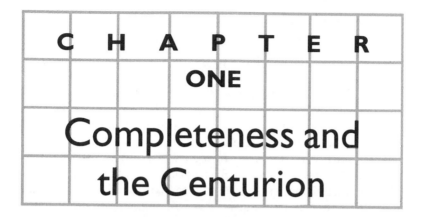

C H A P T E R
ONE

Completeness and
the Centurion

J ust about everything is different as we approach the twenty-first century. It has been said that "the past is not what it used to be," and I think the same is true of the future. Events occur that were unthinkable only a brief moment ago, such as the political changes in Russia and Eastern Europe. An organization must be managed completely with a foundation of zero defects as its operating philosophy. Management must be concerned with wellness and the organization's ability to deal with and overcome whatever evolves. As change is rapid and continuous, the company must be steady and determined. Life in the executive suite will never be the same.

For the first several thousand years of recorded history, management was mostly a matter of dealing with people and animals as they performed low-level labor. Distribution was not much of a problem since businesses concentrated on regional activities. When the industrial revolution came, followed by rapid technical change, management had to deal with steam engines and other equipment, along with people. This century opened with machines doing the work while people fed them; the individual was not too significant a part of the process. As the twentieth century progressed, technology became so complex—with new developments like the semiconductor—that people had to take an active part, in fact the most active and important part. In the twenty-first century we may well be back to managing people who are coping with a technology that has a mind of its own. This time, however, the people will be utilized for their minds and fingers, rather than their backs and hands.

In earlier days management held all the information, while

today much of it is available to all. In the future there will be so much data generated, almost all of it from the bottom of the organization, that it will seem to rise up. Therefore the successful managers will be those who can establish and implement the proper vision, obtaining the best performance of people in the process. Since they will have to battle to install a complete zero-defects philosophy in a new world, I will call them *Centurions.* This was the title given to the Roman officers who led the legions who conquered the world. The alternative to calling them that is to write repeatedly "those who will manage in the twenty-first century." Not only is it shorter, but "Centurions" also indicates that these people will bear little resemblance to their nineteenth- and twentieth-century ancestors. It will be an interesting time period.

There may be a wonderfully different social environment in the next century within which the Centurions and other people will make lives and do business. Basic philosophical alterations in human behavior have been coming about for some time, and they are causing these changes. I am an eternal optimist but this is what it looks like to me:

1. People all over the world will at last obtain the opportunity for the education, health, and living conditions that will enable them to manage their own lives responsibly.
2. Governments will find themselves unwelcome in the lives of their citizens and will reluctantly restrict themselves to doing those tasks that only they can do.
3. Technology will live up to its promise of providing the means of unburdening people's working and social lives, permitting them to be more fulfilling.
4. Religious conversion in the best possible sense will come upon the earth, providing a foundation for genuine peace and understanding.

Whether people will cease their quarreling long enough to take advantage of these trends remains to be seen. And it only takes a madperson or two to upset these predictions, of course. Yet there is hope in that it will be very difficult, if not impossible, for one of them to obtain power over this new citizenry. People are breaking free from political oppression and economic distress; they will not be so vulnerable to the siren songs of would-be dictators. Our personal and professional lives in such a century will provide a combined opportunity and challenge the likes of which no occupants of this earth have seen before. As governments become the helpers of their populace rather than their masters, power will literally be with the people as a whole.

People will have the chance to become educated, informed, independent, well fed, and financially knowledgeable. They will also become somewhat more homogeneous. As real and administrative borders fall there will be migration. Africa and Latin America are growing at twice the rate of the Western nations. We probably will see a France with more of a population mix, like California for instance. All of this could serve to reduce the national tensions that have caused conflict over the years by eliminating identifiable national identity. We have the opportunity to truly see that the worth of the individual will have the chance to shine through all over our "global village." Freedom to travel, obtain a good education, and learn the value of reciprocity in social contact can change everything. The socially unacceptable person will disappear over time. (Boring people, however, will still exist.)

The twenty-first century is going to be dramatically different from all preceding times. History as written has been an uncertain voyage from one set of authoritarian leaderships to another. Judges, Kings, Emperors, Caesars, Dictators, Presidents, General Managers, and other titles have ruled us by our choice. Even democracies record their passage as being controlled or influenced by one person at a time. Monuments are built to pay tribute to those leaders, books are written about them, and their positive or negative attributes are discussed through the years. Whatever happened to people during their lives has been very much influenced and even controlled by the individual who emerged as the leader of that period.

Despots, such as Caligula, Hitler, and Stalin, could do unspeakable things to their subjects without fear of retribution. Considerate leaders who deliberately set out to make life easier for their followers, without thought of their own immortality, have been hard to find in the history books. Many who tried were not appreciated at the time because people wanted quicker results. Solon, for example, solved the problems of Athens and was driven into exile for his trouble. In the past, the only way for a nation to get ahead often was to blackmail, raid, or go to war with a more fortunate neighbor. Armed conflict gave everyone something to do while helping to reduce unemployment and satisfy the restlessness of young males. Similarly, many family fortunes can find their origin in the plunder gained by an ancestor from some unfortunate colleague.

If we begin back in the days of the Old Testament and track mankind's course up to the twentieth century, we see a world population that was generally unlettered, short-lived, and considered—even by themselves—to be incapable of governing or managing their own lives. With a few exceptions nations relied on royalty or a similarly limited group for leadership and continuity. As long as they produced successors and defended the country, their family ran things. There were few laws or agreements written down so that everyone could see them and discuss their fairness. Hardly anyone outside the ruling community could read anyway.

Establishing the "divine right" of these annointed or appointed leaders eliminated a lot of argument. The king was always right, even if not correct (a concept that transferred with no effort to the modern executive suite). The nobility selected by the leadership kept a firm hand on the people and limited their personal growth. An individual knew almost from birth what the future was going to offer, and this turned out to be not much in most cases. As the Western world entered the eighteenth century, people began to lose confidence in such systems. They were beginning to realize that they could probably run things as well, or at least, not much worse than those who had been doing it as their "right." Ever since that realization, people and governments have not been comfortable with each other.

The daily lives of ordinary people did not improve a great deal in the four thousand years between the biblical Abraham and the presidential Abraham. Food supplies were uncertain and unsanitary; almost any disease or injury visited upon a person was fatal; infant mortality exceeded 30 percent and half the population died before age twenty; perhaps 2 percent reached sixty-five; personal sanitation was a hole in the yard, with or without a house around it; cities were crowded, dangerous, and unfriendly (those quaint walking sticks the Victorians carried were for beating off, or spearing, muggers); the financial world, not available to the mass of people, was treacherous to those who could reach it; and communications were primitive. Technology advanced only slightly in all those years: ships still moved by sail for the most part; only a few fires were contained in stoves; guns had replaced spears but were not much more accurate; science was mostly imagination and guessing; everything was made one at a time. Education was not generally available past grade school, even in Europe and the United States. Voting was not something for unlanded or female people to worry about, and for the most part, the large majority throughout the globe had little to say about their lives.

The American and French revolutions made it clear that things had to change, although both were headed more by middle- and upper-class persons than by the underclass, regardless of the impression that has been passed down to us over the years. The American revolt succeeded; the French turbulence produced Napoleon.

Throughout the nineteenth century, leaders of the Western nations struggled to satisfy their populace by organizing stronger countries. Bismarck put Germany together; England gathered up colonies worldwide; Italy united; the United States acquired territory, buying some, and fighting Mexico and Spain for others. National pride became important in itself, rather than just loyalty to the king or government. Japan and China wrapped their cloaks about their people and cut everyone off. It took military action, or its threat, by the Western world to force the opening of trade with the Far East. The British and others invaded China to make the empress permit the trade of opium for the purpose of purchasing tea and silk. The Europeans didn't seem to have anything else the Chinese wanted to buy so they had to be taught to like opium. The world has certainly come full circle on that one.

The First and Second World Wars were the last gasps of world government aspirations by single charismatic leaders. It has been all civil wars since then, at least until the Gulf battle came along. The Vietnam War and the Soviet Afghanistan adventure have made it a lot harder for the super powers to dominate—particularly in situations where their help is unwanted. The fall of communism and the revelations of the dismal life of its victims have converted even some philosophical hardliners.

This is a big change. Even before Socrates laid out the concept of leadership as the responsibility of "the one who knows," autocrats had been taking charge. They ruled, not only in public life, but in private also. The husband and father was master of all he surveyed all those years, at least legally. The Old Testament only counted men; women and children were included with the goats and other household goods.

In an effort to eliminate such oppression and give people their fair share of everything, political philosophers devised socialism and communism. The idea was that the state would run things with the absence of a profit motive and everyone would have a job, along with a bountiful existence. There would be only one class of people, everyone would be educated, and no one would be hungry. Great Britain elected a socialist government after the Second World War, and the nations of Eastern Europe fell under communist domination; other European countries flirted with socialism and communism. West Germany and Japan concentrated on free trade since no one wanted them to have a strong government again. The results, nearly fifty years after the Second World War, have shown that those who chose the least government interference have done the best. (It has been written that socialism is the long, hard road between capitalism and capitalism.)

The United States, where Congress meets continually in order to pull and tug at the social and business structure, has progressed only with difficulty. Japan, where government politely calls businesses every day to see if there is anything they can do to help, has become a world power. The United Kingdom has been trying to get well from its bath of socialism for these forty years and still has not recovered. France, under Mitterand, determined in only one year that its socialistic approach was headed for disaster and backed off, pretending it all had never happened. Many people now realize that socialism and communism just do not work. Governments are evolving their own versions of capitalism and the world is moving on. Latin America and Africa are still being born.

However, we are beginning to reach the time when what governments do or not will be of less importance. We now have the beginning of a world populace that is becoming well aware of what is happening. Satellite transmission has made television available throughout the world, and I'm convinced that the Eastern Europeans of the 1980s, sitting day after day watching free people live well on their television screens, just decided that there had to be a better way. When they heaved their collective sigh of despair the Berlin wall fell and the surrounding communist governments seemed almost to evaporate. Now we are dealing with people who do not want to be led around; they want to be free to do their own thing. They want to prosper personally or be deprived as a result of what they do or do not do themselves. They do not want some mysterious group planning each detail of their lives. They want government and the ruling aristocracy out of their hair.

All of this will come about by what I call a "bottom-up socialism." The people (that's us) will take over the task of making personal and business life better, and governments will be limited to doing the things that they are supposed to do like delivering the mail, communicating with other governments, and providing for defense. This is going to require that we personally understand how to manage our lives for survival and growth in this new world. It will be so different from the past that most of the conventional systems and customs will no longer be applicable. The leaders of all this will be the Centurions—those who understand how to make Completeness happen. There is another reason for giving that title to those who will run successful organizations in the twenty-first century. If we think about it, one hundred people represent about the limit of our personal ability to govern. It is hard to remember names and responsibilities after that point. It is difficult to know what is happening. That could be why we get the correct impression that hardly anyone actually understands his or her executive responsibility enough to do it properly. Today not much comes out the way it is supposed to, even though business leaders live in an environment of almost constant status reviews. The true veterans of this self-examination avoid participating, knowing it is easier to obtain forgiveness than get permission.

Some of the changes we will experience go deep into the fabric of the business, such as new technology; some of them will alter the foundation of our personal life, such as a worldwide religious revival; some of them will be social, such as drugs that can be programmed like software for behavior mod-ification—people will be able to program themselves to experi-ence different emotions or personal patterns (of course, this has always existed in less scientific systems).

The Centurions will have to learn how to manage so that they can deal with whatever happens, and at the same time, anticipate what is coming. They will have to be in a permanent situation of awareness in order to tell the difference between fads and reality. They will have to be able to deal purposefully and effec-tively with people on all levels. They will have to be able to get results, be confident in themselves, learn how to compile and comprehend information, and in short, be complete participants.

A few weeks ago I played a round of golf with a person who is really good at the game. I mean he is one of the best. He hit from the back tees and I used the members tees; this put our drives about the same distance out toward the green. Most of the time I would drive my ball into some place unattractive, like the woods, or the rough. And, less often, so did he. Every time, however, he would somehow manage to get his ball near or on the green from those locations. I did it about half the time.

When we both missed the green he would *always* get the ball into the hole in one or two shots. Once he chipped in from about two feet off the green, and once he sunk one from a sand bunker. I would get into the hole in three shots, and twice it took me four because I flew the ball over the green. Only one time was I up and down in two shots. At the end of the round, which we had played virtually side by side all the way, he had registered twenty-two fewer shots than I had. I was exhausted, while he was going to join his family for a nine-hole stroll and then go to the practice range. I never practice; he does it every day.

The difference was not so much in making shots as it was in management. He knew what he was doing because he takes it seriously. After all, anyone can hit the ball with a putter. He has learned how to stroke a putt so the ball rolls true. And he had trained himself to not make trouble for himself. Without even trying hard, it seemed, he came through with an under par round. His was a game of completeness: He could handle everything. Mine is a game of compartments: I do some things well but have many areas that are not dependable. He deals in the whole;

I do programs and tips. I think about hitting the ball; he thinks about where it is going and what the next shot will be like. We walked around together in the same amount of time, but we were in different worlds.

The next century is not going to be the place for the compartmentalized management concepts of the twentieth, which tended to seek out magic bullets and quick answers in the search for an easy way to the Grail. When executives did find a guru to think out the basics for them, most then proceeded to change these guru-given foundations in a way that detracted from the success of the concepts. This is like tossing a peach into grandma's chicken soup, then questioning grandma's judgment.

The future is going to require a much broader, more determined, more thoughtful, more finished approach. The Centurion is not going to have the luxury of failing as often as those in previous times. Management is really going to have to learn to be good at its job. For one thing, there will not be rows of submanagers to pass things along and sort the burrs from the fabric. There just will not be that many good people available, and expense requirements will be even tighter. Less information filtering will take place because responsibilities will be clearer. The top of the organization chart is going to be dealing directly with the bottom. That means the personal communication strengths of the individual will be basic to managerial success, both corporate and personal.

In trying to describe what the Centurion will have to be doing, it is apparent that hard work will be a given. However, it will have to be work that actually accomplishes something useful. Much of the time modern management invests in churning stuff out is really pretend work. If things were planned and thought out properly, there would be no need for constant telephone calls, late night facsimile transmissions, urgent mail pickups, and all that stuff. It is all playing catch-up because of not getting the real work done right the first time. The Centurion is going to work for the long haul because nothing else will be practical in those days. There will not be many second chances—the competition will be too intense. Those who want to survive will need to concentrate on Completeness. This means that the systems making up the organization must be considered as a whole, and nothing can be taken for granted.

Recently I helped write and produce a new company brochure. Several creative and production people worked on it, doing the layout, writing the copy, taking photographs, assuring accuracy. Hours were spent with the printer to make absolutely certain that the paper was just right, that the colors were accurate. One entire week was spent in the final arrangements and the beginning of the printing. When the copies came off the press everyone was delighted. Brochures were rushed to the executive committee who provided applause and congratulations. We all turned to other tasks.

A few weeks later I ran into an old friend in the lobby of our building who had just been talking to one of our senior people about our doing business together. As we chatted I noticed that he had a brochure under his arm, but it was the old one, the one we had been replacing because it was out of date. As soon as I could decently break away I went to the office of the administrative manager to ask why we were still using the old brochures. It turned out that we still had a few boxes left so they had stacked the new ones behind them. None of the new ones had been sent out to our clients, to our mailing list, to our regional or international offices. They were just sitting there. No one had told the manager anything about the decisions that were made to scrap the old and mail out the new. After a bunch of scrambling the situation was corrected.

This was an example of a lack of completeness. The process of making and distributing a new brochure was not completely managed. The procedures were all there; after all, it had been done well in the past. But the ball was dropped for lack of a piece of direction, and this in a company that really works hard on communicating. Every step necessary had been taken but a link in the chain remained open because it was not thought through. The Centurion has to establish a climate of Completeness in which the urge to cooperate is normal. That requires a different understanding of relationships.

During the twentieth century, relationships between workers and management, workers and workers, the community and companies, and so on, all underwent dramatic change. Workers went from being part of the hardware to having a voice in the operation. Over 30 percent of the ownership of New York Stock Exchange companies today rests in the hands of pension funds owned by workers of companies. Another large percentage is in their personal ownership. This would have been hard to imagine in the era when people worked twelve and fourteen hours a day, seven days a week, with no benefits and little money. This transformation will continue into the twenty-first century. There will be little obvious difference between the people at various levels in an organization in terms of rights and privileges. Those who are more valuable will be paid more, but as bodies we will be much the same.

Agreed-upon procedures, which are a formal cooperation system, will take a different form in this new age. For instance, the dream of a "paperless" office has not been realized to date, because people just have not permitted it. No one trusted the computer system to be reliable, which really meant that they felt their fellow humans would not do their part properly. After all, computers make zero errors all by themselves; they need human help. So people keep file cabinets full of duplicate material and in fact order extra files in the same shipment with the computers. They do not want to be left hanging out in space when someone misses a step.

However, the Centurion will be dealing with generations raised to know computers as a normal part of life. Just as I expect to see a telephone in an office, they are startled if there is no computer. They will create systems to eliminate paper trails altogether. Trees will be safe and forests will be clogged with debris. When everything is in the public or private data bank, there is no need to write it down. The individual communication units we will have on our person will provide us with access to every source of data we will ever need. There will never be any reason to be out of touch. The bad news is that there will be few places to hide.

Another part of this Completeness is communication. The Centurion is going to have to become skilled in the art of personal communication. There are just not going to be enough people to go around who are capable of doing serious work. Employees will need to be selected for life, trained and educated continually, and helped to feel that they are an integral part of the operation. Hiring someone will be like picking a marriage partner. It will be an era of trust and mutual satisfaction; the human resource will be the most important part of the company.

We have come a long way from the days when management used to chain people to machines so they would not slip off to go to the bathroom.

Suppliers, financial sources, the community, business groups, everyone who is part of the enterprise in any way will need to know for sure that the organization not only is supportive but feels kindly toward them. They will have to radiate confidence in the integrity of the company. Dealing with people all over the world will produce a reputation, one way or the other, about the company's ability to perform. Any smudge on that reputation will put the company in a poor competitive position because there will be others in every field waiting for an opportunity to drive a wedge between us and our customers.

Many organizations develop a negative attitude as a normal part of doing business. They do not plan it that way, but it develops relentlessly. Much of this originates from a management whose personality is to see everything in terms of numbers or actions, not noticing the people behind them. People like that began to go out of style in 1990 and will be offstage completely by 2010. The only way such folks can exist is to have control of something so marvelous and unique that people will put up with anything to get it. Those of us who have missed that boat will have to learn to deal with the real world.

During my early years in business I took for granted that the way to do things revolved around detective work. Nothing I received from my sources had all the necessary information or parts that were supposed to be there. So I had to go back up the line of communication, identify the missing ingredients until I found the specific item that needed to be altered. It wasn't very efficient, but it was fun and it worked. The noble feeling gained from this venture was short-lived, because soon the person down the line from me came back to ask me a question about something. When we multiply this a few times we begin to realize what all those people are doing in the hall with papers in their hands and an earnest expression on their faces.

But here in the twenty-first century: we have high-paid, professionally driven, ownership-oriented employees who want things to come to them correctly; we have customers thousands of miles away, whom we may not have even met but to whom we ship things to be used immediately upon arrival; we have competitors who do not speak our language, understand our culture, or even care much about us; and, to add to the equation, both products and services are incredibly complex. Communication becomes our nourishment. As the human body cannot function without refreshed, "up-to-date" blood cells carrying oxygen, so the company needs accurate, reliable, up-to-date, and constantly accessible communications.

To be complete is to have the entire jigsaw puzzle together, each piece fitting exactly as planned. The operation from one end to the other and back again has to be both series and parallel circuits. In modern Christmas tree illumination, when one bulb fails it alone expires and thus can be quickly found and replaced. In the dark ages of my youth, when one bulb went out the entire string died. Then there was a time expenditure for trial and error replacement to find the guilty bulb. If nature was being unusually cruel two of them would fail at the same time. It took forever to figure that out. This was not entirely unrewarding if one happened to be a young boy making games out of things. In fact, my brother and I used to take turns loosening a bulb for the other to find, on a sort of time trial. I often think that many companies have people who go around loosening bulbs. Then they can receive credit for finding the problem and "turning things around." Parallel circuits make things difficult for them.

Business has been run on a compartmentalized basis for centuries. The marketing department doesn't talk much to the sales department, which has little to do with the production department, which could care less about the financial department, which doesn't even know where the shipping department is. We see this even more clearly in service organizations where no one tells the front desk clerk that the maids are changing their hours and thus rooms will be available later instead of as in the past. The absence of this information transmission was not part of a conspiracy to deprive the desk clerk of essential data; rather it was just that no one thought about it. That is also the same reason dad runs out of gas after junior has had the car for an afternoon. And if someone does think about it, they may decide that if they know the desk clerk certainly knows. I have served a lot of time as "boss," and my personal experience has been that the rest of the people think I already know about things, so they don't tell me.

Therefore, all of this communication stuff just cannot be taken for granted. The Centurion has to deliberately build Completeness into the culture of the company so that there is a compulsion to share information. People are not going to realize their personal responsibility for the process as a whole unless they are told about it. Which leads us to caring, or concern. The most successful ventures are those that people ache for, that they take into themselves personally and simply will to success. But they have to feel that the organization cares for them before they will care for it. The concern shown by the management for the employees and all those who touch the enterprise becomes evident. This does not mean everyone has to sit around each day holding hands and staring into each other's eyes. But it does mean that all involved recognize their own individual significance to the whole. They have to realize, for instance, what happens to the rest of the place when they decide to skip a day of work, or goof off on some project. The lack of skilled people, the pressures of world competition, and the complexities of business in general, will make filling their spot a disruptive action.

The Centurion is going to have to be like an orchestra conductor.

Sometimes people wonder why it is necessary to have so many strings or winds in a symphony orchestra. They do not recognize that the group is actually playing many different parts at the same time. Those forty or so string instruments are playing several different parts of the harmony of sound. If the players all do their jobs just exactly right, the audience rises to its feet and gives them ovation after ovation. If a few are not giving it their all, the audience applauds politely. The successful conductor is the one who can convince the musicians to give their all. It is not their talent so much as their skilled participation that matters. Talent emerges in different ways.

Perhaps we need to hang photographs around the office, showing a bearded man wrapped in a white sheet, standing in front of a cave, right hand raised, palm outward, saying: "Worklife is a symphony, my child." It is very hard to get this across because people usually come equipped with poor self-images as standard issue. They have a hard time believing that they are an important part of this machine, that what they do matters all that much. Caring helps them realize that.

The worklife of the Centurion will be a symphony.

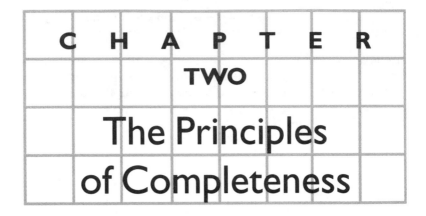

C H A P T E R

TWO

The Principles
of Completeness

The most respected companies of the twentieth century were those that did well financially in comparison with their peers. A consistent profit of 10 percent after tax, for instance, was considered to be a remarkable accomplishment. In other areas of measuring accomplishment an employee turnover level below 15 percent a year accompanied by an absentee rate of less than 3 percent daily would win awards. To increase market share 10 percent each year would be worth a cover on the annual report. But in the future, when companies are faced with worldwide comparison, numbers like that are not going to be enough for the big time, at least for those who take the new century, and Completeness, seriously. The Centurions would expect a minimum return of 20 percent after tax on the bottom line, for instance, and would be surprised to learn that any of their employees not prohibited from doing so by a physician would miss work. They would make certain that their company would be a place where people and management respect each other, work together, and think waste of any kind is old fashioned and quaint. Managements working and thinking along the obsolete concepts of the twentieth century will never make it in the coming decades.

The twenty-first century will offer the greatest opportunity for planned success ever seen. It won't be necessary to discover oil, invent the Bessemer Furnace, develop the telephone, or create the electric light bulb in order to gain wealth and influence. The only absolutely essential management characteristic will be to acquire the ability to run an organization that deliberately gives its customers exactly what they have been led to expect and does it with pleasant efficiency. The key to making that happen is to figure out a way to understand and serve the customer properly while enabling employees to have successful work lives. The single world marketplace will be searching continually for firms that can pull this off routinely. These firms will produce with zero defects as a matter of course. Such companies will not have to advertise or even market. A path will be worn to their door, success will be thrust into their pockets. They will be admired and blessed—and of course, there won't be many of them.

Accomplishing this will take a great deal of concern with what is generally known as morale, but said concern will have to go beyond morale. A unit with proper morale has confidence, submits readily to discipline and leadership, and is filled with hope. General Eisenhower said that morale was the single most important characteristic an army could have. Causing it involves a lot more than having Bob Hope visit once in a while. In the business world morale involves everyone who touches the enterprise and includes suppliers, customers, and the community, in addition to employees. There can be no long-term success without it. Why some managements seem to spend their time deliberately destroying morale rather than building it is something I have never understood. I guess it just shows their own low self-esteem. Yet when I mention this to the offending management they are hurt and defensive to think that someone would question their motives and methods. I always wind up with the story in my head about the boxer who staggered back to his corner to hear his manager encouraging him by saying that the opponent had not "laid a glove on him."

"You'd better keep an eye on the referee," said the wounded one. "Someone is pounding the hell out of me out there."

Everyone wants to be successful, and in that light, let us consider just what success means in an organization, whether it be profit or nonprofit oriented. We must think of this success in terms of achieving agreed upon objectives, all of which are measurable. Objectives such as a steady growth in market share and profitability, a low debt to equity ratio, low employee turnover, a high level of employee voluntary participation, education programs that fit everyone's needs, a management succession plan that works, continuous new product and service development, active support from suppliers, community admiration, and happy and prosperous shareholders. An identification number has to be applied to each of these objectives so they can be measured and understood. Success is a whole bunch of things, all of which are possible when approached properly.

Over the past forty years I have dealt personally with the reality of business life from all levels. I have been the lowest person on the organizational totem and I have been the CEO. In many regards, there is more similarity than difference; neither one of those jobs is in charge of a great deal. Both get yelled at, but usually the hollering is quieter and more discreet at the CEO level. The turnover rate is much higher for CEOs, and there are many pressures and limitations not imagined by those who have not worn velvet handcuffs. In both of these roles, as well as those in between, I learned several lessons. One is that someone must be in charge, and must be willing to make and enforce decisions. It is not possible to run any part of a business without a determination of what is supposed to be happening. I have no illusions that it is at all practical or possible to gather the people together now and then like some congregation to decide what is going to happen each moment. The people as a whole usually have greater common sense than the leaders as individuals, but there is no way to package that truth inside a corporate organization. We can't go to the polls each day on all the pertinent issues, and if we did the people would soon be as disoriented as the leader. Also, it has become very clear to me that organizations of all sizes and purposes make most of their own troubles and inefficiencies. They work hard on the wrong things, they keep everyone upset, and in general there is a lack of the most basic communication. This has been expensive but tolerable in most operations, at least up to now. While a lot of enterprises fail after a while, most do not. Much of corporate success or failure has been a function of how useful the product or service involved is to the customer. Good products and services can survive bad management. Bad ones are going to fail eventually, no matter how marvelous and competent the management proves to be. For this reason, each management team should treat itself to an annual examination by some outside objective source of wisdom. Some person or organization that has nothing to sell should be asked to look at what the company is producing and tell them if it is of any real use to anyone. To qualify as successful in this new league, the Centurion must be able to absorb and implement the principles of Completeness. This chapter offers a general discussion on these principles with the hope of locking them clearly in the reader's mind. An evaluation grid is also provided (in Chapter Four) to let prospective Centurions determine the present status of their organization. Each of the principles is covered in an individual chapter for the purpose of laying out the ingredients involved in their accomplishment. Then, just to make certain that we are communicating, they are woven into cases in the life of a Centurion which attempt to describe daily executive adventures some years from now. Completeness as a way of business and even personal life is well within the grasp of us ordinary people. But it is not something that just pours itself on command—it has to be dragged out of the bottle. Once it is on the plate, though, and available, it adds flavor and consistency to everything it touches, and its container is never empty. The purpose of Completeness is to avoid problems and guarantee success. There are three principles of Completeness:

1. Cause employees to be successful.
2. Cause suppliers to be successful.
3. Cause customers to be successful.

These thoughts may not ring out as concepts with the originality of those found in the Greek classics, but they provide the platform for those who want to cause success in the real world. They apply to the individual as well as the organization. They fit together the way a common and well-balanced meal does; they need each other. Hardly anyone has been able to accomplish all of them to date, primarily because there has been little genuine concern on the part of management with making employees successful. Executives I have met are not necessarily against the thought—it just never occurred to them. They are willing to work on the customers but neglect the employees. However, complete success will not happen in one area without the other. It is possible to walk with one leg and a crutch, but running requires two durable legs. Management has been conditioned to think of employees as a commodity, existing in a sort of ocean stocked with an endless supply of such fish. They come and go, and with a few exceptions, are rather much like each other. If conditions are such that some must be discarded occasionally, then so be it. We just get new (and we hope, more grateful) ones at the proper time. However, this way of viewing our human resource is obsolete. Just as the endless oceans can become "fished out" and weakened from neglect, so the labor pool can wither if it is taken for granted and not properly nourished. Just as fish swimming in polluted waters have only minimal signs of life, most humans in a typical office environment work at less than full speed. They are trained to do it that way because their employer feeds them plastic instead of food.

Making suppliers successful is based on a recognition that everything a company uses comes from some other organization. When these become an integral part of the whole, everything begins to work. When employees and suppliers are successful, they will make the customers successful.

Making the customer successful is a far cry from the vague admonishments of "satisfaction" or "providing customer service" commonly made in today's management conferences. After all, those goals can be accomplished by having an active and effective *rework* capability. Someone who brings a bottle of champagne to the room of an unhappy guest, or repairs an electrical system with a smile, or accepts a warranty charge, or credits an account without argument, is doing rework. Even the people who sit at a desk in the lobby of the hotel wearing tailored suits represent a rework station. They are doing repair on an unsuccessful customer. The customer will remember the problem and inconvenience long after they have forgotten the effectiveness of the repair.

I have a pair of very comfortable casual shoes whose strings are forever coming undone. No matter how many knots I tie in them the bindings eventually work their way loose. Little children notice this and stop me to suggest that I tie my shoes. Once in a while, one of them will kneel down and do the job for me. I never remember that the shoes are going to cause all this problem until I put them on and leave the house. On a recent trip to the shoe store for a different reason I shared this problem with the shoe salesperson.

"Happens all the time on that model," he said. "I have mentioned it to their representative several times, and she has told the company about it, but nothing happens. It seems strange because their policy is to guarantee satisfaction. If you bring them in I'll send the shoes back and you will get a brand-new pair without question. Want to do that?''

"Will they have the same shoe strings?" I asked.

"Oh sure," he said. "They feel that the style of that shoe demands that kind of texture in the string."

So I brought my shoes back in and the exchange was made in just a few days. I gave the new shoes, still in the box, to the Salvation Army. I put a small role of adhesive tape into the box in case the recipient wants to unobtrusively tape the strings down. (I have trouble bending down that low.) As far as the shoe company is concerned, they have chalked up another happy customer on their bulletin board. They can tell stories about how, if someone is not happy, they give them a replacement or a refund, with no questions asked. They miss the point that I didn't come to them in order to obtain that service. I just wanted a pair of comfortable shoes that did not make trouble for me. Meeting those two requirements would have made me a successful customer. Learning to do rework happily has never been a practical formula for success.

The Oxford English Dictionary does not treat the word "succeed" with much reverence. Until we get to the thirteenth definition the word has only to do with following another person or system, like one king succeeding another. In number 13 we read: "Of persons: To obtain a desired end or object; to be successful in an endeavor; to bring one's labour to a happy issue." If we look further forward in the book to "successful," we find: "Of persons: That succeeds or achieves success, that 'gets on.' " (All of this confirms my long-held belief that dictionary definitions are not of much use unless you already have some understanding of what the word means.) I view success along the lines of "obtaining desired ends" and have applied it that way in this book. For the executive, that means determining a way to learn what the customer, and the employee, consider to be those desired ends. Products, services, and lives are quite involved and complex. People are not always clear about what they want, and indeed may not have the slightest idea of what it takes for someone to help them become successful. You can bet they will know it when they see it, however. Before that happy day, someone, perhaps your competitor, will reveal it all to them. Success is not always something large, heavy, or expensive. The highlight of my not very long athletic career came when the grizzled old trainer of the team took time to nod in my direction and mutter, "That wasn't too bad." I would not have known how to order that up, but it makes me feel successful every time I think about it, even today, some forty-five years later. As far as I know, no one else even heard him say it to me.

We will get closer to determining the specifics of making customers and employees successful in the next few chapters, but prior to that time we need to talk about the "climate" of the organization. Without the proper climate many things have no way of happening. The trainer would have never made that remark to me if he had been prohibited by management from talking to the players except when involved in training. In some places there might not even be a trainer, or a locker room, or a team. If an organization is to practice Completeness as its way of doing things, the first ingredient must be to consciously construct this climate of consideration. Consideration is a great deal more than just being nice to each other, but that is not a bad place to begin. I remember the slogan from the Greenbrier hotel on its anniversary which said: "One hundred years of ladies and gentlemen serving ladies and gentlemen." That is a statement containing a lot of instruction and policy. It speaks of respect given and expected. In more practical terms it tells the personnel department something about the type of worker personality to avoid; it lets the employees know much of what management expects of them; it reminds management of its proper role; it puts the guests on their best behavior; and it makes everyone aware that the place cares what it is all about.

THE CLIMATE OF CONSIDERATION

One has to be careful with words. Once when I was running a quality department I made a comment in a brief article about being happy I was a quality manager. That was the title on my business card, one that is generally accepted as a normal part of any manufacturing organization. However, one critic dedicated a whole column to deriding me for a lack of humility in stating that I was a "wonderful" manager. He took the word quality to mean goodness, the conventional interpretation. Apparently he had never heard that there was a whole profession involved in quality, in departments containing dozens of people. I wrote him a dozen nasty notes, tore them all up prior to mailing, and wondered about it for years.

As part of doing that "quality" job, I became very problem oriented. Every time someone from senior management came across me, they would ask about some specific product or system difficulty. No status meeting was complete without my laying out the details of why some failure or other had occurred while trying to be discreet enough to avoid creating enemies. To make certain that I knew what was happening, I had to be involved at all levels of the process. I needed information; nothing was too unimportant to become part of the whole. My detective work was impeccable. I did my homework carefully. It was my custom to come into the plant early each morning, and walk around talking to the inspectors, testers, and the third shift manufacturing supervisors. These people knew all the inside information and loved to share it with me, probably because no one else ever asked them. Promptly at 8 A.M. my staff would gather in my office, and we would have a five-minute stand-up "what's your biggest problem?" session. They all would state their problems so everyone would know about them. There would be no discussion, just clear statements, then everyone would disburse to tackle the day's work. Since I was already loaded with information, I knew more about their problems than they did and would drop in on them during the morning to amaze them with my knowledge. After leaving a few hand grenades on their desks, I would wander about meeting other managers. We would talk about problems and their solutions. My secretary would spend much of the day tracking me down to do the managerial job I was supposedly getting paid to accomplish.

But I was very good at corrective action and my skills were sought out by those who had problems that did not respond to conventional methods. One person even drew a cartoon of me perched on a group engineer's desk with an oversized revolver in my hand, demanding action. Since we all like to do things that make us look useful, I found myself immersed in developing systems to identify and resolve problems. My entire organization responded accordingly and we all were busy killing off the unwanted. Of course, there was an unending supply of these problems. It was like chopping the heads off mythical dragons only to find that each stump grew a dozen more; or the drunk who discovered that the brewery was working three shifts to keep ahead of him. We were never going to get finished.

Problems can only come from a few sources: management, employees, suppliers, customers, the government, competitors, and traces here and there of something else, like the laws of physics. We were busy taking action against all these people and marking it all down on wall charts. Suppliers found to be wanting were dismissed from our approved list; employees were disciplined, retrained, transferred where they could do less harm, or even terminated; customers were double-teamed and treated as though they were wired wrong; the government was given token attention, with the thought that they were not a serious concern, since they changed their minds all the time anyway; competitors were known to be shifty and untruthful, so we built razor wire fences around them. This was the same pattern of activity and concern I found in other companies I visited, so I assumed it must be appropriate.

One evening, at home, I was reading stories to my children. A favorite of theirs was an Irish tale where the wind and the sun have a debate about their respective powers, and which one was the greater. Spotting a man walking up a country lane they made a wager on who could get the man to take his coat off. The wind went first and blew his hardest against the man. The more the wind blew the tighter the coat was clenched against his body. Soon he had it buttoned up so completely that only his nose stuck out. The wind backed off, defeated. The sun, in contrast, smiled warmth upon the traveler. It wasn't very long before the buttons began to be removed from the holes, soon the coat itself was draped over the man's arm and he was wiping his brow with a handkerchief. The parallel was suddenly very clear to me, I was the leader of the wind. The head blower. There was no sun in our operation. Everyone in the company had coat buttoned up tight, and we in the wind factory were doing everything we could short of running around with razors to slice the buttons off. It was a disturbing thought. We were puffing to no permanent avail. No wonder we felt as if it was us against the world. It was apparently my time for fables, because later that evening I ran across an article on Groundhog Day, which pointed out that the animal was only 30 percent correct in predicting how much longer winter was going to last. It dawned on me that the groundhog was not out of line, it was the performance criteria that had the problem. If it were reversed, he would be correct 70 percent of the time. That thought led me to consider prevention of problems rather than detecting and solving them.

The next morning I announced to the assembled 8 A.M. group that we would no longer have a "what's your biggest problem?" meeting each morning. Instead, we would have a "what am I going to do to help someone today?" announcement. Now, people I have worked with over the years have become accustomed to my being somewhat irregular or unusual in my thinking. They take it in stride and just adapt to it or take action to change me around. But these folks stood there, jaws dropping.

"You have any more to say about this?" one asked.

I told them the story about the wind and the sun, threw in thoughts about the groundhog, and closed with how I imagined we might be more effective being helpful than in trying to blast everyone out of their caves. Instead of a climate of retribution, I suggested, why don't we try to be more considerate of others? If we could help others learn not to have problems, we could be in better shape ourselves. Instead of needing a whip and a chair for communication, or having to walk the halls in pairs, we could face the world armed only with a smile and an offered helping hand. They might cooperate with us instead of playing hide-and-seek. We could even help them learn to respect each other.

Since they still weren't reacting, I smiled at them. They stared at me. All of these managers and section chiefs had come up through the ranks. Most of them were college graduates, but the formative impact on their lives, as on mine, came from the day-by-day, hand-to-hand combat necessary to cause production. They were used to dealing with status reports that covered several pages, and going through each of those pages one line at a time (in a marathon session called the "page-in-line" meeting). This was necessary because so many things and their interfaces were involved in the operation that there was an unlimited opportunity for something to go wrong. No wonder there was immediate concern when their gunslinger boss casually dropped in the thought of a lifestyle change the equivalent of switching sides in a civil war. Also, new assignments had caused their lives to become more complicated recently. We as a department were not only involved in the manufacturing operations, we also worked with research and development activities, and with the service and administrative functions. The latter were involved with leasing equipment, developing and printing publications, as well as producing and conducting educational projects. These "nonmanufacturing" people were just being brought to the conclusion that everyone as an individual is in the service business and has a product of some sort.

"Have you written this all out?" asked one.

"Not yet," I replied. "I really don't have the slightest idea of how to go about it. I thought we would start out with this meeting, with each of us listing something we were going to do to help someone today. Then we can see how it works out."

Silence.

I stared at the engineering manager who avoided my eyes. Finally he heaved some sort of sigh and said: "Production control is having a hard time getting their bills of material updated. I think I will go see if they really understand how the configuration control system works."

"Great idea," I enthused.

"Leasing contracts are continually out-of-date," commented another manager. "This means that they are always working overtime in that section and making a lot of errors in the bargain. I will go see if we can't have some classes on situation analysis for that group."

After a few moments each of the participants stated something they were going to do to help and went out to do just that. It was 8:30 instead of 8:05, but we got better at it once the shock wore off. Within a few days, I began receiving calls and notes from other executives commenting on how people from my organization had contributed to their operation. Nothing was ever documented in terms of a procedure or policy, but after a while it became a natural part of the way we worked. You could almost hear the entire company quiet down. Meetings were much more efficient, the problem list began to shrink, and I found myself with much less to worry about. The page-in-line meetings went from twice a day to twice a week. When that happened I began to accept that the groundhog had indeed been right all along.

A couple of years later, when I joined a large international corporation as a corporate officer, the first thing I learned was that everyone hated the corporate staff. They were characterized as being seagulls ("they fly in, eat your food, squawk a lot, crap all over you, and fly away"). It was not only people in field operations who felt this way; the corporate departments even disliked each other. I was determined that my organization would take advantage of that reputation by doing the opposite. So I spent a great deal of time and energy teaching people how to be helpful rather than arrogant and disrespectful. Believe me, arrogant and disrespectful are easier to teach. As the mother of any two-year-old will attest, these traits tend to emerge naturally.

But this is how I turned things around: We learned how to write our reports at the unit and discuss them with local management before sending them on to headquarters. We learned how to help the field operations get better, rather than spending our time adding yet another rock to the pile they already were toting. As a result, everyone was happy to see us, and we were able to get everything we wanted to accomplish done. Once they found that we did not intend to feather our nest by plucking them down to their bleached bones, they cooperated.

As a result of these two experiences, I decided that when I started a company of my own I would make certain to establish this climate of consideration from the beginning. In order to do that it was necessary to orient every person involved and establish policies on how we were going to be nice to each other. "Nice" itself has to be explained.

RELENTLESS EDUCATION

Sitting around explaining things, like "nice," to people on a one-to-one basis is no way to run something. Messages given that way tend to change from day to day, as the explainer is subjected to different experiences. Education is such a serious business that it has to be deliberately structured and induced. It has to be consistent. If meanings and policies are going to change then everyone has to know about it. This is vital in business where the world of knowledge is a loose-leaf notebook. Colleges and universities have less of a problem; they can and do teach the same thing forever in many cases. Born by the need for instructing based on the past they have little to do with the present and the future. The history of economics, like Shakespeare, is well documented and exists as is. None of what happened before is going to change, although views and opinions about it certainly are areas for original thought.

But those who have to make a living by selling something to other people every day have to keep up and keep ahead. We have seen what happens to companies who sit quietly by and ignore the alterations in their industries. People who made large centrally located copiers using special paper, were terrorized when small units using ordinary paper appeared wherever the customer wanted them. Companies who made computers requiring large spaces and special attention were found wanting when everyone could have an equally powerful but much smaller one on the desk. Firms that made television sets needing a great deal of service died when someone came along making sets that just sat there and worked. Old-line retailers watched with bemusement as discount stores took away much of their business.

Management has to keep a close eye on the needs of the customer to make certain that a route is not being constructed around them. The interstate highways destined a lot of small-town businesses to obliteration when their customers suddenly went by at 65 miles per hour, on the other side of the hill. That change was obvious, but most are not.

The skills employees bring to an organization soon will not be sufficient. The half-life of education varies but is rarely more than four years. So those good old reliable people in accounting will be out-of-date before long, which means that the financial management process will steadily become more expensive and less efficient. Imagine what it would cost today to use the fountain pens and manual entries that used to form the foundation of accounting. The quarterly reports necessary for shareholders would soon be months behind.

Education is not just a matter of having classes, of course; it requires establishing a desire for learning. That is a big part of making employees, suppliers, and customers successful.

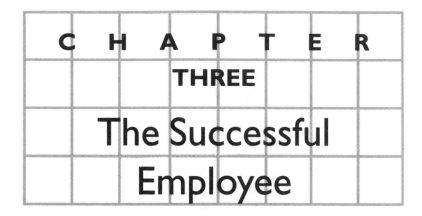

C H A P T E R
THREE
The Successful Employee

Austin Gallagher arrived at the Dean's office with some uneasiness. He had never spoken to an MBA class before, and, in fact, did very little public speaking. He was regretting having accepted the invitation. However, Dr. DePugh, the Dean, and his deputy, Dr. Eleanor Frame, soon put him at ease.

"These students are looking forward to your chat, Mr. Gallagher," said Dr. Frame. "They definitely do not regard it as a lecture; they just want to talk with you."

Austin nodded. "I am honored to be asked to come, but I am not sure that I will be all that helpful. I never went to an MBA school and, in fact, did not study business in college, although I took some classes afterwards."

"In spite of having been denied the advantage of an MBA," smiled Dr. DePugh, "you are very successful by any measurement in both professional and business life. You are recognized as a leader in your field, are president of the company, and have been honored by the community for your generosity and activities."

"You are the first of what the students call the 'real people' series of discussions," continued Eleanor. "It is something the student council conceived. They want to know why people are or are not successful, long range. Obviously, they are looking for role models. The people they have invited so far have not been involved with the fads of business; they have had lifelong success."

"I know you will be open with them, Austin, since that is your customary way," said the Dean. "They see themselves getting ready to go out in the cold cruel world and they do not feel nearly as confident as when they arrived two years ago.''

"How many are in the class?" asked Austin. "Thirty or forty?"

"Actually, we have the whole second-year class," said Eleanor. "There will be more like eight hundred of them, plus the professors."

Austin's calm began to deteriorate. He was beginning to feel the same concern that had accompanied him to his first security analyst's meeting. There he had been faced with people intensely asking questions he felt had little connection with his company or its future. As the Deans talked he recycled that event in his mind and decided that if he had been able to survive there he would somehow muddle through this one. At least he was more experienced than his audience.

"How much time do we have for the presentation?" he asked.

"The session is an hour and a half which can be divided any way you wish. I would recommend forty-five minutes for your comments and the same amount for questions. But it is entirely up to you; there is no reason you can't do questions for the whole time, or just chat. However, they are pretty vocal and will certainly speak up at the first opportunity."

Entering the multilevel auditorium, Austin felt some anxiety again but conjured up the analysts session memory and sat patiently while he was introduced. He received a polite welcome of applause and found himself standing, microphone clipped to tie, next to a lectern. He looked into the earnest faces before him, noting that the professors over to his right all appeared as though they would be just as happy to be somewhere else.

"Good morning," he said creatively, "I have been asked to talk with you about being successful in the long term. If I wanted to finish this right now I would state my formula for success, but I doubt that you would accept it that quickly. So I will state it, take a few moments to explain what I mean, and then we will deal with any questions you have."

He looked around the room, saw no effort to overthrow his plan, so he continued: "The way to be successful, in business as well as in personal life, is to help others be successful. Reward comes from what you give, not from what you get.

"I am president of a company in which I have worked for

eleven years. Before that I was with four other organizations for a total of ten years. At the time I joined my current company, I had become very discouraged with my progress in life and was not doing well financially or professionally. It was generally assumed by those who knew me that I just did not have what it takes to move to the top. I would always make a nice living, it was felt, but I would never be 'important,' and I certainly never would be rich.

"Now there are a great many other things in life besides being successful in business, and they are more significant in many ways. But it was a disappointment for me to realize that I was not considered to be a coming talent. I went along with the opinion reluctantly, only because I could not see any way around it. I felt that there was more to me than was being observed, but it was hard to ignore the evidence. It was apparent that everyone else knew better than I did.

"In my first company, after leaving college, I began in a junior management position. This is where they placed people for training and future advancement. The management was very specific about what we were supposed to do and measured us accordingly. I was found to be 'average' during my first two years and was encouraged to look around, on the outside, for something else. My second employer was in a service business that required work at all hours. They expected their professionals to be out in the field as long as a customer was awake. This meant traveling every week, and required being away from home most of the time. I was only able to deal with this for about eighteen months and had to quit. My supervisor scorned me for such a 'wimpy' attitude, my father gave me an earnest talk about personal responsibility, and my uncle encouraged me to get into his insurance business which he considered 'safe.' My wife did not give up on me, she kept saying that the world was mistaken and that it would all work out one day.

"During the next several years I worked for two more firms with much the same results. I never was able to follow instructions exactly, offered too many contrary suggestions about the way things should be, and in general was not considered too useful. I got a lot of points for being pleasant and bright, but was rated as quite ineffective overall. The funny part of this was that I was really quite effective, it just didn't look like it. I just went ahead and did things without making a big deal of them. This led people to believe, I realized later, that the tasks involved and the resulting accomplishments could not have been too difficult in the first place. If someone just did his job correctly it was assumed that he had been issued a minimum piece of work. I was not experienced enough to see that I needed to market myself better, and that it was up to me to create relationships—no one was going to do it for me. In business, there are no expert writers sitting in a press box watching us work and reporting it in the morning paper. If there were it would be easy for management and the public to tell the difference between the players. If I had learned nothing else it was that management did not have a clue as to who was useful and who was useless.

"At any rate, I found out about my present company, named Achilles Services, quite by accident. A friend told me they were looking for some people who wanted to learn how to be regional representatives. I applied to their personnel office and was interviewed by six different executives over a two-day period. They all were very polite, on time for the appointments, and very concerned that I understood what the firm did for a living. The last interview was with the CEO, Mr. English, who only asked if I had any questions for him. I offered a few, which he answered completely, and then we parted. The next day I received an offer and came to work the following Monday.

"I was placed in a training cycle, first going through a company orientation conducted by Human Resources. This consisted of a film about the company's history, a lecture by one of the executives on what the company did overall, and a visit by Mr. English. He led us into a question and answer session including a discussion on just what the word success meant in both our personal and business worlds."

Austin paused to take a careful look around the auditorium. He did not want to bore his audience, but they seemed to still be with him. However, pausing is a signal in the academic world and a hand was quickly raised in the middle of the group. Austin nodded to the hand, and a young lady stood up.

"What did you all agree that success was?" she asked.

"We asked Mr. English that and he said that success was when all the personal and business objectives you could think of were met through your efforts, and you were recognized as being able to help others achieve theirs. Then you thought up more objectives to go after. He said that success consisted more of a state of mind and relationships with others than an asset count. He also said something that I mentioned earlier, when he reached out to us, physically, and said he was going to share his philosophy of management. He stated: 'Management's job is to make the employees successful; they in turn will make the customers and suppliers successful; and the result of that will be to make the company successful.'

"He told us that in Achilles we would have permission to do things properly, that we would be listened to, that we would be given the opportunity to build up capital through ESOP, Thrift, and other plans. He said that it was not a paternal organization, that now and then people did not produce and were asked to leave."

A hand was raised in the back and Austin signaled to it.

"How much did the company spend on benefits as a percent of compensation?" asked the student.

"I am not sure what it was then, exactly, but today it is forty-four percent of compensation. That includes health care, with emphasis on prevention, child care, pension, education, and company contributions to the thrift plan."

"I just read a report," said the student, "saying that companies who spent more than thirty-five percent of compensation on benefits were bound to have lower profits and possibly none. How does your company do?"

Austin smiled. "Last year our profit was twenty-two percent pretax. The revenues per employee were around three hundred thousand dollars, which is twice what the well-known companies can do. However, spending money for benefits does not necessarily relate to employee efficiency. I know many organizations who spend more than we do and the employees are disgruntled. It would be nice if one could buy effectiveness through generosity, but it doesn't work that way. Benefits show the employees you are serious about helping them have lives, but benefits alone do not guarantee that the employees are going to work hard for you. In many cases people do not realize the money or effort involved in things like pensions, stock plans, and other long-range systems. They do not respond positively to bonuses, for instance, but will be upset if one is reduced or taken away. Most benefits, in fact, only have a down side when it comes to relationships with employees.

"To have successful relationships, management has to generate a culture built on respect for the individual, display consistency in policy and purpose, provide and encourage education for all, and lay out a clear opportunity for growth by the deserving. Consideration and respect cannot be purchased or programmed. They have to be built one brick at a time by management, on purpose. The hard part is getting management to understand and implement this. A study I saw recently showed that the most significant source of stress for employees was the support or lack of it they received from management and fellow workers."

A student stood up. "We hear a lot about company culture and that it needs to be established, Mr. Gallagher," he said. "But I can't seem to find many specifics on how to go about it exactly. Where did your company learn how to do it? It is easy to say that a company should have respect for its employees, for instance, but exactly how does that come about? Everyone may not have the same definition of respect."

Austin was beginning to think that he might be getting in over his head. He decided to cut to the chase: "I do not want to lead you into a path that says there is a series of events or actions for a management to take in order to create this situation. Let me restate your question from the point of view of the employees, the people who have given their professional lives over to the organization. To them respect is the opportunity to be successful and do it every day. It is the elimination of what keeps them from being successful in the first place.

"We have to learn why so many people hate their jobs and their company if we are going to prevent that. We have to think about building the positive atmosphere of a 'great place to work' by eliminating the negatives. This is the basis of what management has to actually go about doing in order to make the good things happen and keep the bad things out.

"The biggest problems we all have in our personal as well as our business lives are in relating to others. Parents and children, husband and wife, friend and friend, supervisor and employee, buyer and seller, there are an infinite number of combinations for our interfaces. We see people who love each other not being able to get along; we see people continually hurting each other without realizing it; we see people making others depressed. There are enough available sources of depression in the world without having to put up with it at work.

"One of the reasons for unhappy work situations is that there are usually no rules or policies that all parties accept and use. However, any determined organization can establish some basic policies and procedures that govern life within that envelope. This is not automatically a great thing; Captain Bligh on the Bounty created rules that caused a lot of problems. Many managements, for reasons clear only to themselves, go out of their way to irritate their employees by establishing regulations that humiliate people. There is a choice. We can recognize, I think, that those in authority are in a position to cause trouble or make things easier. The influence they have on our satisfaction whether they be parents, teachers, bosses, captains, or whatever, is very strong. And if they are insecure themselves, then they will have to build up their own confidence by tearing down that of those they control. I have always felt that the biggest single reason for organization failure is the arrogance of management.

"If we are going to have a climate of consideration in our organization we have to make clear, through the right policies and practices, the way people are going to be treated within it. We are going to have to educate and train everyone in order to make certain they understand this, and then management has to live it every day. There is no cut-and-dried, standard book of procedures; action has to reflect the honest intent of the management. Someone who likes to beat up on people could never accomplish such a climate. So the answer to your question is that there is no program as such, it has to be lived. We would be pleased to get you a copy of our policies and the schedule of the educational sessions we conduct."

One of the professors raised a hand. "Perhaps it would help us, Mr. Gallagher, if you would list a few of the policies your company has, then I would appreciate it if you could tell us about the employee's responsibility for making themselves successful. It surely isn't up to the company to make it all happen."

Austin smiled. "Fine," he said. "We have limited our policies to just a few subjects. The purpose of these policies is to lay out as clearly as possible the company's position on subjects that affect the business and the people involved. For instance, in the policy specifying the way employees are to be treated, there is a section making it clear that no abuse of any kind will be permitted. It always seemed kind of obvious to me that people should not abuse each other, but as you know, there are all kinds of abuse, and they do not always involve physically hurting someone. As part of this policy we have had classes on just what constitutes verbal, sexual, and other kinds of abuse.

"An early policy that Mr. English wrote when the company was founded, stated that the purpose of a company was to help people have lives. It went on to lay out the support services and basic benefit programs that would be required; a parallel policy stated that the employees would be expected to produce for the company and would be measured in an agreed fashion. People can expect to be disciplined if they do not earn their way. Other policies cover the way we deal with suppliers, explain our ethics, and lay out our responsibilities to the community. There are only about six policies in all, but we live by them. Each person attends a class on the policies, and supervisors at all levels, including myself, have a review session each year. It is fatal to assume that policies such as these are going to be implemented automatically. Never a month goes by that there is not a recommendation to alter or eliminate one of them, usually to save money in the short term. Yet money is a very small part of the equation. In our age, it is very expensive to find good employees; it is much better to learn how to keep and develop them. The major cause of turnover, particularly in the ranks of knowledge workers, is mistreatment. When employees feel the company does not care about them or is taking advantage of them, they go somewhere else. Just like customers.

"To address the rest of your question, about personal success. (I got off on the company's side of the deal which is only part of it, of course.) It is possible to give the impression that the company is responsible for dragging people into a successful situation. Actually management's job is to provide an environment in which people can grow without having to deal with barricades and land mines. This includes performance evaluations based on agreed and subjective analysis; education, as I said; clear job requirements definition; and formal encouragement. This also means that the senior management must do the same with the executive level.''

''Do you mean that executives have to be measured, educated, encouraged, and all those things, too?'' asked someone in the front. ''I thought they were supposed to take care of themselves.''

Austin nodded. ''Unfortunately, a company's executives, like the shoemaker's children, are often left out when all the good programs to help employees are instituted. Executives are expected to be self-sufficient, which is a big mistake. Usually that level of people is extremely sensitive to being neglected and require quiet attention. Mr. English used to look out for them personally, I have not done as well. Anyway, lets get back to the question of exactly who is responsible for causing the person's success. Obviously, individual people are responsible for making their own way. If they have the knowledge, understanding, energy—and are given the opportunity—they should be able to be successful, provided no one is stacking the deck against them.

''Yet many who have all the proper characteristics, plus all kinds of opportunities, miss the boat. The main reason, in my experience at least, is that they do not take time to understand what others do for a living. They work inside a large organization for a long time and never dig into it enough to know where things come from and where they go. As a result they do not have a network of information and contacts. They will not be of much help to anyone except themselves.''

There was an audible silence in the auditorium. Austin was beginning to think he had said something that offended them. As he opened his mouth to speak a voice preceded him.

''I thought we were supposed to help ourselves, what do you mean when you say they would not be much help to anyone 'except' themselves. I agree that helping others is worthwhile and an obligation we all have, it is something we should do, but you make it sound like a primary goal.''

Austin was finally beginning to relax; these people were a lot more genuine than the financial analysts. They just wanted to learn, they were not interested in showing him up. He was going to survive.

''Helping others is the primary goal for those who want to

reach their own potential. Just as companies need to make their employees, suppliers, and customers successful, individuals need to do that with their co-workers. They have to recognize that in a very real way fellow workers are their suppliers and customers. Thinking this way also makes life easier. When I went to work at Achilles, my first assignment was to serve as the interface with regional offices. When they had a problem where someone was doing something to them, they would call me and I would try to get it sorted out. Usually I would receive three or four calls or faxes a day from each one of the offices. The problems were usually involved with some violation caused by the central organization, but often it involved something a supplier sent or didn't send. Once in a while, I would be contacted by a customer who was unhappy with something we had done.

"My practice was to take these complaints personally in hand and go see the department that appeared to have caused the problem. I would tell the individuals in that department that my purpose was to find the cause of the situation and then to help make certain that it never happened again. In the process the complainer would be made whole, of course. One of the advantages of the positive attitude of Achilles' employees was that they were willing to accept my statement at face value. Each operation opened itself completely to me, and I was able to help them identify the problems, as well as the preventative solution in most cases.

"I would have the offending department call the region where the complaint originated and explain what was going to happen. This assured them that the true facts would be getting laid out rather than some out-of-line remarks. The regions were pleased with the results, and customers were delighted that their problems were taken seriously. Believe it or not, there are customers who think their problems are not taken seriously. Most of them, as a matter of fact.

"After a few months of this when the complaints had dropped to a few a day, Mr. English came to see me. Now this was an example of the way top management worked there: He came to *my* office to see *me*. He personally called my secretary to see if I was available and then came on down. She wasn't surprised, but I certainly was. I greeted him in the hallway and together we strolled around speaking to each of the persons in that area.

He knew most of them, and they all greeted him with enthusiasm. I am used to people reacting to chairmen with emotions closer to terror than to friendliness.

"He accepted my invitation to sit down and then got right to the point. He had been hearing nothing but good things about the results I had been getting, he said, and he was wondering how come. This particular job had caused several people to be run out of town, or to run out of town, he explained. What was I doing that was different?

"I explained that I was just trying to help these people understand and resolve their problems. The results were good because they felt they were participating and I certainly was not beating up on them. He asked me a few more questions and then wondered what I knew about finance and human resources. I said that I had never worked in either function during my career but was willing to learn. He replied that this was a useful attitude since he wanted me to take on the finance and human resources functions, in addition to this present department. The executives who ran those departments would report to me and I would be a senior vice president. He took a three-by-five card from his pocket and handed it to me. There were five items listed on the card. These were problems in those areas that he worried about, he said, and he would appreciate it if I would give them some attention. All this would take place immediately if I agreed, since he had already run the position and title past the board of directors. They had thought that my results were so unusual they wanted to take advantage of it, and also they wanted to promote me before I realized how good I was. Those were his words—I will always remember them."

"Did you use the same way of working in the new job?" asked the young lady student.

"Yes, ma'am, and I still do."

"We don't teach much about personal relationships in our courses," said one of the professors. "Do you think what you are advocating can be taught? Isn't it a matter of personality more than anything? It could be like trying to teach romance."

Everyone laughed.

"Perhaps we need to think about counseling more than teaching, in this case, professor," said Austin. "I have always felt that people in the business world just didn't realize the importance of getting involved with others in a helpful and unselfish way. The normal career approach people select, if they consciously select one, is more inwardly oriented. They are much more concerned about themselves and learn very little about what others are doing. Perhaps it could be a series of sessions rather than a course but it does need to be discussed.''

When Austin returned to his office he called Harry Endlemen in Human Resources and asked to have a set of policies sent over to the school. He also suggested that the titles of those policies be printed on a wallet card so everyone could carry them. It would have been very helpful to be able to whip that card out for the students rather than stumbling around trying to remember it all. Harry agreed and promised to have it done.

"Speaking of all this," said Harry, "have you noticed that the turnover rate among field people has been rising over the past six months? Let me put it on your screen right now. We have lost some people I thought had real potential, and almost all of them had only been here a short while. Their exit interviews don't show anything significant in terms of reasons, at least they didn't give us any, and there is no pattern I can see. But I am concerned about it."

"It seems to have come on suddenly," noted Austin as he read the data. "What does Helen Black say about it? All the field operations report to her."

"She says that we should be more careful in selecting new people, that the ones we have been hiring in the past year have not been up to our standards, but I don't agree with that. Perhaps you would want to discuss it with her? I'd be glad to participate when you want me."

"I'll call you back," said Austin and punched Helen's code number on the telescreen. Her secretary answered.

"Austin Gallagher, Sally, how are you today?" he said.

"Just fine, Mr. Gallagher," she replied, "what can I do for you?"

"I'd like to drop by and see Helen; is she around?"

"She is in her office right now, and will be there for another hour when she will be off to the airport to visit the western regions. Shall I tell her you will be coming over?" she asked.

"Please do that Sally, I'll be right along."

He worked his way across the building to field operations, chatting with or waving to each employee he met. Over the years he had learned how to have miniconversations and contacts without giving any direction. He was able to pick up a great deal of information this way and at the same time not make trouble for the others by interfering in their work. It was a hard routine to learn for someone who had always been right in the middle of everything.

Helen Black greeted him in her doorway and ushered Austin over to her coffee table. After they brought each other up to date, Austin began.

"I realize you are heading to the airport and that I was not part of your plans, but I wanted to grab the chance to talk with you about employee turnover. Harry is quite concerned, and after looking at the numbers, so am I. Is there anything we need to do about the situation? Do you know why it is happening?" he asked.

Helen nodded and retrieved a folder from her desk. "A lot of it has to do with the fact that we have not been hiring tough enough. Our new people don't have the dedication they used to have. I've been talking with Harry about that. The other reason seems to be the new schedule for field people who are serving customers on projects. They spend most of their time in customers' offices, as you know."

"We have always done that," said Austin. "Getting close to the customer is the key to our service. What is different?"

"What's different," said Helen earnestly, "is that we are requiring our people to be there at the start of the business week, which is nine a.m. Monday morning. Many of them object to that, but we have to serve the customer so I see no way out."

"But that means most of our people will be leaving home Sunday afternoon in order to reach their customers in time. Then they don't get back to the house until late on Friday, or even Saturday morning. That is not the way we have done it before," noted Austin.

"We need more hours in the customer's shop, and I know of no other way to do that," she said. "We have already reduced some of the education and orientation hours that take work time and I am looking for other ways to improve productivity."

Austin flushed. "You reduced education hours? All on your

own? And you changed the hours so people spend less time with their families? What about the company policies on these things? How can you feel you can just ignore them?''

He was upset, and she was alarmed to recognize that. ''I certainly thought I had the authority to take these steps and I am not familiar with policies to the contrary. In my previous company, where I spent ten years, this way of working was customary.''

''If I remember rightly, their annual turnover in field personnel was about forty-five percent and they were not as profitable as we are. Isn't that correct?'' he asked.

''They were looking for a balance between turnover and productivity. Our turnover is about five percent a year; I thought we could handle a little increase along that line. But I don't remember any policies saying we couldn't ask people to come to work when management wanted them to.''

''That point was discussed in the policy classes, don't you remember that?'' Austin asked.

''I was not able to attend those classes when I first came, in fact, I missed most of the orientation because that was when we had the big problem with SEO. I spent the first two months I was here wrapped up in that. I'm afraid I never got back to the class.''

''How did you get permission to skip it?''

''I asked Tommy, he was executive VP at that time, and he said getting the customer's problem solved was more important. But he did tell me to be sure and take the class. I guess I will arrange it next month after the field operations annual conference,'' she stated.

''Tommy has retired,'' said Austin, ''and one of the reasons he did so was his casual attitude about education. I just spent the morning telling a roomful of MBA students that we all lived by our agreed policies, and I find that you have not even been exposed to them. It is not your fault, it is mine. However, I would appreciate it if you would arrange to attend class right now. Postpone your trip. We can't have you going to the annual conference next month uninformed. Also, we will need to retract that direction about traveling on Sunday and the one about eliminating education sessions.''

Now Helen was upset. She stood and began walking around

the room. "I had assumed that I had authority to operate this division in the most efficient manner," she said. "It seems to me that you are recanting on that agreement."

"Your authority is complete, but it is within the limits of the policies of the corporation, just like mine," said Austin. "We have to deal with a set of basics. They can always be challenged and officially changed, as indeed they have. But we have to stick to our principles. That is the agreement we made when you joined us. In fact, we discussed some things along this line in your last performance review," he remembered.

"That's right," she said, "and I am not certain we agreed. I felt that being rock hard on the way we operate sometimes limits our ability to compete. Anyway, there is no way I cannot take this trip in order to go to class, I'll get back to it when I return."

Austin shook his head. "I have not made myself clear. The policy class for executives takes one day a month for three months. You need to schedule all three but if you don't get that first day then your trip is not authorized."

She whirled and stared at him. "You're serious, aren't you?" she asked. "Would you fire me over this?"

"Regretfully, but yes," replied Austin. "And I am going to check with every other executive and make certain they are not on the same path. We cannot let this organization become anarchy."

She paused and continued to look at him, then walked over and touched him on the shoulder. "Point made," she noted. "I'll call Harry and get a special class that begins this afternoon. After that session I would like to sit down with you and see if I think any of these policies are getting out-of-date. Apparently I don't understand them, or their reasons for existing. Okay?"

"Okay," said Austin. "I recognize that you can get another, and perhaps better job just by exciting the telescreen. I would like you to stay here; I just want to make certain we all understand each other. But take all three sessions before we discuss changing things."

They shook hands and Austin worked his way back to his office. There he summoned Harry to talk about assuring that everyone participated in the education program, without exception.

CHAPTER

FOUR

The Successful Customer

First, of course, we have to decide what a customer is. It seems rather obvious, since we are all both customers and suppliers, but then if we can't define our terms, it is difficult to have a useful discussion. To me, a customer is someone we do something for, on purpose. The problem with the conventional use of the word customer is that it is too narrow. The voicing of it brings forth the vision of a person or organization who orders something from some other person or organization. This ordering is done on some sort of form which in turn generates a great many other forms and efforts. Money changes hands formally, usually transmitted by people who never see the product or service that is ordered and used. This is the "customer" who is surveyed, measured, and intoned in business meetings and reports.

As individuals we are that sort of customer on a continual basis. We do dispose of all the compensation we receive in one way or another, even if it is as investment. Sometimes we are known as "consumers." Even if we only place our uncashed checks in safe-deposit boxes we are customers. We deal daily with stores that sell groceries, apparel, gasoline, automobiles, jewelry, electronics, and other things; we purchase services like dentistry, yard care, movies, and so on to a large list. That is the way we think of being customers: giving someone money for what they do for us. Yet each of our families is also a customer demanding our attention and care, and our co-workers are customers wanting us to do our part in the chain that is the organization. These transactions may not involve the transfer of money, but they qualify anyway. All customers are consumers, whether public or private. Whatever they require, buy, or demand, they want it to be as expected. Those who can do that are asked to do it again. Quality, meaning conformance to requirements, is one of the most important parts of making the customers successful. However, that is not what this chapter is about. We have reached the point in business where quality is considered a given, not something that gives the bearer a competitive advantage. If a company, or a person, cannot provide what they said they would provide, then they are dead anyway.

The key to having a successful customer is in determining what that customer wants and then arranging the operation to produce that. The Centurion, dealing with an economy that operates worldwide, is going to have to develop an internal system that performs constant examination of the customer's desires. More is involved than the specific product or service itself; we have to deal with the entire transaction. I stopped using a perfectly satisfactory men's clothing store because they kept getting my son's bill and mine mixed up. The apparel part of the business was without fault; they had always been cooperation plus. Their product is up-to-date, their prices are reasonable, and their sales people are knowledgeable. In the back room a much different attitude prevails; they view the customer as a hindrance to their work. They feel, I think, that customers should be sent to school to learn to obey the store's regulations and procedures. In my case, the accounting people suggested that my son and I remember to carry our charge cards in the future. They could see no other solution for eliminating potential confusion, so they lost a client of thirty years. So much for a tradition of serving succeeding generations.

If there is a secret of making successful customers, it is to be able to determine what they want. This determination really should not be accomplished by the application of some complicated formula able to be translated only by marketing experts. We need something that any normal person can use as a base for laying out the requirements of operating the business. To do any of that, we need to have been exposed to it as a customer. I have always felt that automobile company executives have a hard time dealing with customers because they have never been one. They do not have to take their old car and shop it around to several dealers trying to get an arrangement they like. They get a couple of new ones every year and sell them themselves. Instead of being customers they are minidealers.

For our example we need a business that we know about as a customer and at the same time one that not too many of us have hands-on experience in managing: a hotel that deals primarily with the public traveling by automobile. Our typical customer is a family consisting of two parents and two children. They are on vacation, driving the family car, and have made a reservation at our establishment, planning to arrive in the afternoon. If we gather our team together, we can make up a methodical list of what the customer wants. Later on, as we learn more about the business, we will have the opportunity to add more items. The initial list:

Confirmation of reservation (when made)
Directions to hotel
   Road signs that show how to get to hotel
   Easy determination of where front door is
Help in unloading baggage from car
A place to park car
Clean and pleasant lobby
Easily identifiable reception desk
Someone at desk who is interested in registering them
   Reservation is real
   Quick registration and confirmation of agreed rate
   Acceptance of credit card
Directions and help to room
Key that fits
No one else in room
Comfortable room with bath and facilities
   Sufficient towels, soap, and so on
   Hotel information about food and recreation
   TV set with lots of channels
   Comfortable bed and quiet environment
Quiet area
Clean recreation facilities, such as swimming pool
Places to eat, suitable for children
Wake up call on time
Breakfast
No waiting to pay bill

Directions to next location
Reservation for that night
Pleasant departure

This list can be polished with experience but it forms the basis of establishing how the organization is going to be run. I prefer to ask the team to consider each item in terms of how we would make certain the customer *did not* receive what they wanted. This then lets us learn how to prevent problems by seeing what is necessary to create them. That may sound a little strange, but it really works. Let's take a few of them:

- *Confirmation of reservation.* If reservations are taken in some sort of organized manner, then the customer might obtain a record of it. Therefore we just have to jot them down on a note pad as they come in, and tell the customer verbally that they need not worry.
- *Directions to hotel.* Nothing in writing, of course. Let the telephone operator, who is new to the area, tell them.
- *Road signs that show how to get to hotel.* These should be written so that clever advertising phrases hide the name of the hotel, and then the sign should be placed too close to the exit for the driver to react in time. This also keeps the customer humble.
- *Easy determination of where front door is.* Most hotels purchase two vans so at least one can always be parked in front of the door at all times. Modern designs permit the customer to confuse the conference center door, the banquet center door, and the front door. But this keeps them on their toes; often they are sleepy after a long drive. It is best to not have any signs around the property to give them a clue.
- *Help in unloading baggage from car.* With good timing, it is possible to learn how to arrive at the car just as the customer finishes emptying it. Offer to guard it until he is ready to move it to the room, indicate that tipping is permitted.
- *A place to park car.* Valet parking makes it too easy. The customer has had a long day cramped in an automobile with those dear to him—he could use a brisk walk across a hot parking lot.
- *Clean and pleasant lobby.* Many hotels miss the opportu-

nity to add rooms by shrinking the lobby where no one ever spends much time. Remaining space can be taken by newsstands and bars.

- *Easily identifiable reception desk.* This can be a real challenge, but if signs are omitted or made to blend into the woodwork, the customer can wander from Cashier, to Concierge, to Reception, before arriving at the proper place. Even if business is poor there should be a row of guide rails to keep the customers from storming the desk.

- *Someone at desk who is interested in registering them.* Outside of the obvious ploy of having no one behind the desk at that time, there are more subtle touches available in our plot to disappoint the customer. I particularly like the clerk having a telephone conversation with a loved one on some emotional subject, or being immersed in conversation with the computer so they can avoid looking up. It is also possible to have the clerk speak whatever language the customer does not. The rate structure should vary from day to day so no one ever really knows what it should be.

- *Reservation is real.* It is too simple to book the persons in a room, or rooms, at the agreed rate at the agreed time. There should be a lot of shuffling of paper and pounding of the computer, while the tiring principals lean on the counter and their children whine in the background. I particularly like the empty stare technique, after an energetic session with the computer keys. A real artist can make the tourists feel responsible for the situation. Eventually, we have to give them a room or the rest of the list cannot be considered.

- *Quick registration and confirmation of agreed rate.* They should leave confused as to whether we are doing it right.

- *Acceptance of credit card.* It is best to have the hotel only deal with obscure or regional cards. That lowers the rate and forces the customer to part with the small cash reserve brought along to purchase special gifts for the children.

- *Directions and help to room.* I once received a key to room 3420 and a wave to the elevators where I discovered that the hotel had eleven floors. After a great deal of detective work I realized that the ''3'' stood for the third floor and the ''4'' for the fourth corridor. Since there were only sixteen rooms on that floor (I counted them later), I could only assume that such an imaginative numbering system was deliberately established to irritate me. When I met the manager later, quite by accident, she was apologetic but secretly pleased, I deduced.

- *Key that fits.* The new plastic electronic keys, each of which works in a different way, have added a new characteristic to this bit of trouble. It is possible for the customer to fail even when they are not doing anything wrong. The directions for use can be written small enough to be invisible. If we are part of a chain of hotels, it might be possible to arrange for each to be different. That way the traveler would learn nothing useful each time.

- *No one else in room.* During my ITT days I produced a film titled "Zero Defects—that's good enough." One of the scenes had a hotel guest being shown to a room already occupied by a young lady who screamed at the intrusion. It seemed to me that anytime we showed that film someone came up afterwards to relate a similar experience. Making certain this happens requires real planning.

- *Comfortable room with bath and facilities.* Most hotels have brochures with photographs of rooms and of people seated at well-stocked restaurant tables where none of the food has been disturbed. By placing the camera against the far wall it is possible to give the impression that the rooms are much larger than real life. The furniture does not have to be too special since most people only stay one night.

- *Sufficient towels, soap, and so on.* By careful calculation, we can determine how many towels the typical resident will use and arrange to have a few less. Soap should not be replaced as long as it can produce a foam, and the little items usually found in a bathroom can be avoided. Why waste shampoo and other things on people who should know enough to bring their own? I like the card some hotels use now that says such things are available at the desk should you have forgotten to bring them. We should also make sure that the hotel staff never spends a night in a room, or they may find themselves with a bad case of sympathy for those who do.

* * *

The preceding is probably enough of a listing to make the point. I would encourage the reader to make a session of requirement setting like this into a funny and imaginative time with their management team. The idea of having an opportunity to establish the vital ways of making absolutely certain the customer does not receive what has been promised, will bring out the author in them. They will look at the company in an entirely different way and from a very different point of view; they will be redesigning the system from the customer's needs. Using a negative list the management team can review the operation and as a result establish the positive procedures, training, and systems to make the customer successful every time. When we turn around a specific potential for disappointment, like the lack of instructions for using the electronic key, or having a vague reservation, or supplying inadequate towels, then we can establish our own no-fail way of accomplishing it. By changing emphasis, we can concentrate on having a building full of happy smiling customers who are spending money to enjoy our work. People will form themselves into teams to tackle each area. As they nail down reservations systems that work every time, TV sets with no roll-overs, housekeeping that really keeps house, room service that is snappy, and the fifteen dozen other parts of being successful, they will learn the business. We need to never stop learning—the customers don't.

WORDS HAVE MEANINGS

Some time ago I gave a talk to a group of executives, and after it was over, one of them stopped me to chat. He worked in the hotel business, or as he would say, he "managed properties."

"I noticed that you avoid using the word 'guest' when talking about those who stay at hotels," he commented. "We are very careful to train our people to think of them as they would guests in their own homes. It works out very well for us."

"Have you ever been a guest in anyone's home?" I asked.

"Certainly," he said, "I just finished playing in a member guest tournament with an old friend. My wife and I stayed at their house for a long weekend."

"What time did you get up in the morning while you were at your friend's house?" I asked.

"Breakfast was served at eight-thirty a.m.," he answered.

"What time do you usually eat breakfast?" I persisted.

"Around seven a.m.," he answered. "I like to get up and out early. Waiting until eight-thirty got to be a problem."

"Customers can get up whenever they want," I noted. "Guests have to do what the house does. Which would you rather be?"

"I see what you mean," he said. "We will erase the word 'guest' from our literature and from our minds," he said. "I don't know how any friendship can stand a weekend of guesthood. I hate to think we would do that to our customers."

MAKING IT CLEAR

How about the customer who is not so obvious? What do we do when the sales department, and each individual of the sales team, looks to us to supply them with the up-to-the-minute price list? Here we sit in the center of the operation, gathering data, packaging it, and sending the result out to salespeople who grumble about it all the time. They say that the lists are much too complex, that there are too many special combinations, and that their customers get confused. They also say that the material is out-of-date as soon as they receive it.

"I have tried for several years to satisfy the salespeople," said Kathy Hargiss, "but nothing makes them happy. I think the best thing to do is just accept the fact that they are always going to blame us for all their troubles. As it is, they get something wrong on about every order that comes back. If it isn't the wrong price, then some number or other is transposed."

"Well," replied Harvey Sense, "you should be happy that we do as well as we do. Ours is a price-sensitive business; the customers will switch suppliers in a minute if they think they can pick up a few cents. We receive your lists every couple of weeks, and then we have to determine where the changes have occurred. That takes time, and then we have to update our reference material. While all that is going on the competition is taking the customer to lunch."

"I'm tired of arguing with all of you," said Kathy. "Why don't you just tell me what you would like to have to work with, and I'll see what I can do about it."

The sales people brightened.

"We would like immediate, up-to-the-minute price information on all of our lines, we would like to have a special listing for the incentives that come along, and we would like to know the customer's history whenever we need it."

"And would you like to have access to market information at the same time?" asked Kathy.

"That would be wonderful," they replied, "but how could you do that?"

"Turns out it is not so difficult," said Kathy. "For years we have been writing up a new set of prices twice a month and mailing it to you. Now what we are proposing is that each of you will have a laptop computer with a built-in modem. You can plug into any telephone, even in your customer's office, and come right into my system. That way you will be able to access any price listing or industry information you wish, and it will all be accurate to the last fifteen minutes or so. You can also send in your call reports that way. If you need something printed out, it can be done here and faxed back to you while you're still in the customer's office."

"How about orders?" asked Sam.

"Orders too. They can be filed directly into the loading system, which will also let you check out the status of your customer's previous orders and bills."

"We love you, Kathy."

CUSTOMERS NEED HELP

"This book club is driving me crazy," said Helen. "Every month I get a book and a bill. By the time I pay the bill, I have received two dunning notices and a new bill that is out-of-date. When I try to talk with them on the telephone they put me into some sort of phone mail system where I have to answer a lot of questions correctly before they will let me talk with a human. I am going to cancel out."

"You should try my club," said Carl. "They send me a book

every month and put it on my VISA card so I never get a bill. They also have a special toll-free telephone number I can call if I want to order other books or not accept the one they plan to send me this month. No paper, except in the books.''

"Sounds like they pay attention to their customers. That's my kind of book club.''

THE BOSS AS CUSTOMER

When people make up their list of customers, and we all have several, they often omit one who is very close to them—the boss. All of us have someone to whom we are responsible at work. The chairman has the board to worry about, the truck loader has the shipping supervisor. They are our customers because they lay out what we are going to do and, of course, they have a major role in our compensation and job security. For these reasons, relationships are often tenuous between superior and subordinate. Few of us are ever trained to be supervisors, managers, or executives. No one, except in the military, is ever trained to be a subordinate. That is felt to come naturally. So we lurch through our careers wondering why it is so hard to get things settled. We keep thinking the boss knows what to do and the boss wonders what our problem is.

The successful boss is one who can quietly bask in the glory generated by those who do the actual work. In return he, or she, makes the employees successful by giving them personal recognition and the challenge to develop. This relationship requires that the boss be confident enough to want to help others with their self-image. After all, self-image, or the lack of it, is the largest single personal problem in the world. The employee needs to determine what the boss needs to be successful and then go about accomplishing that. The best way to build it is to avoid destructive action. Building self-image is hard work, tearing it down is child's play. One "you're stupid" will take six months of "you're wonderful" to overcome.

I always made a point of sitting down with a new boss and asking how I was to be measured. Since the boss never had a way to do this I would provide one. Also I learned to stick my head in the boss's office at least twice a week and ask if any problems with me had come up, and if there was anything I could do that would keep the boss happy. About once a month I would drag my boss out of the office and on a tour of my area. This forced communication kept the boss feeling part of my operation. As a result I was left alone.

KEEP IN TOUCH

The using customer, the one who purchases the product or service of our organization, needs similar attention. Some day I am going to run into the CEO of that clothing store, whom I know. He will ask me something about the store, and I will admit I don't go there any more. He will then become concerned and drag the story out of me, then go back and raise the roof. He will then pester me with service and ideas until I finally go back to buying there. But it will never be the same. He could have avoided this particular problem by paying as much attention to the back of the store as to the front. Relationships are supposed to wrap clear around like an overcoat, not just cover strategic spots like a bikini.

Customers cannot be let out of sight. Somehow or other, using a system that relates to our particular situation, we have to keep track of their condition. Every business has horror stories of how customers changed their desires without telling anyone, so that a rock-solid line suddenly dropped off the scope. But in every case, the signs were there; someone knew and didn't care. In the case of the clothing store, I had been complaining about the billing mistakes for two years.

Why do companies keep on doing something their customers do not want them to do? Why do they develop internal systems and attitudes to make life difficult and irritate those who support them? The answer is that hardly any company is truly customer driven. They say they are, but, as is often true, "talk is cheap." Companies use mass advertising in an attempt to communicate with and encourage purchasers. Yet those who buy need only to determine just who will provide what they want. The same amount of money, or less, invested in a serious search to define and offer "want," rather than trying to create "want," would be much more fruitful. People are not all that complex; they will go to the organization that creates the least problem and the most success. Research shows that once they trust a brand they will stick with it. Price alone is not enough to take them away.

PROSPECT, PROSPECT, PROSPECT

"We have a small company," said Thomas Lighthouse. "Our revenues were just under two million dollars last year. We provide a service to business offices, and we are very good at it. We have competition, of course, and there are no technological advantages between us. We are finding it difficult to expand our customer base."

"We have tried direct mail advertising and have a display in the yellow pages," noted his wife, Ellen.

"But that has not done much good," continued Tom. "We have a new multicolored brochure prepared to mail out, and think that will get a good response."

"But we thought that about the other things, too," said Ellen.

"We wondered if you have any ideas. We need customers to build this business."

"Did you have any trouble getting customers when you started?" asked the Swami.

"No, we picked up about twelve right off. Since that time we have lost about four of those and added seven new ones. We have been flat for several months," said Tom.

"Do you know all their names, Tom?" asked the Swami.

"I know most of them but Ellen has been closer to their records. She is the one they call when they have problems."

"Do they have a lot of problems?"

"Now and then, and it is almost always because they have not followed instructions properly. Many of them do not take the training seriously enough. It is hard to keep their attention; these are busy people."

"How about the clients that left you, do you know why they did?"

Tom and Ellen looked at each other. "I don't think there was any specific thing," said Ellen. "They just called up one day and said that they would not be using us any more and that we should send back the records we had. They switched to a competitor. Probably got a better price; some people are willing to do anything to save a few dollars. In the long run, they will not be happy.''

The Swami made some notes. Then he spoke: ''The way to grow, in small business particularly, is to keep and grow the customers now doing business with you, and of course, also sell them other things. Then those customers are the key to obtaining new ones, from references and introductions.

''You folks have been so busy looking for new customers you have not been taking proper care of the old ones. It is not their responsibility to make themselves successful; it is yours. If they do not do the training properly, it means that you are not presenting and managing it right.

''Brochures and ads are not going to make it for you. Get out of the office and go work with the customers. In turn they will work for you.''

''But,'' said Tom, ''our marketing strategy is to reach out to a much broader audience. We will have to hire people to do that if we are spending our time in the customer's shop.''

''I'd suggest you hire people to work with the customers you have now, and work on that relationship,'' countered the Swami. ''Train your new people to concentrate on the customer's success and do it in an obvious way. You can take the introductions of those happy folks and go bring new ones on the scene. It will build rapidly, if you do not walk away from the ones you have.''

''It costs money to hire and train new people.''

''Don't get them until they are going to pay for themselves. But they are going to produce a lot more than brochures and mail outs. Learn how to hold the customer's hand and go back to check them out regularly. Put your eye where the money comes from, not in the dim mists of anticipation.''

''We are making up a business plan so we can borrow money for expansion,'' said Ellen. ''Would you like to see it?''

''Don't expand until the customers demand it,'' said the Swami. ''Never get ahead of the curve. Don't leave your game in the locker room. But that is another story.''

C H A P T E R

FIVE

The Successful Supplier

There is an obvious extension to the principles of making both customers and employees successful. That is the successful supplier. Employees will reach out and bring them into the tent when encouraged to do so. After all, little can happen without them. Traditionally business has maintained an adversarial relationship with suppliers. Price was the only real consideration in any deal, and everyone was felt to be out to do the other in. I lived in that world for years. However, when we begin to think of suppliers as an integral part of whatever we do, then it becomes a different situation.

As I sit here in front of my word processor, I am making a list of things I have provided for myself with no help from others. So far the page is empty. It takes only a moment to recognize that everything around, in, and on me is something that others produced for me to use: the processor, the printer, my glasses, my clothes, watch, glass of milk, books, windows, wood panels, TV and VCR, and of course the dog laying across my made in England shoes. I didn't even have much to do with making me. All of the skills and knowledge I possess came from some other source. Even though I may figure some things out for myself, I have to write it down in a way I was taught—the alphabet came from elsewhere, too.

My life's operating equipment is the product of suppliers. I work to make money to give them, so they can provide the ingredients of my survival and growth in return. It is a relationship essential for both. They have a requirement to give me what they said they would give me, and to keep me informed as to what is available. I have a requirement to use their product or service as I have agreed to do, and to pay them as they expect. They can make my life pleasant and even useful. In return, I can help them be profitable and satisfied.

For the most part these are what are known as sole source suppliers. I only buy from them as long as they do right by me. When traveling out of town, however, I am permitted to use temporary suppliers such as gasoline service stations, restaurants, drug stores, and so on. In many cases I stick to the brands that have taken good care of me in the past. Like any good consumer I take my suppliers seriously; after all, they are responsible for my continued good health and comfort.

However, when it comes to business a different attitude often prevails. The professional buyer in that situation is not dealing with personal considerations, but instead is using company money to purchase things and services for others to use. In most cases the one who buys it will never even see it, let alone use it. Therefore, the evaluation becomes much different. Where the personal consumer may go several blocks out of the way and even pay a bit more to obtain just the right bread for dinner, the professional buyer will not necessarily consider the ''just the right bread'' aspect; it may not even enter into the purchase request. Business buying traditionally deals primarily with the considerations of price and delivery. Appropriate and best are not regular measurements—they are much too difficult to describe. Purchasing departments are not expected to deal in those terms; they have the obligation to reduce things to a minimum of commitment. Managements are reluctant to make any long-term arrangements with suppliers, in case something better— read ''cheaper''—comes along. So where the individual may return to the same grocery store for years, the company switches suppliers regularly, based on price. The result is that the buyer and seller never get to know each other.

In the fast moving twenty-first century, where we will need all the help we can get, suppliers will have to be taken into the tent and embraced. They will have to learn that they can become successful by helping their customers become successful, and customers have to give them that opportunity. People with heart disease don't switch cardiologists based on price, when it comes time for the regular checkup. They are interested in someone who knows their case, understands what has gone on before, and is interested in the long-term outcome of the situation. Constant changes reduce or eliminate the consideration of commitment.

The key to proper selection and management of suppliers lies in two specifics. First, the policy of the company has to be stated clearly: "We will carefully identify suppliers whose products and services fit our needs and whose practices and attitudes are compatible with ours, and we will develop long-term relations that are beneficial to both parties." Something along those lines will do. Implicit in the arrangement is that the supplier will deliver in accordance with our quality policy, which requires the right stuff, on time. To think this is an obvious point, requiring no emphasis, is to court oblivion. Those who place orders have to learn that quality comes first.

Second, we have to reorient and reeducate the people running the purchasing operation. They will need to understand the priorities of the new way of doing business.

1. We need to determine what parts of our products and services we will purchase rather than provide ourselves.

During the twentieth century, many companies utilized vertical integration to eliminate suppliers all together. One cash register manufacturer even made its own screws—they didn't trust anyone. As late as the 1980s, General Motors still produced over 60 percent of its own components. Today, according to Fortune 500 listings, GM has 761,400 employees and revenues of $125,126,000. Toyota, the third largest automaker, has 96,894 employees and revenues of $64,516,000. Toyota set itself up to use suppliers rather than produce components itself. This helps it be a low-cost producer. It also requires that it manage suppliers with great care. IBM is probably the world's largest semiconductor producer, all for internal use. Even in administrative areas, as the need to reduce costs becomes more important, companies have begun using outside sources to perform what had always been internal services: payroll, software, security, and many others. The advantage of vertical integration was seen as better control—even though it didn't work out that way most of the time; the disadvantage was higher cost, because of inherent big-company overhead and questionable attention to quality. It is very difficult for the management of an operation to do much about a sister division that is supplying it with parts or services and not doing a good job in the process. In most cases those supplying organizations received their bonuses based on what went out the door, regardless of whether it could be used. Independent suppliers cannot get away with this for very long, but sister companies can just negotiate. Not necessarily a good way to do business.

2. All supplied items must meet agreed upon requirements every time, be cost competitive, and be delivered as committed.

Thousands of actions and components coming from internal as well as external sources are involved in the most modest of companies. The complexities of a producing organization can be compared to the network of roads and intersections that cover a state (or even a nation, depending on size). An agreed upon set of rules covers the use of these transportation media. For instance, in return for a driver's license, we commit ourselves to bringing our vehicle to a full and complete stop at each and every stop sign we encounter, proceeding only when everything is clear. There can be no allowance for people to have a certain number of times when it is permissible for them not to stop. If collisions didn't get us, the anticipation would. Waiting for someone to swish through the intersection or not, randomly, would be a strain on the nerves and would lead to everything shutting down. People would be afraid to move; they would not cross a street unless it was unoccupied as far as could be seen.

The same thought applies to suppliers. They have to come into the relationship knowing that we are going to actually use their output, whether it be hardware, software, or advice; that, in fact, we are going to depend on it for our survival and prosperity. We do not want to have to check it out; we do not want to have to determine that it is going to work as promised; we want to just go ahead and use it.

3. We do not want to have one drop more inventory of anything than we absolutely need for right now.

When delivery from suppliers is unreliable people begin to hoard. I have been in automobile plants, in the old days, when they had enough inventory to build all the cars they were going to produce for the next three (or sometimes six) months. This was because they usually had to rework the materials delivered from their suppliers. Office staffs will build up closets full of paper clips and other supplies in order to not run out. Those responsible for cost cutting know better than to attack these strongholds unless they can prove absolutely that the office supply place will deliver when summoned. Revolutions have begun for less reason than the absence of typing paper.

    4. A formal program of education and communication will be established with suppliers, to assure that the relationship is soundly based in all concerned.

First of all, we have to educate our own people. (It sometimes may seem to require brain transplants to change the way things have "always been done.") Formal classes and procedures will be necessary, along with working seminars on everything from telephone manners to contractual refinements. We are talking a big cultural change here; a lot of tradition has to be overcome. Once upon a time, for instance, suppliers were deliberately not told how their offering would be used in the customer's system. This was to protect the security of design or procedures. Many of them discovered much later that their product was being misapplied, causing a great deal of hassle, particularly if they had been blamed for nonperformance. Customers learned, usually the hard way, that the supplier knew more about their own output than anyone else and could suggest money-saving and reliability-improving ways of doing things. It became profitable to bring the supplier into the development early enough to make a contribution. This also helped them feel they were part of the family.

If an organization is to communicate with its suppliers and develop positive relationships, it is necessary to reach out and share information with them. At a minimum, an orientation film or audiotape should be supplied to those we plan to do business with. It would explain the principles of the purchasing company, would lay out the expectations, as in number 2, and would explain how to communicate to obtain rapid answers to questions. It would also state clearly that the management of the supplier's organization would be expected to keep their company up-to-date. Realizing that we face the probability of dealing with providers from all around the globe, it may be possible that these tapes will be in several different languages. English will be the international work language worldwide, but usually people who understand another language have better comprehension with their own. If a film or tape seems too elaborate, a neatly laid-out brochure will do the job in most cases. However, the more people know about each other, the better chance they have of working well together.

Suppliers who do a certain amount of business with us, and those with whom we have long-range agreements, would be expected to attend relationship seminars. We can produce these ourselves or have an outside firm do it. Executives of our company would go to various geographical areas and invite the senior people of vendor companies to attend. These must be give-and-take sessions. We, as buyers, have to listen also, and work on ways to open the communication channels that can prevent problems. In the past we often saw multimillion-dollar contracts that were controlled by a low-level buyer and an equally low-level engineer. There was no approved way for the management of the supplier to break through the wall to advise the purchaser of vital information. If someone went around this wall, they could be assured of never having the opportunity to serve that company again. These barriers have to become unnecessary.

5. We will make long-term arrangements with those suppliers who prove themselves to be reliable and interested in our success.

Much of purchasing tradition is based on sending out requests for bids and then selecting the lowest price of those returned. This serves the buyer well because management's primary measure has always been price first, and this system leaves no room for criticism. However, we now know that the lowest price comes from the closest arrangement. When a company has the assurance of business over a long term, it can concentrate on becoming more efficient and productive. This reduces their costs, which can then reduce their price well below that contained in the regular bid process. After all, they know their costs better than any customer ever will. The big Japanese companies created a "tradition" that it was considered polite to bring a slight price reduction along as a present when visiting. This kept them thinking about it.

"Come in Mr. Watkins," said the purchasing manager. "I am glad you were able to stop by this morning on such short notice. I'm Al Bertoni."

Watkins shook Al's hand and sat down in front of the desk.

"Call me Sam, Al," he said. "Actually it all worked out just right. I was in New York for a trade show and it was easy to come by here on the way home. I have a three o'clock plane, but I can adjust that if necessary."

"Do you spend a lot of time on the road, Sam? I would suspect that you get chained to the desk now that you are president of the company."

Sam sighed. "It's good news and bad news, like everything else. I still enjoy traveling, if I can do it in a comfortable manner. That is the only way I can really keep up with what is going on, and I like to see my customers. But the way business is today I just have to rush from here to there."

"You see a change in the way things operate now?" asked Al.

Sam settled back in his chair. "Frankly," he said, "the problem is that it is hard to nail customers down, particularly in our field. There is a great deal of competition—and I don't mind that at all—but information technology is advancing so quickly that the customers get confused. We have a dozen cases right now where they have gotten into systems that are wrong for them and have come to get us to bail them out. So we have surges and relapses."

Al nodded. "We have experienced some of the same things, Sam," he said. "In fact, that is why I was hoping you could come by this morning. We would like to see if we could work out an arrangement with your firm on a continuing basis. I thought you and I could discuss the possibilities, and then we will join Jim Karking, our president, for lunch. At that time we could determine if this is a good idea.''

Sam was delighted. ''You mean we would actually agree that we were going to do business together over an extended period of time, provided everyone produced as they said they would?'' Sam said in amazement. ''You could get into the hall of fame with an idea like that. We would be thrilled, and I am certain that it will turn out to be much less expensive for both of us.''

''I'm glad to see you like the idea,'' noted Al. ''We weren't quite sure how our key suppliers would react to it. They could consider themselves as being 'locked up.' ''

''I'll take 'locked up' to 'locked out' every time,'' Sam said, smiling. ''Most management people do not realize that their suppliers are as important to them as their employees. They do not deal with the real world of putting things together and sending them somewhere in a box or an envelope. How do you plan to manage these accounts?''

''We have some ideas,'' said Al, ''but the real reason I wanted to see you was to ask what sort of system you would recommend we work out. How do you like to communicate with us as your customer and with other customers?''

''I think the key to proper communication is to begin as early in the process as possible. If our advanced systems people can work with the proper folks in your organization, we can prevent most of the problems from happening. Also, there has to be a central source of information and control in both companies. One person or group does all the arranging. Our company has five or six times the number of employees you do. We could overwhelm you in a few weeks if everyone wanted information. Then you would be sorry you got involved with us.''

Al smiled. ''That can happen. So both of us would work through one contact point. Also, we would need to sign nondisclosure arrangements, I suspect.''

Sam nodded. Al checked his watch and suggested that they go on up to Jim Karking's office, leaving Sam's coat and briefcase where they were.

''We are really delighted you could drop by, Sam,'' said Karking. ''This is something new for us, but we feel it is the future. Our objective, outside of the obvious business of running our company, is to make you and our other key suppliers successful. We want to be part of your growth and prosperity, with the thought that we will benefit, too. I am thinking of setting up one department to handle relationships with those suppliers classified as 'key.' ''

''You can be certain we will cooperate all the way, Jim,'' commented Sam. ''But let me suggest that the interface might be more difficult than it appears. Supplying companies are very different from each other. Trying to have a group of folks deal with all of them might complicate things. It is practical to have one place—we were just talking about it—but they should only coordinate. Let me give you an example.

''When I was starving as an engineer, I used to work in a men's clothing store, part time. I sold shirts, ties, and the stuff that is in the showcases around the floor. If a customer said he was also going to go buy some shoes, I would walk him over to the shoe department and introduce him to a salesperson. If a suit salesperson had a customer who wanted a shirt, he would bring him over to me and I would take care of shirt and tie needs.

''Then one day the boss decided that we should all be—and this is the word he used—'key' salespeople. We would pick up the customer wherever we found him and take him throughout the store. That way I could sell shoes, suits, shirts, and whatever else was necessary. It sounded like a great idea.

''Within a week the inventory in the back rooms was a complete mess. None of the other people knew where the ties or shirts were, for instance, and they mixed everything up. The suits and jackets were in the wrong size areas; no one was speaking to anyone else. We found that knowing how to size shoes did not provide an understanding about fitting suits. It took a long time of education and forced cooperation to get to where we could roam the store to the customer's satisfaction. But the relationships were never there again.''

Jim and Al thought about this.

''I get your point, Sam,'' replied Jim. ''We need to get a firm agreement on what each party is going to do, set up communication control points with no contractual authority, and leave the technical stuff to those who understand these systems.''

''I think that would prevent problems and keep both of us from building a new bureaucracy, of which we need no more.''

"Let's go to lunch," said Al. "I promised Sam he could catch his plane this afternoon."

"Good," said Jim, rising. "I asked a couple other people to join us. If you don't mind, Sam, tell that clothing story again. It is a good way to help them get the idea that we are cooperating rather than regulating."

"Oh, I've got a better one than that," said Sam, laughing. "Let's go."

Someone working in the bowels of an organization may think of suppliers as being those trucks backed up to the unloading dock. Often it is possible to omit the supplier equation completely from our job. Certainly computer paper, pens, electricity, and other components of our work come from outside sources. But we do not deal with them; there is a department somewhere that does it all. One could get to thinking that one does not have any real suppliers.

Yet where does the information we process come from? Who makes up the invoices we are mailing? Who provides the telephone listing we use as reference? Who creates the software that runs the computer? Who stocks the shelves with more shoes so I do not run out? Who creates my paycheck? Suppliers are all around us—people who work for the company, people who may sit at the next desk. We have an obligation to seek them out and make certain they understand exactly what we need from them. Then we have to help them eliminate roadblocks that keep them from doing just that.

Everyone in the world is a customer (a potential one, anyway) or a supplier. That does not necessarily make them tax deductible, but it is the beginning of a relationship.

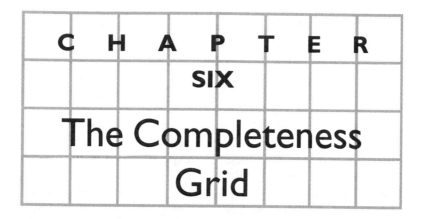

CHAPTER
SIX
The Completeness Grid

Discussing different management styles becomes a bit easier when systems can be compared with each other. For that reason I have included a grid to help put things in perspective. Actually, it is only a courtesy to refer to management styles as systems; what really goes on is an extension of the personality of the dominant individual. It is hard to tell the difference in the way places work unless we know what actually goes on inside. Those viewing from a private box, such as the board of directors usually occupies, often cannot tell the difference between the useful and the disastrous. You have to be there, as they say. For example, the goals chosen by all the management styles can come out sounding about the same—something along the lines of the following:

- Increase earnings and revenues each year
- Have the best quality in our business sector
- Develop people to their maximum
- Create and market new products or services each year

It is hard to quarrel with such stated objectives; any management team aspiring to meet them could surely be considered as candidates for the "best managed" award. However, goals (even those that are not easily measured, like the last three) are one thing; the way you go about achieving them is quite another. There is nothing in that list about ethics, respect, concern, or a hundred other aspects that affect the managerial climate. One major league baseball team used to increase its revenues each year by selling off the current star, thus routinely finishing last in performance and first in finance. A large company I know, with a reputation for innovation, picks up a product or two each year by snatching it from some unwary developer. I had the honor once of being one of their involuntary contributors. Many employee "development" programs are designed to keep employees working in lower-level pay grades, while expecting higher-rating work from them. And quality is the easiest of all "measurements" to rationalize, since few companies are willing to measure it financially; they much prefer subjective evaluation.

The "system" of management that is applied to a company determines its long range success probability. Dictatorships (political or corporate) crumble inevitably, for instance, if only because no number two authority figure is ever permitted to emerge in such an environment. Paternal and forgiving cultures crumble just as certainly, although for different reasons. Lethargy and fear produce the same result, which is that people lose interest in what is happening. They become self-focused, either in hopes of surviving or of attaining even more benefits.

Companies have climates just as geographical regions do, but the characteristics of the corporate climate are policy, requirements, education, measurement, and purpose. They represent the choice of freedom, repression, excitement, depression, and other qualities resulting from the relationships between the leaders and the led. The grid is intended to help us in determining our location in this regard.

Five different climate-establishing systems are listed, all selected with an author's liberty, of course. They relate to the kind of internal world where making the employees and the customers successful is or is not the primary objective. The purpose of this quick review is to help the reader determine what sort of managerial environment dominates his or her own work and/or family life, and to provide a framework for the issues discussed in the rest of the book.

"THIRD REICH"

Not all dictators can be easily identified as the leader in the center of a group of uniformed attendants watching thundering armies pass by with waving banners. Some of these despots wear aprons, or three-piece suits, but they all share one identifying characteristic: insisting on total power. They alone get to decide who is going to do what, and they alone are the judges of how well things get done. They use intimidation, a lack of conscience, and naked power to get what they want. Absolutely nothing gets done unless they have blessed it. They create a difficult workplace yet continually state that they wish others would do something so they could step back from their daily toil.

MANAGEMENT SYSTEMS GRID

	Third Reich	Banana Republic	Constitutional Monarchy	American Republic	21st-Century Completeness
Organizational Policy	The Boss makes it up each day	Might makes right	Rule by the elite	The balance of power	Consent of the governed
Requirements Definition	The Boss announces it each day	No one knows for sure	Governed by agreements of leadership	Described in depth	Clear description
Education	Teaching people to serve the organization	Not much of a concern	Available by class	Available to all as capable	Everyone keeps learning
Performance Measurement	What makes the Boss happy	Stay useful and alive	Those who serve well	Meet requirements	Climate of consideration
Purpose of Organization	To glorify the leader	To make the junta rich	To have an orderly life	To keep people free	To make citizens successful

© Copyright, Philip B. Crosby, 1991.

Policy. Forget it. Policy is made every day, and those involved better be sensitive to the changes. There is no long and thoughtful process, just whatever the boss feels at that moment. Yesterday's priority item can today be considered a wasteful and disobedient effort with one twitch of the eyebrow. Practices formerly held to be vital and absolute suddenly become crimes against the company, family, or state. Those living in such an environment concentrate all their efforts on determining the latest policy swing.

Requirements. No memory exists of those that used to be applicable. Everyone has to wait until the new word comes down. Inconsistency is the only consistent thing around. The leader often has obscure personal objectives, but does not reveal these. He or she may eliminate an entire function or organization just because the head of that operation is becoming too visible. Customers are expected to have their requirements defined for them and are abused if they fail to appreciate this.

Education. Certainly we need to train people to serve the organization. The leader will decide what schools they will attend and how they will be indoctrinated (rather than educated). They learn how to act, not how to reason. In families this control is absolute from the beginning; in nations it takes a little longer. The latter cases require the extermination of conventional education first.

Performance measurement. Glorification of the leader to the exclusion of all else. Careful attention is paid to make certain that no negative words or attitudes exist. The leader takes quick and dramatic action to discipline those who do not show the proper adoration.

Purpose of the organization. To carry out the mission of the leader, who may be the only one who knows it.

Prognosis. Destruction is inevitable as individuals are robbed of their ability to think and act on their own. Just as those who abuse their children come from abusing families, so it is with the citizens of a "Third Reich" type organization. Relationships will never get better.

"BANANA REPUBLIC"

The main characteristic of this management system is a concentration on control and privilege. There is no thought of assuring the organization's growth or building respect in the minds of the populace. No one is safe who shows any signs of being a problem to the leadership. The governing group is concerned with building their own fortunes, and in generating a secure base. In business they create private prerequisites, bonuses, and cash flows; in the family they deprive others of their share; in government they loot the treasury without concern.

Policy. Whatever the junta agrees on, at least until an overpowering boss emerges. Then policy becomes whatever is spoken by the boss at that moment.

Requirements. No thought of writing or publishing anything; therefore, people have to make them up as they go along. Customs develop, most of which are defensive in nature.

Education. Children must be taught to learn enough to become good soldiers and workers; higher education is unnecessary. Those with advanced degrees or professional status must be eliminated.

Performance measurement. Blind obedience is a good place to start. Those who show ambition of any sort are viewed very suspiciously, and are considered to be plotting against the leadership.

Purpose of organization. To control and loot.

Prognosis. Will be overthrown, usually by those concerned that they are not receiving their share.

"CONSTITUTIONAL MONARCHY"

One of the oldest forms of stable government is to appoint a ruler and then limit the power that can be exercised. Families do this all the time; the ruler supplies a constant presence, and the parliamentary body determines what is going to happen or not happen.

Policy. Created by an elite portion of the populace who usually have the favor of the ruler. While the ruler may not have the right to make policy directly, it certainly comes under the influence of that personage because of his or her influence with the public. The ruler provides stability, while elected leaders come and go. In the family, for example, great grandma is consulted when a determination is to be made.

Requirements. These same members of the elite, although often differing on what requirements are needed, issue them reaching a compromise. Usually these reflect policies that everyone accepts, but at the same time considers not aggressive enough. The requirements are rarely innovative, but they are useful. Often there actually is no written constitution in a "constitutional monarchy."

Education. By being classified at birth people often know what level of education they will be able to receive. People are aimed at certain careers early in life whether they like it or not. In corporations the education obtained before being hired often preordains the career levels that will be gained in an organization. Very little is offered by the company.

Performance measurement. Those who fall out of line with these requirements and customs are dealt with in many ways, although usually not physically. They may be denied something having to do with their place, or be sent off to a less desirable life.

Purpose of organization. To provide all with an orderly and safe life by keeping any really detrimental way of government from emerging.

Prognosis. Lasts a long time, but the limited input to policy and requirements keeps the organization from growing beyond a certain level. Life for the people sort of averages out, with hardly anyone living lavishly and very few living poorly. Generates a lot of quiet infighting over privilege and progress.

"AMERICAN REPUBLIC"

This form of government provides maximum freedom to the citizenry but also permits unusual power to special interests who have the capability of influencing leadership. Bosses are chosen by, and thus required to listen to, the electors, which keeps them attentive. Bosses can be removed easily, unlike the previous three systems.

Policy. Made by elected officials in accordance with the desires of those who voted for them. Unfortunately many policies are not well thought out and do not produce their desired effect. However, overall, the system works because of the balance of powers inherent in the structure.

Requirements. Laws and other government or company documents describe requirements in great depth. Changes are orderly.

Education. Available to all who want it, with no consideration as to class or social status. However, the worth of it varies from place to place depending on local mores and politics.

Performance measurement. Conformance to requirements is considered important. Public image establishes the perceived worth of the individual.

Purpose of organization. Freedom of the individual and the market combined with protection from outside forces.

Prognosis. Since the citizens want the organization to prosper they will make it do so. However, special interest at all levels can run the system off the track. This is not only true of corporate or political efforts but also of splinter groups who want to deny the majority their rights. As Winston Churchill said of democracy, it is the worst system except for all the others.

"TWENTY-FIRST-CENTURY COMPLETENESS"

Modern communication systems will let the management know and understand the will of the people. For that reason misunderstandings will be avoided, special interest groups will be easily identified, measurement will be obvious, and things will be well thought out. The idea will be to plan and create something so well that it immediately becomes effective.

Policy. Made by the leadership with the consent of the governed.

Requirements. Provided in a way that makes them understood by all.

Education. Everyone keeps learning due to the availability of material and freedom of choice.

Performance measurement. A culture of consideration.

Purpose of organization. To help individuals be successful in every aspect of their lives.

Prognosis. Should prosper forever as long as its citizens do not become complacent and by doing so ignite the ambitions of those who would turn it into a Third Reich.

You might think that once we find ourselves living in one particular management style we are stuck there forever. While a complete dictatorship might force us to tunnel our way out in real life, business systems can be slunk away from. Some of my colleagues have even managed to get themselves fired from unpleasant situations, walking away with cash payments for agreeing to keep quiet. They are the fortunate ones.

Most people in difficult work situations are not able to get out without a great deal of cost to pride and pocketbook. These are folks without options. I would like to relate some of the experiences I have personally had or witnessed in this regard. All of the names have been changed to protect the guilty. My career in business has been a long one and covered a great many jobs from the bottom up. There is not much I have not seen or been around, in places all over the world. It has been a great learning opportunity. I have met some wonderful people as well as some complete jerks; I have learned that most management cannot tell the difference between the two. But I must say that, if I had not needed to work, I would have been just as happy to spend my time writing and teaching instead of going to all those meetings, plants, and offices.

My first exposure to the Third Reich form of government came when I was assigned to an off-site hospital run by the military for the military. After being recalled to the Navy for the Korean War as a Hospitalman third class, I went to the Norfolk Naval Base for orientation, testing, and all the things that go along with it. Between wars I had graduated from college and was eligible to become an officer, which would have required agreeing to stay in for five years, rather than for the fourteen months left in my reserve enlistment.

"We have all the results of your tests, Phil," said the Lieutenant, "and realize that you do not want to apply for a commission. We would like to make you a Chief Petty Officer and have you teach in the Hospital Corps School here in Norfolk."

"You can have base housing, and bring your wife down," said the Ensign. "Would you like to do that? We realize that you have been ordered to the Second Marines, but that can be changed."

I happily agreed and went back to the barracks, where the Master at Arms told me that my orders had arrived and I was to be on the bus to Camp Lejeune, North Carolina, that evening. I explained how I was going to be a Chief Petty Officer, teach at the Corps school, and live on the base. He said if I wasn't on the bus when it left they would probably shoot me. I dashed back to the office only to find that the officers were gone, and the place was empty. I left them a note, packed, and caught the bus. It has been almost forty years, and I still have not heard from those people.

After Marine field training I was assigned to the regiment and spent a few months in exercises invading North Carolina and Puerto Rico. Living the life of a Marine in the woods and on the beaches is not the worst thing that can happen to a person. It is not the best either. The Marines are a good outfit in which the officers experience the same conditions as the troops and people take care of each other. I enjoyed it, at least until I was transferred to the offsite medical unit. Most of the regiment went to Korea, but I didn't have enough time left to complete a tour properly, so the group decided to send me to the place where cooks, bakers, and mechanics were trained. I would work in sick bay over there for the next several months until I was released.

"Would it be possible to take a week's leave?" I asked the administrative officer. "I'd like to bring my wife down for the last part of my stay, particularly since I won't be shipping out."

"No problem," he said. "I'll just make the orders so your time at Point Montford begins with your return from leave." I packed up my gear and sent it over to the new place, hopped in the car and headed for Pennsylvania, driving all night, as was the custom. When I arrived at my in-laws' home there was an urgent message for me to call the base. I dialed the unfamiliar number and reported in.

"You're supposed to be over here this morning," said the voice. "What the @#$@#$&% are you doing in Pittsburgh?"

"I'm on leave for a week," I answered. "Who is this?"

"This is Chief Warrant Officer Tracey, your direct superior who is about to put you on report. Now you get back here by tomorrow morning, or it is going to cost you a stripe and maybe a few days in the brig."

He hung up.

I called the administrative officer who had authorized my leave and asked for his help. He said he would see what he could do, but that Tracey ran his own show over there, and I might as well see if I couldn't get back. I questioned the integrity of his operation, but he was obviously more concerned about Tracey than me and wasn't even insulted by my inferences. So we packed up and drove back to New Bern, North Carolina, and I went on down to Camp Lejeune, reporting in to the installation. Tracey, I learned, had gone off on a trip for a couple of days and had left word to let him know if I didn't show up. I immediately went back to my original base, obtained copies of my leave papers, and returned to New Bern to help move into the little apartment I had rented.

Tracey was not impressed by my orders and laid out to me the rules and regulations of the station. Essentially this was that he ran the place, we did what he said, and that was the end of it. Also we were to purchase any capital items, such as tires, from him. If you can imagine Sgt. Bilko crossed with a Mafia Don, that was Tracey. He made my life miserable for six months, and there was nothing to do about it. The place did not exist for the patients, the Navy, the Marine Corps, or the nation. It only existed for Tracey. The brass thought he was wonderful, he passed every inspection with honors, he did not cause them a bit of trouble, and he could lay his hands on anything they wanted. He had contacts everywhere and used them to the maximum. With one telephone call he could have you transferred, demoted, and probably hung. He was absolute master of the operation, ruling by terror and intimidation. His hold on me was to deny me the ability to go home to New Bern, forty-five minutes away, anytime I was "difficult." When I finally was released from my service commitment I carried my gear out to the car and packed it away. Tracey offered his hand, and I just stared at him.

"I've never told you that my brother-in-law is being appointed special assistant to the Secretary of the Navy next month," I lied. "I am going to make absolutely certain he knows every detail of the job you are doing here." Tracey beamed in anticipation, and for the first time I realized that he had no idea of the kind of operation he was running. He didn't realize how difficult life was for those who worked there. He thought that if his bosses were happy that must be all there was to it. That is a typical pattern of the Third Reich system.

Since that time I have always checked out the person who was to be my supervisor in any position, before agreeing to go there. Four other Traceys have crossed my path. One was the chief operating officer of a large corporation I was about to join. A lunch with him wiped that potential relationship out completely. He exhibited a clear Tracey-like sign right off the bat by verbally abusing all the dining room employees he met. Once the Centurion is able to identify a Tracey, it's important to make absolutely certain not to let anyone work for that person. It is much the same as keeping a child molester away from children.

Banana Republic companies are easy to identify—they are the ones where no one you meet is in charge of anything, and hardly anything gets done without the boss's personal participation. There are no systems and very little direction. Actually most of the Savings and Loan organizations that fell apart were typical BRs. Decisions were made based on the waves of the moment, and the desires of the management, rather than on facts. People were loaned money only because of what they could do, or had done, for that management. My favorite example was the one in which the bank loaned a developer the money needed for the next four years, plus the interest that would have to be paid, and then took the four years of interest payments (which had not been given back yet) as profit. Many Latin American dictators probably shook their heads in admiration at that ploy. For details of Banana Republic banks in action read Martin Mayer's book, *The Greatest Ever Bank Robbery*.

Constitutional Monarchies are found throughout the corporate world—in the U.S., Europe, and the Far East. They are characterized by the reign of a single person who amasses a large staff to carry out agreed plans. Like Britain, where the King or Queen has only a ceremonial role, in these organizations the master is sort of above the fray. As in Britain there is a carefully crafted aristocracy that runs the place. My first real exposure to this was found when I joined ITT's corporate operation and was introduced to Mr. Geneen's concept of management. Simply put, it was to know everything so that decisions could be based on reality rather than impulse. Knowing everything meant gathering information relentlessly and having resident experts from every field who could translate it into something we could all understand and take action on. There was a series of planned meetings in order to make certain everything was considered.

In the early part of the year financial projections for the next several years were developed. The product line managers ran these sessions and made it possible to know what every number in the area of revenues, inventory, profits, personnel, accounts receivable, and such would be. They mounted guard over the meetings and the resulting data.

Functional groups, such as Marketing, laid out their plans for the upcoming several years based on the projections determined in financial planning. The operating units then had the obligation of developing business plans to show how all these goals would be met during a five-year period. The result of this planning was a large notebook, sometimes two of them, containing the exact actions necessary. Everyone who was anyone received a copy of this book in midyear, to study in preparation for the business plan meetings.

Business plan meetings were held throughout the fall in New York and Brussels. The management of each unit would come to headquarters to present their plan and suffer questioning from the staffs and, of course, the senior executives. All of these were conducted very formally and taken quite seriously. The planning department kept close control on everything, from who sat where to who got what information.

After all the plans were agreed upon, the headquarters staffs were responsible for seeing that the units performed. To do this they required that each unit send in a weekly telex listing in an agreed format the status of its operation. They held onsite operations reviews and immediately pounced on any transgression. The culmination of all this was the monthly meeting schedule that reviewed status. Each unit manager sent a letter to the chairman, and the planning department then compiled them into sets of two books each, which were distributed to the senior people. The books were meant to be read and the boss did just that. A three-day meeting in New York, followed by a one-week session in Brussels, brought the participants and the information together. I always felt it to be a sort of House of Commons layout, only more polite. It was hard to get a lot of work done if one actually went to all the meetings required.

The atmosphere of all this was positive and for the most part nonpolitical. Management treated their people well, but it was clear who was and was not aristocracy. The system was effective for controlling the many products and services produced by the corporation. It did make both growing and innovating a little difficult since a consensus was required on most things. Mr.

Geneen was a strong leader who also made a point of listening. He wanted everyone to be part of the whole, although it would have been quite easy and acceptable for him to make all the decisions on his own. In most cases he reigned, but once in a while he would insist on something he wanted. He was never around when heads were removed.

It was a good place to work and to learn. Succeeding ITT management dismantled the system, along with the staff, as the world of business changed. This may have produced some advantages but it couldn't be nearly as interesting as watching people squirm their way through all those meetings.

When Philip Crosby Associates, Inc. (PCA) began, I intended to avoid the three types of situations just described and try to have an "American Republic." All of them require a domineering leader who, one way or another, tends to smother personal development. All of them require constant indecision on the part of management in order to keep people off balance. I wanted everyone to know what was happening and to have the opportunity to speak up. Much of this strategy was described in an earlier book, *Running Things*, so I won't lay it all out here. It is enough to say that the result of managing this way was to produce an organization of people who liked each other, who routinely did things right the first time, and who generated a great deal of revenue per employee. The customers appreciated them also.

To date I have not seen a company that would qualify as a Completeness organization, and I suspect that it will require a twenty-first-century environment to develop one. Very few executives have enough self-confidence to let that happen.

Look up your organization on the grid and see where you stand. When I was a caddy I learned to always look for a ball about fifteen yards short of where the golfer thought it had been hit. Use the grid with this in mind.

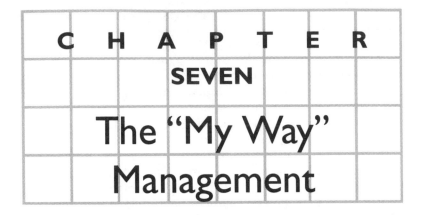

CHAPTER SEVEN

The "My Way" Management

" **A** rrogance" is not a nice word; it produces a negative reaction. Yet it is exactly the word to describe the behavior of many executives and managers worldwide. These are leaders who have to do everything their way for their benefit. These are the ones who drive everyone to distraction, whether they are running a baseball team or an investment firm.

I have been trying—so far, without success—to think of a business failure that was *not* caused by the specific arrogance of an individual or the cultural arrogance of a group. If you read business magazines or even newspapers regularly, you've seen many such folks in action. They overexpand; they try to force their customers to obey; they consider themselves to be above the system. When people will not listen to others, when they are in love with their own knowledge, when they abuse power, they are arrogant. Such people make life miserable for those beneath them, and they disappoint those who deal with them. They ruin companies; they take first-place teams and drag them into last.

Often the arrogant are difficult to recognize at first because they do not exhibit this behavior to those who are important to them. It is only when they feel the need to intimidate that their true character emerges. In the process they are difficult and disrespectful. They may never yell, pound tables or scream, they may be smooth and cultured, they may not even use foul language, but they're just holding their anger inside. They think only of themselves and their own goals. They know that they need others, but no one is ever good enough for them—at least not for long.

There are no programs, systems, or even business philosophies that will make much of a dent in these people. We just need to deprive them of the ability to control. When Hitler was appointed Chancellor he organized an election to give his party legitimacy. Before the voting began the Nazis killed, or otherwise dismantled, all the other parties and politicians. Then they won the vote and did exactly as they wished until there was nothing left to govern. Arrogant executives, using junk bonds instead of tanks, did the same thing to many corporations in the 1980s. They were permitted to do so by those who should have known better because it all looked as though it would turn out to be for everyone's benefit. The opportunity to make such expensive and destructive mistakes is going to be much greater in the coming century because of the speed of communications and the intensity of competition.

But my concern with arrogance is not concentrated on the megabomb individuals and groups alone. I worry about the regular managers and executives in all areas because the effect they can have on people is out of proportion to their importance. The difference in whether people enjoy their jobs or cringe when it is time to go to work lies in the way they are treated. Arrogant managers or management teams make life miserable for people without good reason. They just have such little respect for others—and, it seems to me, themselves—that they need to do this. They deliberately change their minds so often that their subordinates cannot lay down solid plans, giving them yet another thing to criticize. It is destructive behavior, and it generates a high turnover rate and reduces the probability that really good people will ever join the organization. Executives in particular have to help each other guard against such attitudes. I like to require one hundred percent agreement on policies and decisions by the executive committee in order to avoid these kinds of excesses.

As a chief executive I went to great lengths to make certain I did not fall into this trap. When you are the founder and the creator of most of the organization's products, it is easy to begin to assume omnipotence. People will let you be right all the time if you insist, even if you are not. For this reason senior executives, particularly CEOs, have to be like professional athletes and learn when it is time to step down. Going out when everyone loves you and wants you to stay is much better than seeing the organization leave you.

I can remember the day when I decided to take the succession plan seriously. There was a discussion in the executive committee about expansion, and plans were laid out for an office in Singapore. I immediately became less than enthusiastic. While pouring out reasons, I realized, in the back of my mind, that I just did not want to look forward to regular 20-hour sessions on an airplane. The rest of the committee caved in right away, but started up again in a few weeks when I made it clear that I would not be in authority by the time Singapore could be established.

As I was writing this chapter, I had the sudden feeling that I was being watched. Looking up from my word processor I saw a portly figure standing there, arms akimbo, as they used to say. He was dressed in a business suit, blue, jacket open, cigarette in one hand and clipboard in the other. He waved the cigarette at me.

"I think you are all wrong about this 'incomplete boss' thing," he snarled. "I do a lot of announcing, and once in a while I yell, and a strong word or two comes out regularly, but that is the only language these people understand. And I do not consider myself to be incomplete in any fashion."

"Huh?" I replied creatively.

"You heard me," he insisted. "Not everything out there is peaches and cream like you write about. Everyone is so reasonable and positive in your books, it's sickening. Why don't you get out into the real world and see what it is like? Our company would fall apart in a month if I ever did all that stuff."

"I thought I lived in the real world," I stated lamely.

"All you see is the good stuff. When you go anywhere they are all polite, and they pretend to listen to everything you say. They pretend to listen to me, too, but I drag the information out of them."

"What would you suggest?" I asked. "How do I get acquainted with your version of the real world?"

"Come spend a few hours in my office, and then we'll meet with some of my people. You can find out for yourself. I want you to hear about our Atlanta office, which is doing great. Well, are you coming or not?" he growled.

I leaped from my chair. Fantasy is one thing writers can deal with.

Suddenly we were standing in the reception room of his office. A young lady wearing an attractive suit and an earnest expression approached us with a clipboard in her hand. They traded boards.

"Your ten o'clock meeting with the planning committee is ready in the conference room, Mr. Wills," she said. "They are all in there now."

Wills harrumphed and lifted the board to his reading range, glancing at the names. "They can wait awhile. Most of them don't have to be there anyway," he said. "This is Mr. Crosby, Heather. He writes fiction books."

We shook hands and Heather smiled at me. Wills brushed past her abruptly, and we went into his office. As I gingerly sat down on the couch, he shuffled a few papers around on his desk. The room was elegantly furnished and very large by anyone's standards. However, there did not seem to be anything very personal—no photos, no awards, no debris.

"Are you always mad?" I asked.

His face got red—redder, actually. "Mad? I'm not mad, I'm never mad. In fact, I am in a good mood today. You can't let people think you are easy. They'll take advantage of you if you let them. Remember, this is the real world."

He picked another clipboard off his desk and walked over to the table area, sitting down heavily across from me on a chair. He lit a cigarette and gestured with the board. "This room is the last place in the building, except for the executive dining room, where you can smoke. One of our employees sued the company on smoking in the workplace and won. I don't need to tell you that he is no longer with us. But that is the way it is today. They don't have any respect for management. Take this planning meeting. I don't know what the agenda is, it isn't on the schedule here, but the last time we met they had a proposal to issue policy manuals and set up a procedure control group. It's crap like that keeps overhead up."

"But if a company doesn't do some systems integrity things like that, how are they going to know who is responsible for what and how things are to be done?" I protested.

"Sure, you make a good living putting out that stuff, and guys like me, here in the trenches, have to keep tossing water on it. Hell, before long we won't have anyone working, just people doing paper things. Well, let's go to this so-called planning meeting and after that we can drive over to the catalog office. You'll like that better than the Atlanta office. I think I am going to close that down anyway, it doesn't do worth a damn.''

"But you said it was doing great," I whined.

"It's never going to amount to anything—that's plain now. But don't say anything about it during this meeting."

"My lips are sealed," I assured him. "Besides, you may change your mind again, later."

He scowled and we went down the hall. When we entered the room, everyone stood up until Wills had taken his seat at the head of the table. As they sat down I noticed that each person had a clipboard lying in front of them. The attendee nearest me looked me over and asked if I was who she thought I was. I nodded, and we shook hands as we laughed about it. Wills didn't think it was funny.

"Crosby is here taking a break from his work to look at reality," he said. "After this very short meeting, he and I are going over to the catalog operation, and that will be short, too. Who has the items for discussion? I have searched my board from top to bottom and can't find an agenda. I thought I had made it clear that every meeting had to have an agenda issued in advance of the meeting."

There was an embarrassed silence. Then one of the attendees passed a sheet over to Wills. "The agenda was sent out several days ago, Mr. Wills. I got your copy back with a comment on it to take the procedure discussion off the menu. Anyway, the first item concerns facilities for the new educational programs. Jon Smathers has the report."

"Facilities for the educational programs?" said Wills. "Do we always need something brand new? Why can't we use some of the space we already have?"

Smathers laid some material on the projections machine. "You had directed that we use existing space, Mr. Wills, and that is what we have done. The projection here is of the Riverview building, which currently holds some of the catalog inventory. Their new program of having suppliers drop-ship to customers will make it available. Here is the calculation of how much it will cost to make it into classrooms."

He laid another viewgraph which showed the cost of transformation and maintenance. Wills grimaced. "That drop-ship stuff is a pipe dream. Those vendors are unreliable, and there is no way to control them except by spending an arm and a leg for a new computer system. That expenditure on top of what you people want will bankrupt the company. The analysts will kill us.

"What do you plan to teach in that building?"

"It is all laid out in the proposal," said Smathers, "but I will be glad to give you an outline now."

"If you can't explain it in a few words, you obviously don't understand it, Smathers," said Wills. "Is there anyone here who can tell me what we are going to do in this new and very expensive program? Also, I'd like to know what the bottom line is going to get out of it. That's what we live for, you know, although it seems to me that I am going to have to have it tattooed on your foreheads."

He gazed around the table. One person cleared her throat after a moment. "The program covers what is accepted as standard in most companies now, Mr. Wills: employee orientation, executive and managerial competence in making customers successful, training on Completeness for knowledge and skilled workers, and various special subjects. Everyone in the company will be required to attend classes regularly. We will use our own instructors who have been trained by the Crosby people. All of the material, except some that is special to our company, came from that source. When you brought him in today, we thought you knew all about it. Otherwise, we would have explained it all up front."

"I'm trying to straighten him out, not get him more business," growled Wills. "How much does it cost and what do we get out of it? That's all I want to know. Can you tell me?"

She nodded. "It will cost us about $200 per employee per year; the projections and the experience of other companies show that we can plan on reducing waste by one-third in the first year. That would have the effect of increasing pre-tax profit by $16,000 per employee. It sounds like a marvelous return on investment. Also, we will have a company that will be a lot easier to manage."

Wills stared at her. "I've heard that song before," he said. "But go ahead with it, and I'll hold you responsible for that profit increase. That is the end of this meeting."

He got up and walked out. I followed, shaking hands with most of the attendees on the way. They did not look like a group that had just gotten their own way.

"What do you all do with these clipboards?" I asked, not able to help myself.

There was a sigh. "They are to remind management that time is precious. Also, we fill out time slips on everything we do and turn them in to Heather. When they start paying attention, we will get rid of them."

"That went out in the 1950s," I noted.

"Tell me about it," said Smathers.

Heather materialized at my elbow and escorted me back to Wills' office, where he was standing impatiently, ready to go on to the next phase.

"See, I'm not such a big bad wolf as you make out," he said. "They got the program they wanted, and we are going to spend the shareholders' money on a building so they can all entertain themselves doing the programs you invent."

I shook my head and motioned him to a seat. "Does it occur to you," I asked, "that although they did indeed get permission to do something the company needs in order to keep it ahead of the competition, that they have no satisfaction in the matter? They are all ticked off at this moment. You have accepted their proposal and irritated them at the same time. I would be surprised if many of them stay around to do the program.

"You could have had exactly the same result, treated everyone like mature adults, and sent them out eager to do the job. I can't tell if your attitude is some sort of strategy of intimidation or if it is that you just don't know any better. Is there any particular reason that you make so much trouble for yourself?"

Wills jumped to his feet, red all over.

"Who do you think you are, coming in here and questioning the way I run this company? I am the CEO here, and this company has had record growth since I took over. These wimps of mine would spend us out of business if I let them. I just keep control, I don't intimidate anyone. Business is like football, no place for sissies—it is all hand-to-hand combat."

He paced the floor in an effort to calm himself.

"You'd better watch your blood pressure," I said. "Heavy people have a tendency for it to rise when they get excited. You are younger than I am, so you have a chance to learn how to stay well."

" 'Wellness,' " he muttered. "That is another one of those code words. I know that you think it refers to prevention and proper management and all that. But I don't buy it. My way is to have a very effective emergency room. You get sick—we find out, we fix you. I have a special SWAT team that continually analyzes if something is wrong and then takes care of the hurting operation immediately. They don't even have to ask. Right now they are in the catalog division. You will get to see them in action."

" 'SWAT'?" I asked.

"Special Workout Acceleration Team." He smiled. "I created the name myself. I thought it would let people relate to the police SWAT teams, everyone knows about them."

"Fascinating," I replied, not meaning it. "They can move into any operation they want where they feel control is being lost or efficiency is being compromised? That sounds like a Gestapo sort of concept."

As we walked to the door, the ever-present Heather handed him a new clipboard and some telephone messages.

"Tell me about the calls as we walk, Heather," he said.

"There are ten of them, eight from various operational locations asking for specific direction on one subject or another."

He nodded. "I'll call them from home tonight after dinner. They pester me with the smallest detail that they should be able to handle themselves." He shook his head at their helplessness.

"How do they know you are interested in those details?" I wondered aloud, although I already knew.

"I read their weekly reports and communicate through them to ask questions now and then, that's all."

"Don't you have senior people in charge of those areas?" I asked. "Why don't you ask them the questions?"

"They never tell you the truth, and most times they don't even know the truth. I find out a lot of things they don't know about. What else, girl?"

He turned to the blushing Heather.

"Your granddaughter wanted to know if you are going to be able to come to her piano recital tonight at six p.m."

"Wouldn't miss it. Send her a corsage and let her know that we will be there in the first row."

Elston Smith, head of the catalog operations, greeted us in front of the building and seated us in the backseat of his car.

"How are things going at Catalog, Elston?" asked Wills, winking at me. "I understand the SWAT team took over three or four of your departments. How are they doing?"

Elston winced, and his neck turned bright red. "Everything is pretty much of a mess right now, Mr. Wills," he said. "The order input has been backlogged for the last ten days. You know that we promise the customers they will receive their order within two days of the time we get their input. Actually, we had been doing it the next day. But now the whole thing is jammed up."

Wills sat forward on the seat.

"Better get the SWAT people onto that right away; your people obviously can't handle it," he sputtered.

"They are in there, Mr. Wills," Elston noted, "that is why nothing can get out. They are going over each order one at a time, manually; they have shut off the computer. Everything comes in, nothing goes out."

Silence fell on the car.

I asked Wills, "How do you deal with functional areas like human resources, administration, and facilities? I assume you have departments to handle that?"

"Only reluctantly. We have to have some of that because we do have several thousand people. But I keep them lean, they are always complaining about not having enough staff. Our turnover is considered high by everyone but me, but I tell them to use headhunters when recruiting. That way we don't build up any more noncontributors."

"You consider those areas to be noncontributors? Is that because they don't make sales?" I wondered.

"Exactly. The real people in our company are those out there with the customers, like Smith's people. I see very little value in other functions. I keep them off the bonus rolls, too."

I took a sheet of paper from my pocket. "Since all of this is in my imagination," I noted, "I have the financial results presented at your last board meeting. Revenues are rising but profits are declining. The internal waste is going up every year, turn-over is eating the company up, and customers are dropping out because of the continual conflict the company gives them. That is from the audit firm's report.''

He waved it aside, contemptuously. "Crap, all crap," Wills said. "One of the investment firms brought that up at the ana-lysts' meeting the next day. I don't know where they got it—there is a leak somewhere in our management group."

"And what did you tell them?" I asked.

"That is was none of their business. I don't know why they consider it an important measurement. I told them that if they don't like the way I run the company, they should sell their stock."

"According to this other sheet, they did. And in fact, the stock price is the lowest it has been for several years."

"I get out here," said Smith, bringing the car to a stop. "I don't want to go back and watch my catalog operation be com-pletely destroyed, so I am going to work for the Overland Com-pany. This is their building. You can drive yourself the rest of the way, Mr. Wills. This is a company car."

Smith got out, saluted us, and walked into the building. I patted Wills on the arm, smiled at him, and then got out myself.

"Hey, Elston," I said, "wait for me."

The Centurion will be too busy surviving and growing to tol-erate the waste that comes from arrogance. It is extremely ex-pensive and destructive, and it takes no prisoners. It is also preventable. No one can be permitted to become all powerful. The organization should not develop different levels of treat-ment. Everyone should fly the same class, have appropriately sized offices, get paid for what they actually do, and have the same opportunity to be successful.

In the case of a public company, the board of directors has a duty, which they rarely observe, to watch for arrogance on the part of management. It is not necessary to require complete humility, but it doesn't hurt to have a little. In every case where power was abused that I knew about personally, the board knew about it but did nothing. They apparently did not feel they could raise the question and still keep their seats. Why they would want to keep them under those circumstances is beyond me. But we must be clear that there is little the employees can do about it. Customers can leave, and do; suppliers can often leave, and do; employees can only leave, or do as little as possible, so as to keep out of trouble.

Managerial arrogance is the tragedy of an open business society. With the exception of those who were born to the job, senior executives usually arrive at their positions through merit and hard work. But as Lord Acton said: "Power corrupts, and absolute power corrupts absolutely." In Western management organizations particularly, the CEO gets to do what the CEO wants, and the perks pile up. Other executives join in and soon everything seems justified. The whole package becomes irresistible and at the same time impossible to kick. All drugs do not come in little vials.

The signs of arrogance are not subtle:

1. The boss dominates all meetings.
2. The boss is usually late.
3. The boss is out of touch.
4. The boss has different rules from everyone else.
5. The boss rejects those who do not agree continually.

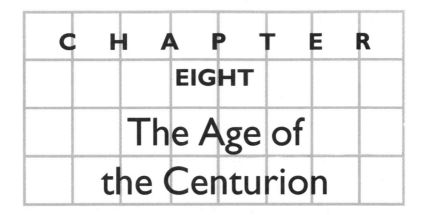

CHAPTER
EIGHT
The Age of the Centurion

Executives of the twenty-first century are going to have to be smarter and more thorough about dealing with the real world than their twentieth-century counterparts. There will be less room to wiggle out of poorly conceived and ill-planned situations. Proposals and plans will have to be based on candor. Employees, customers, and suppliers will be less tolerant of incompleteness. They will expect professional, ego-free leadership. This will require a different type of person, the Centurion, who will have the opportunity to help shape the most dynamic and successful time in the world's history.

In the current age, the executives who have won the recognition of their superiors, of the media, and of the business philosophers are those whose primary management characteristic is being resourceful. This means that the person can indeed spin silk scarfs when presented with the ears of swine. By being knowledgeable, energetic, brave, and relentless, the executive snatches victory from the jaws of defeat on a regular basis. Many of those I have known also made a significant contribution to placing the situation into those jaws in the first place. But that is the kind of leader companies have wanted: someone with solutions, and action. Their time is past.

The Centurion will have to deal with the business jigsaw as a complete entity and will not be permitted to pound pieces in place with a hammer or purchase waivers that will authorize placing a size-ten foot into a size-nine shoe. The Centurion will realize that all things must be considered and worked out before the project is launched. The Centurion will realize that people are the most critical asset to success and will carefully select, encourage, and raise them. The Centurion will establish a philosophy of operating that is consistent with Completeness and human dignity. It will not vary each time a new book appears or a seminar is attended. He or she will recognize that quality is the skeleton of an organization, finance the nourishment, and relationships the soul. The Centurion will be an adult, yet will have the urge for innovation and adventure of a child. A Centurion will be fun to work for and work with. It is very important that organizations be headed by such a person if they are to survive. This is not going to be the age of consensus, but the age of the individual leader, the Centurion. Socrates, who said that democracy was not the proper system for organizations that wanted to accomplish something, will be vindicated in the business world.

During the recession of 1982, our company, of which I was chairman and chief executive, suddenly found itself in a cash crunch. At that time our primary product was conducting weeklong seminars on quality management for executives and managers. We were just beginning to develop and produce film and workshop–oriented courses for the employees of the companies sending their senior people to our Quality College. This required an expenditure of several hundred thousand dollars. As we expanded our classrooms in Winter Park to meet the demand, and began to write and film the fifteen sessions of the Quality Education System, the business world suddenly shut down.

Companies large and small placed an immediate brake on such frivolous things as education and advertising. This had an effect on PCA. Our revenues for the first half of the year were around six million dollars, but the second half was to produce less than three million. Meanwhile expenses continued. We had plenty of assets, since we owned a building and a lot where we planned to establish future operations, but we had no cash. The bank was unsympathetic and rumbled down on us. Everyone agreed to a 20 percent pay cut in order to avoid laying off people, and we cut back on everything. But we kept producing the new product. After eight agonizing months we emerged into the black again and since that time have grown to a public company with over $70 million in revenue, no debt, and worldwide operations.

I received, and continue to receive, congratulations for my

"management courage and skill" in saving the company during that period. The truth is that the company should never have been placed in such a vulnerable position. A more experienced and less involved board might have tossed me out on my ear for letting this happen. There was no need for us to spend capital on a building, for instance; we could have leased as we do now. There was no need to build classrooms ahead of the growth curve; we could have been a little rushed and crowded for a while. There was no need to add employees who would spend a year being trained to be consultants at that time; they used money without producing. It was from that experience that I began to develop the concepts of Completeness that are discussed in this book.

This is a case where a company that has served many people well almost died because its management was blinded to the real world by the assurance of success. How many others were not able to snap back and actually entered the grave? We have to manage at all times as though a recession, or a competitor, is about to devour us. We should never be fat or out on a limb. I have never met anyone who did not agree with this concept.

So why do companies lurch from peak to valley to peak? Why are they so surprised every time something happens to the market place? Who is it that does these terrible things to us? The answer is not much of a mystery. Most victims of crime or other violence know the perpetrator; the vast majority of personal assaults are the result of impulse rather than conspiracy. Family, friends, acquaintances, customers, and others are the ones who do most of the harm to us. Police officers and home owners suffer more from their own guns than from those owned by criminals. Shoplifting, or "shrinkage" as it is known, is mostly done by the employees. After all, they know where everything is. And most of the difficulties companies and other organizations have are caused by their own management. All those songs about hurting the ones we love have a basis in fact.

On the other hand, the people who do the very best things to us are also those we love. They are close to us and we trust them. They show by their actions that they respect and love us. We do well together. Yet they are no further away than those who would make our life difficult. There is no obvious physical difference between those who do us well and those who do us bad. It isn't as though one set is blue and the other gray. They all look the same to us; it is only by their actions that we know them.

Business parallels real life in this regard. Many of the executives I have worked with as well as for spent a large amount of their time terrorizing the employees of their organization. This style usually produces a negative result, which in turn infuriates the terrorizer. Of course, there are companies where the employees would die for the management. This fact makes it clear that despite all the well-developed systems and concepts of management, the reality is that almost every company is operated according to the formula formed in the mind and actions of one person. Even the consensus-driven companies of the Far East succumb to this pattern. It goes way back in history. We have worked that way up to now, from Abraham's trip out on his own, to Lee Iacocca running Chrysler.

Certainly there are always individuals who get into those jobs who are incompetent or destructive or both. That probably happens at least a third of the time. Those who are terrible leaders never seem to understand that they have that reputation. The worst executive I ever knew, bar none, asked me to help him write a book about his management style, so others could copy it. I wanted to tell him that *Mein Kampf* had already been written, but demurred. A great many people are hurt by these executives, and many previously fine companies, even industries, are destroyed through their efforts. Many of us have had the pain of working for such persons. Often we have to wait it out patiently or just go elsewhere. Either way, someone is affecting our lives in a manner we did not plan, and we will feel eternal resentment about it. Bad bosses seem to last as long as good ones—primarily because most executives concentrate on looking upward in the organization chart and do not notice the carnage being wreaked below them by their peers. Bad companies have bosses that are incomplete. They think they are without fault, and they are not interested in learning. They want to find some magic system that causes everyone else to be as smart and effective as they are. They do not discuss, they announce. For instance, they announce that the company is going to open a branch office in Atlanta without telling the executive who runs North American operations. Or they announce that Joe is going to run the office, without discussing it with Joe. They announce that the office will be in a certain building, without telling the facilities department. They announce that specific services will be conducted in that office, and they announce that the budget will be such an amount. No one knows about this until the statements are made. Then the boss becomes very upset when things do not go just right.

Unlike the Centurion, these people snarl a lot, use obscene language regularly, do not listen to anyone, and make all the decisions (and change them rapidly). Their evaluation of any individual's performance varies drastically day by day. They do not trust anyone else's opinion for long; they think that they are articulate but repeat themselves continually; they do not recognize talent when they see it; and they do not understand why their people do not love the company. They take personal advantage of the facilities, services, and funds of the company. They raise the roof over the travel expenses of others but live like royalty when they are on the road. They live a separate life from everyone else, at least as far as the rules are concerned.

This type of person does not have to be the chief executive. There are thousands of incomplete managers who have not made it to that level yet. Of all those who are in charge of us, probably four out of five are inadequate as bosses, and probably only a third of those are willing to learn how to become outstanding or even adequate. The remainder do not recognize their problems and will do nothing. An unusual number of these people become senior executives because they tend to take credit for the accomplishments of others. (These figures are my own estimates and not the result of a carefully controlled study.)

As a quality management practitioner for twenty-five years, a CEO for ten, and a lecturer/author all that while, I have met perhaps two thousand bosses at all levels. Some I worked for, some worked for me, some I advised, some I taught, some I just met. Out of all these folks there were about a dozen whom I consider outstanding bosses and leaders. And there were about a hundred whom I consider not too harmful; most of them wanted to be good at their work and were diligent about learning what it took. The rest wanted their people to become more cooperative, and the customers to be more understanding. As they saw it, the sandbox belonged to them. But in fact, the organizations would have been better off if these bosses' offices had been left empty and they had never existed; the workers would have done better if left alone with an inflated dummy in the corner office.

When I left the U.S. Navy in 1952, after being recalled for the Korean War ("join the reserves, Phil—we aren't going to have any more conflict"), the first real job I had was a junior technician working on an airborne fire-control system. All of what we were doing was beyond my experience; I had studied medicine, not electronics. But science is science, and I soon caught on to the tests we were conducting. I did not understand how electronics worked, but neither did anyone else in that area. However, I was able to recognize when I was doing something the hard way. In one procedure we would test a small electric motor as it drove a gear train. Before running it we would mount the motor on the box, safety-wire it in place, and then move it to the test bed. If the motor was defective I had to undo all that wire and replace the item. I accumulated a great many cuts and scratches on my hands. Safety wire is a true invention of the devil, as anyone who has worked with it will attest.

When the general foreman strolled by, I suggested to him that it would make more sense to test the motors before they were mounted. That way no assembly or disassembly would be required if there was a problem. Since about a third failed, I pointed out, this would save us a lot of time. His response was that I should concentrate on my own job, that we had industrial engineers who worried about that sort of thing, and that he had not asked me for advice. My direct boss gave me a lecture on the folly of speaking to my betters, and my co-workers let me know that they did not appreciate getting the brass all fired up. I learned my lesson on that one. To this day I never give anyone advice unless they ask me, and I usually charge them for it. That way I am sure they will listen even if they do not act on it.

While working in a corporate headquarters some years later, I visited a subsidiary company and was invited to listen to their monthly status review. As each department head rose to speak, the division president would interrupt to tell me what was really happening in that area, what the problems were, how the department head was not handling it properly, and how swift action by himself had prevented further problems. When finished, the embarrassed manager would fumble through the prepared viewgraphs and get offstage as quickly as possible. If I asked anyone a question the boss answered it. After a couple of hours we adjourned for lunch, where the main conversation was the boss talking about a pet project.

Later he confided in me that he hoped he was being considered for a group executive position since he had done such a good job of building a team in this operation. I pointed out that during the status review it was shown that sales and profits were below budget, while inventory and compensation were higher than the goals. I also mentioned that his team, at least it seemed to me, did not get the opportunity to say much. He exploded in a tirade about headquarters people who come out and harass honest, hard-working souls who produce profit for the company. He thought no one understood, but his real problem was that they did indeed understand.

When I was a retail clerk we used to receive a sack of change each day to place in our cash register drawer. (To give you an idea of how long ago that was, the amount of the change added up to $15.00.) At the end of the day we would tabulate the transactions. If there was more money in the drawer than there was supposed to be, the company kept it. If there was less than required, the difference was deducted from my salary. Usually the variation was under fifty cents and it only happened a couple of times a month. I often wondered if the executives who gave us occasional lectures on having a good attitude and treating the customers properly knew about that. Everyone hated the company.

During my quality engineering days, a general manager decided that it was necessary to reduce overhead. Inspectors and testers were considered overhead, while line workers were accounted as direct labor. So she decided to make the manufacturing supervisors responsible for inspection and laid off all the indirect quality people. The acceptance stamps were transferred to manufacturing; no training was permitted because that would cost money. Within three months the customer (the U.S. Government) came in and threatened to close the place down because of all the nonconforming material they were receiving. The company replaced the general manager, put the inspectors back, and got a new quality manager. One person's whim had almost destroyed a business. She did all that without asking anyone for advice.

The head of a large service firm decided that a new system was needed for financial data. Without mentioning it to her comptroller or her information systems people, she hired a consulting group to create a company-wide database software system. They moved in a new computer system and began to convert the existing data to that format. Suddenly the comptroller found himself without the ability to pay bills or payrolls, or even to know how much money was in the bank. The consultants wouldn't talk to anyone except the boss, and she felt that the others were just complaining because they felt left out. She encouraged them to be patient and adapt their operations until the development job was done; then they would all make a great leap forward. Protests were met with a resolution worthy of a wartime leader.

When it came time for the monthly management meeting, the financial people were unable to provide a status report that they were willing to certify as accurate. There was no clear understanding of revenues or billings because that was all being done by hand. The software development representative assured the staff that everything possible was being done and commented that more cooperation was required. Completion dates were still vague, but confidence was expressed that it would all be in good shape soon.

The result of this affair was a complete disorientation of the operation, the resignation of several key people, and the eventual replacement of the leader, who to this day insists that she was sabotaged. After several years the system still does not work properly, and the most accurate information is produced by the senior accountant on her laptop computer.

I have watched several executives destroy their areas of responsibility in order not to appear wrong. Eastern Airlines is a good example. The union and the management fought each other so relentlessly that they did the operation in while the customers stood by helplessly. These people got so involved with wanting to make their version of the company happen that they forgot all about the business and the people who used it. Now everyone is suffering and the company is gone.

The Centurion, whether running a company or a union, will not be able to make such casual choices, nor will one want to. Senior management will be watching and be watched much more closely than is possible now. There will no longer be the automatic assumption that the leader is correct and the people are misinformed. Centurions will no longer view the opinions of the people as being irrelevant. They will recognize that in the twenty-first century information flows up the organization, not down as in the twentieth century.

When a client company was being acquired, I was asked to go have lunch with the management team and the new CEO. The acquired firm had a reputation for treating its employees with respect, had almost no turnover, and boasted revenues and profit per employee well above that of any comparable company, including the one that was buying them. During lunch, the boss of the acquiring company led the conversation around to the subject of "pampering" employees. He cited unnecessary and expensive things that should be "looked into," such as the child-care program and "longer than normal" vacations. He talked about how employees should be made to account for their time on a task-by-task basis, to become more efficient, and how training time should be reduced in order to give people more time to work.

By the time lunch was over, everyone except him was depressed. I wondered aloud to him why he had invited me to come to the session. He said that he felt my ideas and the services our company offered could help get these people in touch with reality, and he wanted to hire us for that purpose. I noted that we had been working with the company for some time and that they were running better than any operation of that size I knew. I suggested that they didn't need much help and that we probably would not be interested in meeting his scenario. Making a lot of unnecessary changes would seem, I noted, like building a latrine in a rose garden. He didn't get that point. In the next two years, he managed to destroy the morale and uniqueness of that company. Turnover rose to 30 percent a year, most of the better people left, and clients were resistant to the new aggressiveness. He still didn't get the point, and his hand-picked board never notices what is happening.

The savings and loan debacle that occurred in the United States in the 1980s was a crime of incomplete bosses. I always felt that the only difference between the Mafia and the executives who looted these institutions was the width of the pinstripes on their suits. These were knowledgeable people, experienced enough to know that Congress had opened the lid of the cookie jar, and they enthusiastically gorged themselves on the cookies. An entire industry was offered a bonanza, and about a third gobbled it up. They thought about themselves and their friends, with no consideration for the institutions, depositors, or employees.

There are also bright, hard-working, success-oriented executives who do *not* steal from their companies but cause as much disruption and loss of worth as if they did. They keep irritating people over things that are not remotely important. They remove the foundations of their firms by constantly tinkering with whatever they consider to be incorrect or inadequate at that moment. This is the key to the incomplete boss syndrome: their belief that the only things that matter are those they want to do.

The Centurion will recognize the need to provide a complete concept as a reliable framework for running an organization. Executives, managers, supervisors, professionals, employees, suppliers, and even customers will know where they stand. Change will come from thoughtful action rather than impulse; policies will not vacillate by whim; action will be taken quickly by the appropriate people; there will be no surprises. And yet the boss will know what is going on. A lot of leaders do not like this kind of world, and they're the ones who will not be able to manage in the coming age. Their antics and demands will be greeted with puzzled eyes and ears. They will not be dealing with the submissive mass we became in twentieth century business. Vest-pocket Hitlers will not be able to intimidate their employees because the employees will have choices. Other firms will be after them.

Because of this, the Centurions will be selected by natural qualifications. They will find people willing to work for them enthusiastically; they will learn to lead, not direct. At the same time they must be the best informed and most involved—like the captain of a ship who stands calmly staring out at the horizon knowing exactly what is happening all over the craft at that moment. Department heads have been carefully selected for their ability to produce according to the ship's agreed strategy. If the captain insists on personally selecting the menu, cleaning the heads, and steering all the while, the transit will be difficult. Mutiny is one of the least things that can happen in such a case.

Why are such otherwise smart people so difficult? Why do they harass those whom they need? Why do they feel the requirement to demonstrate authority when everyone already knows that they have it? Why do they have a hard time letting other flowers bloom? They do these things because they do not know of any other glue with which to bind the organization. They may understand intellectually that their subordinates will operate much better when they are bound to a common cause with a common process, but they just don't know how to bring it off. They are basically individual contributors, not leaders. They got where they are by being good at something. The leader, however, doesn't "do" anything. So, in order to show that they are in charge, they run around being in charge—driving everyone nuts in the process. Most of these folks can be saved, and that is what Completeness is all about.

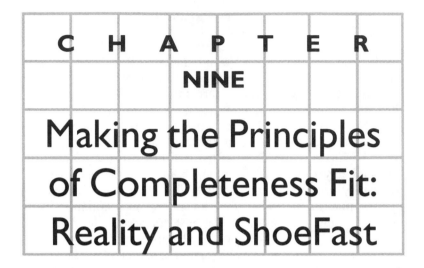

CHAPTER

NINE

Making the Principles of Completeness Fit: Reality and ShoeFast

The ShoeFast Corp. owns and operates fifty "perfect fit" shoe stores located across North America. They are trying to add two new locations each year, and plan to enter the European market soon. The company's product line and marketing strategy have been successful so far, primarily because of the company's technological advantage. However, competition is beginning to appear, despite an energetic legal program to defend the company's turf and copyrights. ShoeFast dominates its special market with a share of 75 percent. However, management is worried because other companies have blown similar leads before.

The company's product is both unusual and practical. Using laser technology to measure seventy-three characteristics of the customer's feet, ShoeFast then manufactures a pair of shoes that fits exactly, and does it within one hour right there in the store. This has an added advantage because there is no large finished goods inventory requiring storage space, or creating the need for a clearance sale every quarter. The problems of a conventional retail shoe store are eliminated. In a ShoeFast store the customer places his or her feet in an attractive enclosure and looks down into it. The various styles of shoes are imaged on the customer's feet until selections are made. Then the clerk transmits the sales information to the laboratory, which is displayed behind a glass wall, and the shoes are manufactured by technicians. Since fit is not a variable, the customer does not have to parade around the store while trying to match comfort and style. At ShoeFast the shoes are priced at a 20 percent premium above traditional stores, and fit is guaranteed or your money back. The customers love the product, particularly because they can order new shoes by mail once they have been calibrated by the machine—it is a rare day when someone wants money back.

The bad news is that each store requires a capital investment of at least $4 million for the measuring technology and manufacturing equipment. ShoeFast thus finds itself with a debt almost equal to its assets, but the cash flow is strong. Even though stores are busy, the company does not make much money. That fact encouraged the management team to come together in a special meeting.

They asked an older consultant, Campbell (Cam) Delta, to come and conduct a "reality session," to get the management team to take a realistic look into their organization and how it is run. Cam had been a chief executive for many years, and now, semiretired, he consulted at senior levels of companies. He delighted in forcing executives to understand their own mission statements and policy notes. The executive committee of ShoeFast gathered one Thursday morning to meet with Cam. The CEO wanted to do it over a weekend but Delta said retired people did not work on weekends. The members of the committee were Harold Bronson, president and CEO; Doris Homeri, director of operations; Betty Valiant, from Materials and Inventory; Jack Ortoni, from Advertising and Direct Mail; Earnest Hupman, comptroller; Ellen Prosynzki, a doctor of podiatric medicine; and Sam Levy, from Human Resources.

"We are in the customer service business," said CEO Harold Bronson. "One day everyone will have the same laser equipment and our only advantage will be customer service. We need to learn how to please the customer."

"Let me understand more about your business," said Cam. "I would appreciate it if each of you would just tell me your biggest problem in just a few words. We'll start over here on my left with Betty Valiant. If you wouldn't mind, state your part of the business first so I can be certain I know what everyone does."

"Certainly," Betty said, smiling. "I am in charge of worldwide inventory, which is mostly unfinished material since we do our processing on site. My biggest problem is material that is damaged during shipment and storage.''

"I'm Sam Levy and I manage human resources," said the next executive, "and my biggest problem is finding and training new personnel.''

"If you are growing by two stores a year that must be quite a challenge," said Cam. "How many employees are there in a store?''

"Usually about twenty people in order to cover all the hours we are open. Five or six are doing the shoe manufacturing, and the rest are selling or supporting. Worldwide we have close to fifteen hundred people. We hire and train about sixty people each month to cover both growth and personnel turnover.''

The next person waited to make certain that conversation was complete and then introduced himself.

"Jack Ortoni," he said. "I am in charge of advertising and direct mail. My biggest problem is keeping the mailing list up-to-date. Often the clerks do not write customers' names completely or at all. They are very sloppy about that.''

"Ernest Hupman, Finance. My biggest problem is gathering up cash from all the stores. It is only a small part of our sales, since customers mostly use credit cards, but a great deal of money can be sitting around in drawers instead of being invested.''

Cam signaled to the next person.

"I am Dr. Prosynzki, the podiatrist. My biggest problem is in making certain that the design of the shoes is not harmful to the customer. Fit is only one characteristic of wearing a shoe; there are leverage forces also.''

"Do you do orthopedic shoes?" asked Delta.

The doctor shook her head.

"No, that is not our business, although there is a market for them. Our equipment can measure the customer's foot exactly, but only as it is. To design orthopedic shoes is another technology altogether. However, our customer base consists mostly of people who have trouble being fitted for shoes in conventional patterns. Usually people settle on one size and that works out for them throughout their adult life. However, probably twenty percent of the population does not mesh with the traditional measurement system of shoes. Their feet are in between—

instead of being a nine and a half, for instance, they are nine and five-eighths. They will never be completely comfortable in conventional shoes.''

"Does that mean ShoeFast can never have one hundred percent of the market?'' asked the consultant.

The president smiled. "We'd settle for one hundred percent of the twenty percent,'' he said. "That would be a billion people worldwide, two hundred million in our current market.''

"So you are dealing with people who have been uncomfortable?''

"That's right,'' said the doctor. "They are very pleased to have their shoes fit and also be fashionable. We can provide a great number of designs.''

"I am Doris Homeri, and I head operations, which means that all the stores report to me through some regional executives. My biggest problem is finding managers.''

"My biggest problem,'' said the president at his turn, "is that we are not as profitable as we could be.''

"Are your expenses too high or your revenues too low?'' asked Cam.

"All of the above,'' said the president.

Cam Delta nodded.

"In order to approach this in a systematic way,'' said Cam, "I would like to suggest that we examine our operating practices and policies in terms of the principles of Completeness. The first of these is 'make the employees successful.' We have a high turnover rate. Do you have an annual percentage on that, Sam?''

"It is engraved on my forehead,'' Sam replied. "I'm surprised you can't see it there. Overall our turnover is forty-seven percent, mostly at the lower levels of the organization. In our defense, let me say that we have benchmarked against other personal performance companies and find that we are on the low end when compared with the fast-food industry, but much higher than department stores and such.''

"I think our turnover is about right,'' said Bronson. "A certain amount is healthy, and to reduce it dramatically we would have to pay people a great deal more. That would raise the expense rate, which is killing us already.''

Cam asked, "How much does it cost to replace half of the staff each year? Have you ever figured it out?"

The finance director grimaced. "We have not done so in exactly those terms," he reported. "It is hard to identify all the costs. There is the matter of separating the person who is leaving, searching for the new ones, training them, and of course there is a gap while they learn. As a result, we certainly have more people than we really need at any given time. But my rough estimate is that it costs about a half-year's average salary to replace, hire, train, and support each new employee."

"Our average payroll cost per person is about forty-five thousand with benefits," said the CEO. "Are you saying that we are spending sixteen million dollars a year on turnover and training? I never heard that number before. That is three times our profit. You must be wrong; I'd like to see your figures."

Hupman shook his head. "I may be off a little, but the number is essentially correct. Even if it were half as much, it would be enormous. We have asked the auditing firm to study this for us, and their report is supposed to be ready next week. Then we will know for sure."

"If you all don't mind," said the consultant, "I would like to assume that the numbers are correct for our purposes. My thought is that you apparently pay your people an acceptable amount, your benefit program is as good as what your competition offers, and yet the employees apparently do not feel successful enough to make a career with ShoeFast. Could we discuss that?"

"What do you mean by 'successful'?" asked the doctor. "There could be a lot of definitions of that."

"Successful is as successful does," said the human resources director. "If they stay for a career and are happy with their job, and have an acceptable lifestyle, then that is probably successful. The philosophers say that people have an absolute need for food, sex, and a sense of purpose. In most cases they expect to obtain their most significant sense of purpose from work. We don't do much about that."

"They don't feel very professional?" asked Cam. "After all, they get to use all that laser equipment, and many of them manufacture shoes with their own hands. I would think that would give you a great opportunity to have a success ladder of sorts."

There was a silence.

"Are you saying that we need to provide our employees with a way of feeling good about their job and life on a continual basis?" asked Betty. "I would think that their life is their own problem. I know I feel that way about mine."

The facilitator shrugged. "If you cut the turnover in half you could come close to tripling the company's profit. Taking steps to make that happen would seem to me like a sensible business decision," he replied.

"We might wind up running a psychology clinic if we take that seriously," noted the finance director.

Cam waited for some more comments, and receiving none, continued.

"We will certainly come back to this, but let's take a moment to briefly consider the next principle of Completeness, which is 'make the suppliers successful.' "

He turned to Betty.

"You were talking about problems with damaged materials. Are the suppliers involved in that?"

"Absolutely," she said. "All our material comes from suppliers, as well as the tools we use to build our shoes. We do well with them in terms of price, but overall, we have a lot of trouble with suppliers being reliable. They don't seem to take us very seriously. We have a long list of them and deal with a great many."

"Do you know how much the handling and other damage costs each year?" he asked.

Betty turned toward Ernest. "Finance and I have been working on this," she said. "So far the calculations are not complete but it comes to about twenty-five percent of the material that is discarded or reworked. Our material costs are right at two hundred million dollars a year, which gives us a potential shrinkage of fifty million. It isn't that much, I'm sure, because a lot of the reworked material is used."

"I would say that is a pretty impressive number," noted Cam. "What are the main causes of this shrinkage?"

"There are three main causes, I think," Betty said. "A small part is the material that is left over after things are cut to make a shoe. That is probably ten percent of the waste, and could be considered as planned. A larger part is material that deteriorates in storage or becomes obsolete; but the main part is physical damage done in handling by the suppliers or by our people.''

''That is really ridiculous, to have that kind of damage these days,'' said Jack Ortoni, from direct mail. ''I keep reading about 'just in time' inventory and things along that line. Don't we do any of that?''

''I think the suppliers have not wanted to go along with such a system, but I'm not sure,'' replied Betty.

''Who is in charge of suppliers?'' the consultant asked.

''It is in my department; Tim Watson does the buying, the stores order from a standard list they get from marketing, everything goes into the database, and my inventory group monitors the status.''

''Tim isn't here?''

''Tim wouldn't normally be involved with this particular group,'' said Bronson. ''If it would be helpful we could ask him to come by for the afternoon session.''

''Good idea,'' replied the workshop leader. ''In the meantime, why don't we go on to the next principle, which involves making the customer successful. We probably should begin by defining that phrase. Just what is a 'successful customer'? And before you answer remember that this is a discussion about reality. Don't think of some abstract person—think of *yourself* as a customer. We should rule out the word 'satisfied.' ''

''But everyone says 'satisfied,' '' commented Sam. ''That is all I hear. Why don't you want to use it?''

''It just isn't enough; people can be satisfied if you give them the goods for free. We need them to be successful, to have achieved all the things they wanted from their purchase. Then they will tell their friends and also come back. Do we have any idea of the repeat rate of our customers? How many do come back? Would your mailing list tell that, Jack?''

Jack grimaced. ''My mailing list has so many duplicates and errors that I am ashamed to even talk about it. Since we enter every customer's name in the computer we should be able to know exactly how often they return. And we follow up by mailing them literature after they purchase. I would guess that seventy-five percent of them come back to us.''

''How do the clerks know how to make the entry that gives you the customer's name and address?''

"The store managers tell them about it," said Jack. "It is part of their on-the-job training."

"Is there some sort of instruction sheet? Is there a video about it? How do they know it is important? Do they know where the entry they make goes?"

Jack looked over at Sam, who nodded and replied: "I would say they probably do not know how important the list is, and there is no room in the training budget for videos. It would be a good idea. Actually there are computer programs that teach now; we could put them in each store for a few hundred dollars a location."

"Why haven't we done that?" asked the CEO.

Jack smiled. "The training budget gets cut every time the profit goes down. We are at rock bottom right now. It would require a thirty percent increase to get us up to a minimum level of training. The quality improvement program, for instance, is on hold because of the need for training materials."

"I thought all that stuff came from the consulting firm who trained the management," said the doctor.

"It does, it does," replied Sam. "But they don't give it away. We already paid for the most expensive part—sending management to school. Now we are hung up on something that costs us about three hundred dollars a person."

"That is about four hundred fifty thousand dollars," noted Ernest. "It's a big number."

"Perhaps we should discuss this at the executive committee meeting next week," suggested Bronson.

"This is a reality session," said Cam, "and this is as real a subject as you are going to get. Apparently, there is a disagreement about the value of training. That indicates that the matter may not have been presented from a long-range viewpoint. It is like cutting out the fourth grade and giving kids a year off in order to save money."

"Do you think a lack of seriousness about training has something to do with our turnover rate?" asked Betty.

"I would have to toss that back to all of you," he replied. "I have only been in two of your stores. I was processed differently in each store. And from my conversations during those visits, I got the impression that the clerks were there only until something better came along."

"I thought those looked like our shoes on your feet," said Jack. "What locations did you visit?"

"One was Pittsburgh, and the other in London, Ontario," he replied.

"Two different cultures," said Bronson.

"Same company," said the consultant. "But let's take a look at making the customers successful. Is that all up to the product?"

"We take a great deal of care in designing the stores so they are attractive and comfortable," said Doris Homeri, head of operations. "We make it easy for the customers to get to us, and we encourage our people to be nice to them. I would define a successful customer as one who bought shoes they liked, that fit as they had imagined, and that cost what they were willing to pay."

"These customers are driven to you by the difficulty they had in being fitted by regular shoe lines?" asked Cam.

"That seems to be the prime reason, and many of them are quite suspicious about our claims," noted Bronson. "We find many of them coming in sort of hostile. But afterwards they are happy. They don't even seem to mind paying more than other stores charge."

"Have you thought about raising that price level?" asked Cam.

"Why yes," replied Bronson. "As a matter of fact we are working that out now. It sure would help profit."

"Have you thought about lowering the price level?"

Another silence.

"Why would we want to do that?" asked Bronson.

"We hardly make any money now," added the financial director.

"I was just thinking that the market open to you is limited under your current strategy," said Cam, "because you only get people with troubles. How about all those who would like the feel and prestige of custom-made shoes?"

"There certainly are a lot more of those," noted Betty. "But it would be very difficult to reduce our prices unless we were able to slice expenses dramatically."

"We need to have our lunch break now," said Cam, "but after lunch I would like to suggest that we tackle some of the main problem areas—which are employee turnover, supplier participation, limited customer base, inadequate training, and profitability.

"We need to think about things in a different way. For instance, your pricing has been developed by figuring how much it costs to make shoes, what the overhead is, and then adding a margin. Unfortunately, the overhead keeps sneaking up and is shrinking the margin.

"You need to turn that around and figure what price would be necessary in order to attract those people who want custom fits but don't want to pay premium prices. You need to get at the same level, or below that of the regular stores.

"So we identify the price, subtract the profitability, and what is left is what we have to design the system to utilize. We must bring our suppliers into the fold and get better prices from them by offering longer-term relationships. We can eliminate material handling damage. It will be like starting over."

"But we have spent a lot of time making the decisions that run this company. We'd have to do that all over again," said Ortoni.

Cam nodded. "Doing them over will be a revelation to you. Very few management decisions are made on the basis of fact. Actually they are the result, almost every time, of some accommodation. In order not to disrupt some group or person, we do not take the hard course. After a while the organization is soft. We have to ask ourselves to identify the real reason behind every policy and practice. The *real* reason."

They were all staring at Campbell. Then Bronson spoke.

"I think you are on the right track, Cam. We need to stop patching up the system. We need a blank sheet of paper. I'm ready. Let's work right through lunch."

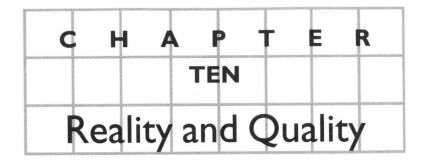

C H A P T E R

TEN

Reality and Quality

The president and the human resources director were having lunch in the neighborhood diner. HR was nervous because she had been essentially yanked out of her office by the boss and set down in a place where the special was hot chili. She watched as her leader pumped hot sauce into the mixture and happily began spooning it down.

"I'm sorry to drag you off like this, Carol," he said, "but I wanted to talk about something where we couldn't be interrupted. It concerns quality."

"Quality," she repeated.

"Right," he said, nodding as though she had said something remarkable.

"I believe this concept that the boss should concentrate on finance, relationships, and quality. We are realigning the organization, as you certainly know, to deal with that. It has certainly made my life easier, more enjoyable, and much more productive. Also, we are learning to prevent problems, at least in finance and relationships. We are not doing well in quality at all."

Carol straightened in surprise.

"But Clay," she noted, "we have had all that TQM training, you created the post of vice president of quality for Al, and we are making application for the Baldrige award. Everyone is happy and enthusiastic. I thought quality was doing well."

"Have you looked at customer complaints? Have you looked at the financial numbers I had Bruce put together? It shows our price of nonconformance is actually rising. We are getting worse and thinking everything is wonderful."

Carol put down her spoon.

"This is quite disturbing to me," she said, "and I can see that it bothers you. What would you like me to do?"

Clay put his spoon down, too, but only to reach for some more Tabasco.

"I think the problem is that we just do not understand what quality is really all about," he said. "I want to have a meeting on it, and I want you to set it up as part of something or other. Our quality VP works his tail off, and I don't want him to think I don't have confidence in him—even though I don't."

Carol thought a moment. "We have been talking about having some internal management round tables. The thought was to invite a couple outside experts on some subject, put them together with our people, and then just sit around for a period discussing it. Hopefully we would examine our approach and see if there was anything that could be learned."

"Perfect," he said, "perfect. I would like to do it as soon as possible. Get Al to invite the consultant he has been using, and I will ask Frances Wilson to come. Travel Services, Inc. has had dramatic improvement in quality, and they don't even have a quality department. I checked your people, and they said that in the past year Frances's people have not had a single error in our account."

"And that represents a lot of trips, hotels, and rental cars," agreed Carol. "They have been terrific ever since Frances became president."

She pulled a notebook out of her purse. "Okay. I have Frances, you, myself, Al, the consultant, and how about the operations director and comptroller?"

"Good thinking," Clay said, handing over the bill. "I believe in being 'politically correct' in all things. So to show I don't discriminate I am going to let you pay the bill."

"I will agree to that," Carol said. "But I still expect accompanying males to open doors for me, and to pull chairs out. Do I detect that you are concerned about what is real and what is 'politically correct' in this quality business?"

"No comment," Clay replied. "I'll keep on opening doors, but I haven't made up my mind on the other stuff yet."

A few days later Carol called the first Management Round Table to order. Tracey Axton, the operations director, and Bruce Weston, the comptroller, came as promised. Al introduced Ellery Thomas, the TQM consultant.

"I am delighted that all of you could come," began Carol. "We particularly appreciate Frances and Ellery working us into their schedules. When Frances is out of the office it cuts the working people by twenty percent, so we will try to get her back as soon as possible.

"Let me ask Clay Whiteside, our president, to begin the discussion. Clay?"

After stating the purpose of the sessions and thanking everyone for coming, Clay got right to the point.

"We are putting a lot of effort into our TQM program," he said, "and Al here has been working very hard. He has been to every part of our company and has taught courses day and night. Ellery, I know your company has been very supportive supplying material and consulting help, and we appreciate that."

Ellery smiled and nodded.

"Tracey and I are responsible for running the company," Clay continued. "He does most of the day-to-day, and I watch out for longer range—but in reality we confer continually. Would you like to make a few comments, Tracey?"

"Thank you, Clay," he said. "I have a concern, which is that we have trained all our people and we are doing the actions laid out in the material but nothing seems to be happening. We still have as much nonconformance as ever, and we still have a great many customer complaints. I think that we just do not understand this quality business as well as we should."

He paused and Al responded. "I think it takes a little longer than we have had, Tracey. Let me ask Ellery to share his experience with us."

"Thank you," said Ellery. "This is a comment I hear regularly. It takes awhile to turn a company around; I like to compare it to an oil tanker. Just turning the wheel doesn't make things happen quickly. As your people internalize TQM, you will begin to see rapid results. Right now you are almost qualified to apply for the Baldrige award. There has been a very rapid progress along that line."

"I get a little confused about TQM, Ellery," said Clay. "Could you give me a quick understanding of just what it is?"

Ellery smiled. He had been through this many times.

"Certainly," he said, "TQM refers to a company's approach to quality. It means that we are committed to take actions in every level of the organization to make sure that quality is met.''

''Then perhaps,'' said Clay, ''I just don't understand what quality itself is. I have been looking at quality as being the foundation of our company. But if it is not in place, then we have no foundation. What is quality, really?''

There was a pause and Ellery looked at Al.

''Quality,'' said Al, ''is driven by the customer.''

''What does that mean?'' asked Clay. ''It sounds like a vehicle of some sort.''

''It means,'' said Ellery, ''that the customer determines just what quality is, and no one else does. Many companies think they can dictate quality to the customer but they find that not to be so.''

Al nodded in agreement, while Clay looked blank.

Tracey spoke up. ''I certainly think customers have to decide what they want, and our job is to listen to them and then obey. However, I don't quite understand how the customers do this 'driving.' If I am working in purchasing, say, how do I know what to order so the customers will receive what they want?''

''It is the job of the company to determine that,'' said Ellery. ''Everyone has to know the customers.''

''Suppose I examine my customers and I discover that they want quality, but they can't tell me what that is. How do I proceed?''

Ellery nodded in agreement. ''That is the hard part of all this. Quality is quite nebulous, a matter of opinion in many cases. It is really better to plan on exceeding the customer's expectations in order to be sure.''

''Does that mean,'' asked Clay, ''that if they want one scoop of ice cream, I should give them two?''

''How about if they want one hole drilled, should I do two, or even three?'' asked Tracey.

Al raised a hand. ''This is a complicated subject. We are preparing a course on quality philosophy to present to management soon. It will help your understanding.''

Tracey shook his head. ''I have been reading TQM material, and I have gone to several conferences, and I still don't understand exactly what it is. Also, after listening to the speakers and walking through the exhibits, I have concluded that none of them understands, either.''

"It takes awhile," said Ellery.

"The best definition I have heard so far," said Tracey, "is that quality means 'conformance to requirements.' That means we find out what the customer wants, write it down, train everyone how to accomplish it, and then deliver that to the customer on time."

"That is a definition that is overly simple, we have found," said Al. "It doesn't take into consideration the value aspects of quality."

"But aren't the value aspects, as well as all others, included in the requirements?" asked Clay. "Isn't that the primary form of communication between the management, the people, and the customers?"

"It can be done that way, of course," said Ellery. "But conformance implies that there is a restriction on individual freedom. It tends to discourage creativity."

Clay turned to Frances. "You have been sitting there very patiently, Frances," he noted. "What is your feeling on conformance to agreed upon requirements versus creativity?"

"They go together," she said. "We found that once we all agreed on how we were going to do things, we were able to do almost all of our work without confusion. Then we could depend on each other, and we didn't have to keep checking up."

"And how about creativity?" asked Carol.

"Once we as a group determined that people would do what they said they were going to do, it became possible to create, particularly on things that made the job easier. And when we have a problem we don't talk about quality, we talk about the requirements. 'What were the requirements?' people say. It has been a big help to us."

"You must have been at this awhile," said Ellery. "When did you begin your program?"

"About a year ago," said Frances. "But we have been like this since the first week. Everyone caught right on and we just took off."

"That is possible in a small company," said Ellery, "but when there are a lot of people it is much more difficult to get their attitudes changed."

"I think the key item here," noted Tracey, "is that at Frances's shop they all understood quality to mean the same thing—'get the requirements clear and then conform to them.' That is what we are lacking in our company.''

There was a pause.

''While we absorb the definition question,'' said Clay, ''let's talk about the system of quality. We have been concentrating on measurement, I understand.''

''That's true,'' said Al. ''We have put all of our people through statistical process control classes and we have reporting from almost all areas now.''

''How about financial reporting,'' asked Tracey, ''what used to be called the cost of quality? As far as I know we don't do that.''

Ellery nodded. ''That has been found to not be too meaningful to the employees, so we discourage it. As a matter of fact, it usually just confuses them.''

''We have done a little of it,'' said Al. ''Perhaps Bruce might want to talk about it.'' He nodded to the comptroller.

''Al sent me a paper on the subject a few months ago,'' reported Bruce, ''and I had some of our folks brainstorm it. We have only been doing it on a procedural basis so far, but the results are enough to scare you. We were able to go back a few years because of the computer programs and look at the non-conformance costs as a percent of operating costs.''

''How much improvement have we seen?'' asked Al.

''Actually,'' said Bruce, ''it has gotten a little worse, particularly in the customer service areas. They attribute that to people's increased awareness concerning quality.''

''Are you certain those numbers are meaningful?'' asked Ellery. ''We have never seen much interest in measuring quality that way.''

''We measure everything else that way,'' said Clay. ''Management spends all its time peering at charts full of financial numbers.''

Another silence.

''Let's talk about a performance standard for quality,'' said Clay. ''What we have been using is 'get better continually.' I'm not sure what that means exactly.''

''It is a very practical standard and goal at the same time,'' said Ellery. ''People recognize that they can't reach perfection right away, and so they don't get discouraged.''

"We went to the reality of 'defect-free' in a week," said Frances. "I never thought getting better slowly was much of a way to do things."

"A lot of people put a great deal of thought into creating that standard," said Ellery. "People with a lot of experience in teaching quality management. One well-thought out standard is more technical; it is 'six sigma' and refers to statistically determined standard deviations. In layman terms it means that we can expect three-point-seven deviations per one million opportunities. That is pretty good performance."

"I don't see how you can ever explain to the people that so many do not have to do things as agreed. It just doesn't make sense," said Tracey. "Look, we all agree to stop at every stop sign when we get our driver's license. Now if we were to say that three-point-seven signs per million could just be passed each day, it would destroy the integrity of the whole highway system. Who would say which people and which signs? It would just not be reasonable. How can these people recommend that for a business?"

"Did these folks ever actually have to work at making quality happen?" asked Tracey. "Have they always been teachers, or have they worked in the real world?"

"They have been at it for a long time and are well known. Their books are read everywhere," remarked Al.

"Why are they against 'defect-free,' or 'right the first time'?" asked Clay.

"They think it is impractical," said Ellery.

"What do you think about it personally, Ellery? Do you think expecting everyone to do things right the first time is impractical?"

"I haven't really thought about it in that way. I have always assumed that it was against the basic instinct people have and that it takes a long time to change their minds."

"But," said Clay, "we seem to believe that management is the problem, not the people. We feel that employees get their bad habits from management's direction or lack of it.

"I send my children to drivers' training class at the high school. But when they graduated, took the state test, and received their licenses, I found that they really did not know much about actually driving the car. I had to teach them. What they learned in class was how to pass the test. Are you sure that our quality program is not set up so we can pass a test? It doesn't seem to have much to do with making the customers, suppliers, or employees successful.''

Al cleared his throat. "What we have been doing, Clay,'' he said, "is the accepted program of Total Quality Management. You have raised some very pertinent questions about it. Frankly, I have not questioned the program itself, since there are so many well-known companies going along that road. My background is marketing as you know. Perhaps we need to study it some more.''

"I think we need to get real about it,'' noted Tracey. "We have been treating quality as though it were something beyond management's ability to comprehend. Management has been following along on that same assumption. However, we can't have something in the philosophy of the company that its management can't deal with.''

"Are you saying,'' asked Ellery, "that you feel TQM is a case of the emperor's new clothes? That everyone pretends to understand it? How do you explain all the progress that has been made in other companies?''

"I don't see much real progress,'' said Clay. "Do you know of any company, anywhere, that routinely delivers defect-free products and services to their customers? I have found about ten, and all of them have a very realistic quality philosophy that I can understand. They believe that management's job is to develop clear requirements that the employees, suppliers, and customers understand. Then they train and supply everyone with everything needed to be able and willing to meet those requirements, every time. All the management are educated to become examples of prevention; the performance standard is defect-free, and quality is reported by the finance department just like every other function. These companies just weave quality into the fabric of the organization; in fact, it *is* the fabric.''

"I never understood what the word 'total' was for,'' said Tracey. "Is there a 'partial quality management' or something along that line?''

Ellery smiled. "I have to agree with you folks that some of the program approaches do not appear to be too real. But that is the way most companies want them. Senior management in most cases just wants some education, and some flag-waving. They don't understand, as you do, that quality is the structure of the company. I feel we have let you down, but I must say that we felt we were giving you what you wanted. We can change it all with no problem.''

"I think you *were* giving us what we said we wanted, Ellery; we need to review our approach on all this,'' said Al. "We'll discuss it and then get back to you in a few days.''

Clay nodded in agreement and the meeting disbanded. Tracey, Al, and Clay went back to Clay's office.

"We all signed up with our eyes wide open, Al,'' said Clay. "You gave us what we thought we wanted. Now, I think we know better. We have to get real—we have no alternative. We have wasted a lot of time working on the wrong things.

"What we need is a process for quality that will fit in with the other work we are doing on Completeness, rather than just confusing it. It needs to be an integral part, not something like a United Fund drive. Find out how we do that before our meeting next week, Al.''

"Actually, Clay,'' noted Al, "a process does exist that will give us that, and it is the most-used in the business. Those companies you identified as doing well are all part of that philosophy.''

Tracey was puzzled. "How come we are not using that supplier, and that process, if we know it is better?''

Al was embarrassed.

"I really need to know, Al,'' said Tracey.

"Well,'' replied Al, "when we were selecting consultants, those folks were higher by about sixty percent. You eliminated them and we bought Ellery and his group on their lower price.''

"I remember that,'' said Tracey. "I thought they all were the same and that it was a matter of price. I'm sorry about that.''

"Let's get them back, Al, if they will take us,'' said Clay. "At least we can see how they define and teach quality. We can't expect this company to survive if we do not get this in hand.''

"I have a lot more experience now than when I took this job,'' said Al. "I think a lot more is involved besides getting the right consultant. For instance, one of the reasons we turned down the other firm was that they wanted the executives to go away to class for a couple of days. Ellery said he could do it in an hour.''

"You are saying," stated Clay, "that we weren't serious about it. I have to admit that is a fair statement. I guess we thought it was enough to pour something into the water."

"We know that doesn't work," said Tracey. "We do not even have a quality policy yet. The executive committee is still wiggling around about that one. The last effort I saw was a page-and-a-half long and had all kinds of escape clauses. Do you know what it should be, Al?''

"I do, exactly," said Al. "In fact, I have one all written out, if you want to sign it today we can put this part of our task to bed. It has been difficult trying to do quality by consensus.''

"What does it say?" asked Tracey.

"Simple and clear: 'We will deliver defect-free products and services to our customers and co-workers, on time.' ''

"I'll sign that and even make a speech about it at the meeting tomorrow. We need to get moving. I'm sorry we put you into this situation without proper support and participation, Al. We'll do better now.''

"I'll accept that," said Al. "Particularly if we can all relate to the thought that you two didn't delegate quality to me—you are just expecting me to manage the process for you.''

"That makes sense," said Clay. "We certainly didn't delegate the responsibility for finance to Bruce, or relationships to Carol. You let us know if we slip.''

"I won't have to let you know, it will be apparent. Bruce and I are putting the price of nonconformance into the accounting system at this very moment. That means you will have a daily status on what it costs us to do things wrong and specifically where those expenses occurred. It will also give us trend charts for the executive committee sessions. I would appreciate it if you would put quality first on the agenda, instead of dealing with it if there is time left over.''

Clay and Tracey glanced at each other.

"I think he's got us," said Clay. "Okay, we will go at this properly. I see no reason why an oil tanker can't turn around quickly, provided it has tugs like us pushing and pulling.''

CHAPTER

ELEVEN

The Life of the Centurion: Communicating

The executive committee of Dean and Samoline, Inc., gathered each Monday morning for a status review. Everett Brown, chairman and CEO, conducted the meeting exactly as he had learned from those who had held that same position over the years. After a brief financial update, each member talked about the events that had occurred during the past week in their area, problems were noted, and action decisions were handed out as agreed. It worked well for them, and "D-Sam," as the firm was known to clients, competitors, and employees, had been around for many years. They had a reputation for performing effective work on behalf of their clients, and also one for being insensitive to the fate of employees and suppliers of said clients. Everett Brown thought that this latter opinion was a bum rap.

"We have to take the fall for doing what the client wants done, sometimes. But we help people get other jobs and in the long run we develop a sounder business for everyone involved," he would say. All this was true, of course, but was of little satisfaction to those who had been fired or whose jobs had been reduced by the D-Sam effort. But people cost money, and most of D-Sam's clients were struggling to become properly profitable when they asked for help.

D-Sam made companies efficient, for a fee. They married and combined companies throughout the world, for other fees. They would bring companies together, arrange the financing, educate the management, and even put an equity offering together. No one could do it like D-Sam.

"However," Everett was telling the executive committee, "things are beginning to slip a little bit. This is the first year that sales have not increased at least fifteen percent; we are only up five percent. We have more clients than before, but they do not do as much work with us. I feel we are not quite as close to them as we were. Are we still in contact with each of our principals each day? They are all being talked to regularly, aren't they?"

The members nodded as one.

"We talk on the communicators to each of them every day, chief, or we have a fax; we are right inside the contract with them at all times," said Helene Gonzalez. "However, our spread is getting a little wider all the time and we have to rely on the principals to tell us if the client is satisfied or not."

"How many contracts do we have going at this moment?" he asked. Everyone looked blank except his assistant, Tammi Hope, who addressed the minicommunicator dish on her notebook. "We have three thousand two hundred seventy-eight contracts in force at this moment, Mr. Brown," she answered. "They represent three hundred ninety-three thousand, three hundred sixty professional weeks of commitment, and are being handled by four hundred ninety-one principals, who are supervising a total of nine thousand seven hundred thirty-six professionals, each of whom is working on an average of forty-point-two weeks backlog. That is down from an average of fifty-six-point-three weeks of backlog in the last fiscal year."

"Thank you, Tammi," Brown said, nodding proudly to his fellow executives.

"I have that somewhere in my reports," he noted, "but Tammi can get it much faster from her machines. It is easier to ask her than to look it up."

"Everett, I think we need to get a better understanding of why clients aren't committing to quite as much work now," said Clarence Buckworth. "I haven't heard anything that would indicate they were losing faith in us, or something along that line."

"We're just not meeting their needs somehow, Clarence," said Helene. "They get flighty now and then and, of course, there is a lot of new competition."

"We have always done continual research on client needs, but I don't recall any reports on that lately," said Brown. "Tammi, is there anything in your magic machine about client dissatisfaction?"

"Client complaints have risen from four-point-five per thousand work hours to eleven-point-three over the last year. The biggest single item is the feeling that we ourselves are not efficient. We spend too much time on situations; the second biggest item is that they feel we are making work for ourselves—which is kind of like the first one."

"They both sound like the same thing," said Clarence. "Stretch work and make work are the two curses of the consultant. Are our people still going through the same educational program? We have a lot of new ones, I know. Have we let down on training?"

"I think we need to review this whole thing," said Everett. "Helene, would you pull the information together so we can come to some conclusions next Monday?"

Helene nodded in agreement, asked if she could borrow Tammi for a while, and then went on to the next subject. After the meeting Brown returned to his office and addressed the folders of correspondence lying on his desk. At ten o'clock he would place communications to three different principals around the circuit, in order to see how they were conducting themselves today. He insisted on keeping a "string" on what he called real-world activity in order to assure that he would not get out-of-date. His predecessor had completely lost touch with the clients and the professionals over the years; Everett did not want that happening to him. At the appointed hour he pressed the preset dialing button.

"Tim Watson here," came the cheery voice.

"Hi Tim, Everett Brown, how are you today?"

"Good shape, Mr. Brown," replied Tim. "Is everything going to suit you?"

"No problems. Any day you can get up and out is a good day. How is the Turton job going? Have they agreed to your new proposal yet? It sure would be a big leap for us if they would let us work out their Latin American offices."

"They're still stalling, Mr. Brown. Their CEO asked me some questions about our resources in Peru and Brazil. I have notified

New York to send me the information. It should be here by express telephoto in about three days.''

''What do they want to know?''

''Who our people are down there, what kind of experience they have, what sort of facilities we can offer, what financial relationships we have, and how long we have had them. Stuff like that.'' Tim paused.

Brown thought a moment.

''We have never had questions like that before. Our reputation takes care of that. Where do you suppose they got the idea to ask those questions?''

''Oh, there is no mystery about that, Mr. Brown,'' replied Tim. ''They have a proposal from Smedley which includes all that as back up; our proposal is just on the work to be done. Smedley has all the resources listed by world computer code so the client can check them out.''

''That must be a big book, Tim,'' noted Brown. ''Smedley must be paying a fortune for proposals.''

''I don't think so, Chief. They sent them a letter of proposal and a modem number. Turton's people just call up the Smedley data bank on the computer, introduce a code number, and they can look over all the bios of their people, the list of banks with telephone and account numbers, the private line numbers of several satisfied clients, and an invitation to meet with the Smedley senior execs.''

''All that from one code number?'' asked Brown.

''And more, it is a complete data bank. If they get the job they will let Turton tap into their status reporting line on a daily basis so the Turton execs can know what the Smedley execs know about the job.''

''How could they do that? It would take an army of clerks to keep those reports up-to-date. I thought Smedley was smarter than that; they will be building up overhead that will make them uncompetitive,'' mused Brown.

''I don't know about that, Mr. Brown,'' said Tim. ''The costs they are offering are lower than ours. Besides, the people on the job just 'speak in' their daily status according to an agreed format and it is right into the data bank on a real-time basis. They even know who is eating lunch with whom. No clerks are involved. It only takes a few moments a couple of times a day.

That is the primary way they communicate, anyway. They don't do these daily communication calls.''

"How do they keep up? What do you mean 'speak in'?''

"Each of their professionals has a little computer input card, they just take out their pocket phone, wipe the card across the input notch, and then talk about the status. What they say is picked up on the central computer and the data folds right into the bank,'' Tim replied, obviously enjoying the opportunity to inform the big boss.

When the conversation was complete Brown sat back in his chair as a wave of depression passed over him. Could it be that he was getting passed by, just like the previous chairman? Everett remembered when the subject of establishing branch offices in Europe and the Far East was enough to send the older man into convulsions. But it was just that action that caused the board to suggest that it might be time to hand over the reins to someone ready for a world market. That someone turned out to be Everett. Now the business appeared to be changing rapidly, but no one in the company was insisting that it was time to change their ways, or offering something innovative . . . except, he thought after a moment, Tammi, the information junkie.

He dialed the phone and asked Tammi to come see him when she had a moment. True to her way of doing things she popped through the door almost immediately. Her forte was information systems, but she was also serving as assistant to the chairman until they found the right slot for her. Brown liked to hire bright young people and then let them search out jobs in the organization. Many of the middle management folks had come from that source.

"Yes, sir,'' said Tammi. "What can I do for you?''

"Sit down, please,'' replied Brown. "You've got too much energy standing, I want to get you on my level. Let's talk about information. Our competitors, I find, are putting all their information on computers and using that data bank to communicate with each other and their clients. We are putting everything on paper and sending it back and forth. Also, we burn up the airwaves using our phones to keep each other informed. Are we falling behind? And if we are, how come no one is in here beating up on me about it? Do you know the answers to these questions?''

Tammi smiled, nodded, and swallowed several times. She was not used to such direct interrogation from her chairman.

"Actually, we are falling behind because we do not have an up-to-date, useable, growing data system. No one is beating on you for a better one because all approaches so far have failed to raise much response. It is felt that neither you, nor the executive committee, are interested in such systems."

There was a pause.

"But I am interested in them. I am always asking you for information, and you usually come up with it. What's wrong with that?"

Tammi blushed for some reason and then remembering her "old girls network" classes, settled down.

"Well, sir, I guess they feel that if the senior executives do not think these systems are appropriate for us then we must not need them. You do not have a data terminal in your office, and neither does anyone else on the executive committee. There is no documented communication from the field operations because it is all done over the phone. No one knows what is happening out there except those in that circuit, and they only know what they have talked about. The information I gave you this morning is probably a month old."

"And it could be up-to-date?"

"It could be no older than a few moments, and it could also relate to other information all around the company. The technology is available to provide each person with all the information needed to run the job, and do it on a continuing basis. In fact, we have a great deal of that equipment here right now; it is a matter of using it for the proper purposes," replied Tammi.

"Here we are in the year two thousand twenty—one hundred years after my grandfather was born, as a matter of fact—and we are still operating with twentieth-century data. What would you need to get us into the twenty-first century?" asked Brown.

"Some new software and a few million world dollars worth of additional equipment would take care of the technology end. The biggest problem would be educating management to understand and use it. Everyone else would be routine to teach," she said.

"Why would management be such a problem?" asked Brown,

becoming a little irritated. "Are we all water buffalos or something?"

Tammi smiled and shifted in her seat, took a breath, and went bravely on.

"It's just that this is not the type of information system that has been typical in this company or any like it. Our executives are very proud of their ability to keep their fingers on the pulse of the company, so to speak. We will have to have a very clear permission to change things."

"Why hasn't this just evolved as a sort of progression until now? What keeps this type of system from just becoming part of the way a company is run? The accounting system is all computerized."

Tammi nodded and sat back in the chair for the first time.

"Being computerized has little to do with it. The computer system is just a way of handling data. I notice that you keep everything you consider important in that little breast pocket calendar. I am always amazed at how much you can get out of it."

"I keep a lot in my head, too," noted Everett, "and that is not always reliable. We stick with what makes us comfortable. How do we know what to put into the data system?"

"The easiest way is to begin with the questions you want to ask. The data systems are ultrafriendly now—it isn't even necessary to have keyboards. You just ask your dish for the information you want and it is displayed on the screen. Or you can have a conversation with the system: You ask, it answers. Some will even provide opinions if you want—like the one that is supposed to be in the White House basement."

"And our system could be fixed to include all this?" asked the chairman.

"All it takes to come up to speed is money and a little time. I can take care of that," she said. "Getting the senior executives to use it is your problem. They wouldn't even have to make those daily phone calls with all of this being available."

Brown smiled. "They might not know what to do without them. How long would it take you to be ready to explain all this to the executive committee and then the board? The board has to approve capital expenditures of this caliber, and they are a lot harder sell than I am. How long do you need? The next board meeting is in two weeks.''

Tammi thought for a moment. "We'll be ready for a demonstration. (It would take a few weeks to introduce all the real information necessary in a working database.) How about having the meeting in the fourth floor conference room instead of the board room itself? There arc not enough power accesses or space in there to do what we need. If that is all right I need to know how many will be at the meeting.''

''We'll have the session wherever you wish,'' he replied, ''and there will be nine of us at the board meeting. The executive committee is also nine, although the other eight are not on the board. That makes seventeen different people in two meetings. The eight board members are all outside directors; none of them works for the company. All of the executive committee members are employees. I assume you know all that, but you asked.''

''Could we have the executive committee meeting the day before the board meeting? That would give us a chance to practice. We could meet in the same room.''

''Done,'' said the chairman. ''I will make the arrangements from this end, and I will tell everyone to let you do whatever you want to do. But it better work, because with these people you only get one shot.''

They shook hands and Tammi scurried down to her department to arrange the meetings. Brown went back to his mail, which he liked because of its consistency. He could dispose of each piece in any of several manners. It took no more than lifting his transcriber and saying a few words to have a letter produced. Or he could forward a document on to another, knowing that proper action would be taken. In a world of stampeding technology, it was comforting to sit and "do" the mail much the way it was handled a generation ago. He realized that there were paperless ways of doing things now. But he liked it this way.

The problem of information was both that there was an enormous amount of it, and that one never knew which part was accurate and which was off-center. Everett read, for instance, all of the business magazines (mostly in their video formats). He subscribed to a continuous news resource that let him learn about any subject whenever he wished. It was only a matter of speaking the name of the situation or person into the receiver and the information came promptly over the video. Yet it was confusing because the whole story was rarely known, and ever since it became possible to construct photographs and films through computer alteration there was no assurance of integrity in those areas. One little adjustment and they can put anyone in bed with anyone else, in the photo, anyway.

He remembered a few events in which he had personally participated that became news stories. He had been frustrated as he realized that the whole truth did not appear. This was not due to dishonesty of the media but to the impossibility of getting a complete story out of everyone involved and then understanding it. Also the media and the public lost interest after awhile. In one case a close friend had been identified as soliciting a kickback from a supplier. The charges were reported widely in the popular as well as the business media. After a complete investigation showed that the executive had nothing to do with the situation, the charges were dropped with apology. However, the stigma hung on because the wide coverage was not repeated. When it came to news, getting the complete story was not easy. Nor was it easy when it came to running a company, he had decided. No matter how many reports he read, how many meetings he conducted, or how many telephone calls he made, there was always something he didn't know about. Information was like running water—one could only drink so much at a time, and during the necessary pause for breath, tons of the fluid rushed by. What was needed was some way of having it all processed into a package. Then questions could be raised either by the system or the executive. Executives would work on thinking up the questions rather than memorizing the data.

Back in the 1990s, when his college days were ending and his career was beginning, Everett had worked as a summer intern for a bank. He was assigned to open the mail, sort it by address or department, and deliver it to the proper place. In order to learn, while easing a boring task, he began to pay special attention to customer complaints. The bank president was interested in the quality wave that was sweeping the nation and had installed the procedure of including a postage paid suggestion card in each status mailing to customers. The customers could make their comments on the card and mail it back to the president's attention.

Everett noticed that the cards just stayed in their box in the president's office. Once in a while someone would thumb through them, but no planned analysis seemed to be taking place. He asked the administrative assistant if it was all right for him to take the cards and see what was on them. She was delighted to get rid of them. He placed them in a folder and took them home that night.

Everett sorted the 174 cards into piles based on the main comment, then he broke those comments down into the areas he guessed were responsible for doing something about it. All of this was done at the kitchen table while his younger sisters tried to help him. He finally had them bring their workboard downstairs and let them make check marks as he called off the complaint. When he was done the list looked like this:

1. Long lines at the tellers' windows during lunchtime. (83)
2. Rude people on the telephone. (42)
3. Getting parking ticket stamped is complicated and humbling. (16)

All the rest were varied but he listed them all. He decided that the biggest opportunity lay with the teller lines. Deciding to attack that situation first, he went to the lobby on his lunchtime to observe the situation. It didn't take long to see that the complainants had been correct in their statements. Beginning at 11:30 A.M., and extending through 1 P.M., there were never less than ten people in line, waiting for a teller. After one o'clock the line diminished, and for the rest of the afternoon it was possible to reach a teller with no more than a one-person wait. He kept dropping into the lobby all day to see how this was going. That night he dug out his operations research book and prepared to do a statistical analysis of the problem. He laid out crowd processing plans on the workboard and even got all the salt and pepper shakers lined up in order to create his own bank lobby. His little sisters enjoyed this part of the work, but despite their eager help nothing seemed to make much sense.

The next day, during lunchtime, he stopped at a pay phone and placed a call to the status room of the bank, to check on the other main complaint, about rude people on the phone.

"Good morning, status room, this is Harold, how may I help you?"

So far so good, he thought.

"My name is Brown, Everett Brown. I would like to verify the credit amount on my BankCard."

"That is on your monthly report, Mr. Brown. If you need it more often than that, please send your inquiry to us, along with a self-addressed envelope, and we will get it right back to you."

"You could have checked it out in the time it took to make that speech," said Everett, indignantly.

"I just work here," replied Harold and disconnected.

Returning to the bank, he stationed himself in the lobby again and watched the crowd. There were fourteen people in the positioning gate and two at tellers' windows. At this moment, he realized that there were actually six windows but only two had tellers in them. With the excitement of discovery growing in him, he summoned courage to walk into the back office and approach the fearsome head teller, Ethyl Marks.

"Where are all the tellers?" he blurted.

She looked at him with pity.

"They are at lunch, dummy. Don't you interns have anything to do? I've seen you hanging around the lobby instead of working. Go back to where you are supposed to be. Get." She returned to her work.

That night at the workboard Everett decided that the lines were long during lunchtime because the tellers took their lunch at the same time as the customers were rushing over—during the only time off they had—to make some transaction. Along with this discovery came the realization that seemingly complex problems have simple solutions if the problem can be understood. If he told someone about this, the head teller would put out a contract on him. The status people worked for her also, and it was easy to see where they picked up their telephone manners. But it all was a problem that didn't speak well for the bank and needed to be corrected.

He prepared the analysis of the customer complaints with his suggested solutions and decided to face the problem directly.

His grandfather had often said, "An honest man can't make a bank transaction, get his teeth fixed, buy a suit, or do any of those nine-to-five things. Everything is open while he is supposed to be at work." He had also said that if you wanted to shut off a gushing fire hydrant, you had to put a wrench on the top of it and get wet in the process. Knowing his grandfather would not voluntarily appear within 300 feet of a gushing fire hydrant did not make this any less useful. Taking his mental wrench with him he went to call on Ms. Marks. She was not thrilled to see him.

"I wanted to show you this report, Ms. Marks, if you will take a moment. I analyzed the customer complaints that come to the president's office, and thought you might be interested in the results. I haven't shown it to anyone else."

She took the paper in her hand.

"What am I supposed to get out of this?"

"Well," he replied, "it says that the customers think our biggest problem is long lines at the lunch hour."

"That's part of banking. Every bank has long lines at lunch hour. That's when everyone wants to come in and cash a check, making a deposit, get traveler's checks, and do all those little things. That's part of banking."

"Yes, ma'am," he said. "I noticed that there are fewer windows open at that time than at any other time, because the tellers are at lunch."

"So?"

"Well, if the tellers took their lunchtimes when the customers were not here, instead of when they are here, then there would be no lines when they are here."

He paused and she stared at him.

" 'Out of the mouths of babes,' " she quoted.

"Ma'am?"

She stood up and slapped him on the shoulder.

"It takes someone who doesn't know a thing about the business to find the simple cause of these problems; we have worried about that for years. What else have you got on that list?"

"We aren't very polite on the telephone," he muttered.

"So what can we do about that? Sometimes the customers aren't very polite either. What are you suggesting?"

"The telephone company has a manners class. I know because my girlfriend is interning there this summer. They come and explain how to answer the phone and how to deal with people on the other end without getting everyone upset.''

Everett flushed to himself as he remembered how Ms. Marks had told the president about his work and how proud he was when the lunchtime lines disappeared. Several months later, Ms. Marks had called him at school and asked him to drop by at lunchtime one day that week. He was surprised to see that lines of three or four people were in existence.

''The word has gotten around that you can get in here at noon and we have had a surge of new accounts,'' she said. ''Now you figure how we keep the lines short again. We will pay you the standard consultant's fee. Go to it.''

During that stay he did an analysis of what the customers actually wanted during that bank visit by asking them as they stood in line. He discovered that most of their needs could be handled by installing a ''host'' who would question the customers and either direct them to the special desks set up during the rush time or just take their transactions from them. Transactions not involving the transfer of cash could be handled quickly there. In addition, the bank installed automatic tellers for people who just wanted to take some cash out or put some in.

That experience convinced him that he wanted to be a consultant as a career. After graduation he searched around and eventually joined the firm of Dean and Samoline, Inc. He discovered that he soon was teaching the art of operations research analysis to his new employer. He was able to create a new and very profitable way of working. The firm appreciated it so much that today, instead of dealing with the hands-on excitement, he was back to sorting mail. Now he was able to do it sitting down at least. That was some sort of progress.

When the Executive Committee arrived at the meeting room they found that each of them had a display dish at their place. Looking like a piece of plate glass, and apparently connected to nothing, the disc just lay there. Tammi waited patiently for all of them to take their assigned seats and then picked up her plate.

''I know all of you are familiar with the display dish,'' she said, giving them the benefit of her optimism. ''The one you have in front of you has been tuned to your personal correlation; it will not respond to anyone else. The display is connected to the central data bank, which in turn is hooked to thirty-two different data centers around the world. D-Sam operations data is not entered, of course, just the financial material, but we will be able to begin entering operations quickly if you decide to implement the system.''

''What is the idea of being connected to the thirty-two different data centers?'' asked Clarence. ''Do we need all that to run our business?''

''That connection lets you gain the answer to just about any question of what is going on in the world at that moment, or what has happened in the past, or what is known about practically anything. All you have to do is ask,'' she replied. ''It provides a background of information that lets our business data sit in a real world. For instance, to take something very basic, if we were going to schedule someone for a trip to Paris we would need to know where Paris is, how long it takes to get there, what it would cost, and a dozen other things.

''These systems contain the Paris phone book, street locations, businesses, and the names of their people—every one of their people—the compete history of the city, and—where you can buy popcorn! Every bit of financial, social, and other information is in there.''

''What was Babe Ruth's lifetime batting average?'' asked Clarence.

''Three-oh-six,'' said the display dish.

''Who was Babe Ruth?'' asked Tammi.

Clarence winced.

''A baseball player who popularized the game during the nineteen-twenties and thirties,'' said Tammi's dish, before Clarence could speak. ''A full biography is being printed out in your office. You can get it when the meeting is over.''

Joseph DiCarlo, the financial officer, nodded eagerly.

''I have been trying to get this group interested in database management for some time, Tammi. They are just plain scared of it. Is that common?''

''I guess people are always concerned about the unfamiliar, Mr. DiCarlo,'' replied Tammi. ''However, we all are used to the personal communicators we carry with us, so it isn't the device itself that bothers them. I really think it is the belief that central data lack integrity. We trust the information we gather ourselves rather than something that comes from elsewhere."

"I think people don't recognize the value of all that information. I know I haven't until recently. Complex organizations like ours require constant measurement and evaluation, just like any whole body does," said Everett. "It has taken society a long time to realize that disasters, for instance, don't just happen in one moment. They build up over time, and the clues are there for us to see."

"You mean like a war, or a building falling down, or a business going to pot," asked Helene, "those kinds of disasters?"

"Those," nodded Everett, "and the less gigantic ones, like an automobile engine running out of oil and burning. That takes a long time getting ready to happen. Or when people used to smoke all their lives and get lung cancer, the signs and the information were there all along to be recognized. All of this comes under the concept of Completeness, which has to do with taking care of every aspect and knowing that you are doing so. The San Francisco earthquake of 1989 is a good example. The majority of deaths occurred because of design failures in the second deck of a freeway. These were design inadequacies that had been known about for years. The buildings that were damaged in the Marina area were erected on soft land fill—everyone knew that."

"I always thought our company was pretty 'complete,' " said Helene. "Our customers have been pleased with us all these years."

"Now don't start getting defensive, Helene," said Clarence. "You know as well as I do that running this business is like pushing a safe across the sand."

"What kind of current data would we get from the field?" asked Helene. "Would it be everything we get now?"

"You can have whatever you would like, certainly a lot more than now," replied Tammi. "Let me demonstrate. We have obtained a package that was used by a car leasing firm. As you know they manufacture their own vehicles, provide them to individuals, and even have their own car train system between major cities. Their customers just hop on and off the train, riding in their car most of the way. They use a magnetic levitated propulsion system, and even subcontract the train path out for others to use. In addition to being innovative, they are good managers. They control prices and services closely and keep in constant touch with their customers.''

''How can they keep in constant touch when their customers are in cars, or on a train, or wherever?'' asked Everett.

''Sensors are part of it,'' said Tammi. ''Every car has a mood sensor in it for one thing—if a negative mood hits a car, the client gets a call from the control unit. They take care of everything and do it right now.''

''I'd be anxious to see some of that,'' said Helene.

''Okay.'' Tammi nodded. ''What we have here is a recorded exchange between the midwest region manager of systems integrity and the information center. The written matter will be displayed on your dish, but we will put it on audio so you can hear it.''

The group was silent as Tammi signaled her dish, then a voice spoke. Everything sounded very natural. The voice was making contact with information central.

''This is John Butte, location 3279, personal code 3918.''

''Go ahead Mr. Butte, how may I help you?''

''How many of our cars that are in the midwest region today did not originate in this region?''

''As of eleven a.m. there are twenty-three thousand ninety cars in this region that did not originate there. Five thousand forty-three arrived by train, four thousand five hundred seventy-six by ferries, and the rest drove into the area.''

''Have we had any operational complaints?''

''Service has been performed on eighty-nine nonregional cars today, and we have had one hundred thirty-four calls for information or service.''

''Are those eighty-nine included in the one hundred thirty-four?''

''No, they are different incidents. I'm sorry, I should have made that clear, it will not occur again.''

''What have been the main service problems? And what vehicles were they on?''

''Eleven of the services concerned irregularities in the communication system, and all of the rest were concentrated in power units. Of the information calls, ninety-three referenced the power unit; I will display the remaining data on your dish.''

"Have we had any reports of those difficulties in the regionally based cars recently?"

"No, sir, it has been seven hundred thirty-four days since we have had a power unit difficulty."

"And how many units are there in the region, those that are based there?"

"Three million five hundred seventy-four thousand, nine hundred eight at this time. We project an addition one thousand six hundred forty-five units will be contracted by the end of the day."

"The cars whose power units required work, where were they made?"

"All but one of the cars were made in plant fifty-six, which is in Phoenix, Arizona. The power units themselves came from an oil company supplier, all from the same location which is tower E-four-five in the Persian Gulf. I will display their serial numbers."

"Do we have information on these E-four-five units from the past?"

"Yes, a total of seven hundred thirty-nine units were identified by the systems integrity evaluation as being potentially unable to retain nuclear power energy after three years. The E-four-five management designated them as short-lived and delivered the units to Phoenix for assembly."

"Are there any others in that category worldwide?"

"No, these are the only ones."

"Get the plant manager of E-four-five for me."

"Simpson speaking."

"This is John Butte. Are you aware of these seven hundred thirty-nine power units with the short time span?"

"Yes, we reported them as soon as the information came to light. The units are being replaced as quickly as we can get the car lessors to bring the units to our shops."

"Do you know of anything else along these lines that is going to come and bother our customers?"

"No, this is the only situation like that."

"What happened to the people who made that short-range decision?"

"This happened a year ago, and they have all been back to system integrity school and learned the error of their ways. This really was a random incident and should never have happened."

"Had these people been to school before they made this decision?"

"Well, no, and that is the problem. My predecessor felt there wasn't enough time to send them. But they have been there now."

"Is there anyone in your organization who has not been to class?"

"None that I know of, but we will check immediately and get back to you."

"Don't bother, I can do it from here." Addressing the information system, Butte continued, "Do we have anyone in the whole system anywhere who has not been through the SI courses and the rest of their required education? If so, how many are or have been in E-four-five?"

"There are one thousand two hundred ninety-seven employees who have not completed their basic education. Of those sixty-three are in E-four-five."

"Notify their individual management immediately and place the list on my dish memory. We will need a report on the status and causes tomorrow. Close."

The group paused to think about this. The interrogating experience was completely new to them.

"I could have gotten the same information and held the same communications," said Clarence. "It would have taken six months, but I could have probably done it."

"By then it would have been out-of-date," murmured Helene.

"Could we actually do this?" asked DiCarlo. "Wouldn't it be incredibly expensive?"

"It would cost a lot of money initially," said Tammi. "But once the system is in and employees learn how to make their regular data inputs, then it takes care of itself."

"What kind of money are we talking about?" asked Clarence.

"We have put together an estimate based on a company very much our size and configuration," replied Tammi. "The financial data are displayed on your dish at this moment."

"Wow, is that everything?" asked Helene. "Won't there be another sixty percent later?"

"No ma'am," said Tammi. "Mr. Brown said to get it all out and it is all out, nothing more to do."

"The real question," said Everett, "is whether we can live *without* it. Can we function in the future as we are doing now? Will our information and action sources keep us in business? Or will we become uninformed and slip quietly behind our competition?"

"I feel we should recommend that the board approve this action and expenditure or sell the company to someone who will," said Helene. "Anybody who doesn't want to do this?"

"One question," said Clarence. "How did we slip behind like this? Is it because we stopped listening?"

"Self-answering questions don't count," replied Everett. "Motion passed."

"We will present the proposition to the board tomorrow. I am certain they will recognize this need," said Everett. "I will recommend implementing the system to them, and we will all get back together after that meeting tomorrow to press the go button if they agree."

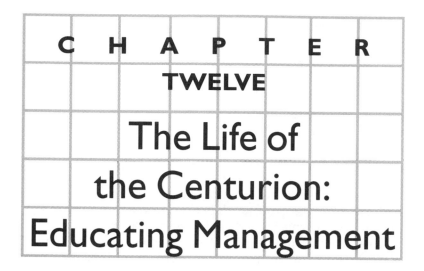

C H A P T E R
TWELVE
The Life of
the Centurion:
Educating Management

The board of directors meeting of this era was not the usual passive gathering known to CEOs in the past of old and carefully selected friends. Everett was the one "inside" member, as a D-Sam employee, while the other eight directors were all "outside," meaning that they were not employed by the company. The directors were all senior executives in their own right and served on the D-Sam board because they had accepted a responsibility to the shareholders of that company.

This new way of managing had come about when the stock exchanges required, in 2006, that all equity corporations have no inside directors on their boards except the chairman and the chief executive, who might be two different people. The governments of the participating countries had passed supporting legislation requiring that these directors be fully informed by the companies. In turn, the directors were required to assure that the public was given all pertinent information. The companies themselves were required to purchase insurance policies protecting the shareholders from the directors, and vice versa.

All of this had come about because of the Boxan scandal. Boxan was, like most large companies by the turn of the century, a conglomerate with many different businesses throughout the world. The Boxan management had set up subsidiary boards in each of their operations and placed themselves as members. Each board then voted themselves significant directors' fees and stock options. The subsidiaries were all taken public individually, with

Boxan retaining 60 percent of the stock. By reporting the revenue and profit figures enthusiastically, the management group was able to drive all the share prices higher and take personal advantage of the results. Naturally, they all became very wealthy individuals. Just as naturally, some of the shareholders took offense at the actions and sued. When the case was dismissed because the executives had done nothing illegal, other corporations began to set up the same questionable arrangements.

But the publicity hurt Boxan's core business by convincing customers that the company didn't care about them and was, in fact, taking advantage of their business. The resulting loss of revenue, combined with lack of management attention, put the company into receivership. Many people were hurt financially by this action, and a fine old company was essentially destroyed. The reaction of the financial community and the public was to attack the traditionally cozy board systems practiced in corporations. The demand was made for the independent selection and election of directors, and for action to replace those directors who were also employees of the company. The Exchanges published a list of individuals who would be considered acceptable as directors, and the various companies invited people from that publication and welcomed the participation of major investors also. Individuals or groups with large ownership positions were also eligible for election provided they were not employees of the corporation. Everett was on two boards himself. One of the restrictions was that people couldn't serve on each other's boards. This created competition between companies for the really good directors. The result of all this had been excellent for the companies in terms of integrity, but had often reduced their ability to react quickly. Also, the directors wanted to know a great deal more about the operations than they had in the past, and that required companies to become more sophisticated in their status systems.

Preparing for the meeting, Everett reviewed the list of directors, trying to determine where he could have problems with his capital needs proposal. His board had been very cooperative and understanding to date, but now he was talking about changing the basic way the business was managed. It was also going to be necessary to become much more involved in employee education, and that was also going to cost money. He had asked

Sam Cross, the education manager, to present his new program and wish list to the board. Sam's view of education was that it went on all the time anyway, and it was up to us to direct and supplement it.

He returned to the list:

- Hi Cho, 57, chairman of the Shanghai/Boston Bank. Hi knew more about financing than anyone Everett had ever met. Originally he had been coaxed onto the board because D-Sam felt his contacts and introductions would be a big help in the Far East. He had indeed provided valuable assistance there, but as chairman of the Audit Committee, he had also helped D-Sam avoid large tax penalties. He would have an open mind.
- Alden Foster, 41, publisher of sports fashion magazines. Alden had accepted an invitation to the board for the purpose of learning more about business. He felt he was having trouble managing his operations and was always willing to listen. Since he produced twenty or so magazines around the world with a very small staff, Everett had to wonder how much more he could expect to learn here.
- Luther Jacobson, 50, president of Industrial Fabrication, Inc. Luther was a "nuts and bolts" man to his toes. He was the last person Everett knew who did not carry a personal communicator. He was going to be a hard sell on this project.
- Booker Johnson, 62, chairman of United Agriculture. Booker's company supplied 10 percent of the total foodstuffs in the United States and a larger proportion in Latin America. He looked rural but was a keen investor who understood markets worldwide—the commodities business bred tough, quick-acting executives. Booker would make up his mind in the first ten minutes.
- Grace Moroski, 54, former ambassador to the United Nations, former United States senator, currently a partner in the world's largest public accounting firm. Grace looked at everything in reference to its effect on people. She will like all the things we are going to present.
- Courtney Simmons, 29, trustee, Samoline Foundation, and corporate vice president of World Autos. Courtney is the

granddaughter of our founder, who placed most of his stock in the Samoline Foundation. A well-educated, business-sharp young woman, she has been the moving force behind our "expanded community" program. She will be all for this new effort.
- Nathan Weinstein, 67, chairman emeritus of Southeast University. Nathan has tried to resign from the board several times, but the other directors, as well as myself, just won't let him. He has been the voice of reason so many times he would be sorely missed.
- Barry McPhearson, 45, chairman of the Scottish Investment Trust. Barry's trust has a big investment in D-Sam and he takes his role on the board seriously. He will be difficult because he seems to think that money once spent is lost forever. He would not be missed if he were to decide that the monthly trip to our meeting is too much trouble.

The compensation and audit committees met that morning, as usual without the chairman, who was not a member. Everett guessed that no one was really safe as long as the compensation committee was in session. He had managed to keep McPhearson off of it—so far, anyway.

As the members assembled for the postluncheon meeting, Everett called the session to order.

"We have a few routine agenda items," he said, "and then we need to have a lengthy discussion of taking the company into the reality of today."

"That sounds expensive," commented Booker. "It sounds starry-eyed."

"You think everything is expensive, Booker" said Courtney, "particularly 'reality.' I remember you talking about giving up golf when they raised the price of balls."

"He changed courses, got a place with no water," said Nathan. "Now he still has the same ball."

"Had it for years." Booker smiled.

Everett tapped his gavel on the block and nodded everyone into place. As he was about to begin, Hi Cho spoke.

"If we have an item that will require a lengthy discussion, Mr. Chairman, I recommend that we go directly to it. We can deal with other things later."

Everett glanced around the table for consensus, and upon receiving it, nodded in agreement with Hi's suggestion.

"Good idea, Hi. Let me make a few comments on the items, and then I will invite the two young people who are going to make presentations to join us.

"These subjects concern the company's database, or lack of it, and the educational program for our employees, suppliers, and customers. We have slipped behind in both areas. The growth in available technology has been so rapid that it is only necessary to take one's eyes off it for a brief moment and it has zipped by. New firms entering the field as our competitors start up with the current technology, while older organizations such as ours have to deal with the past in order to get to the future. We need to leapfrog, not fight our way out of the brush.

"We have begun to realize that our way of keeping up with the status of client projects is old-fashioned. We rely on our senior people, who have a great deal of experience, to talk regularly with the field people. The information they receive is shared in our staff meetings; also they can give advice and counsel to those who are out working. Unfortunately, this cumbersome way of managing reduces our reaction time and raises the cost to the customer.

"In applying our long-proven techniques to ourselves, we find that we need to be current, we need instant status around the clock. There is a way of doing that. You all have noticed the communication dishes at your place. They are bound up with several information systems and our own financial network. They are tuned to your personal frequency. These dishes will play an important part in the demonstration today. But before I bring Tammi Hope and Sam Cross in, I want to show you how much money we are going to ask you to appropriate. The total will now appear on your screen."

Each of the directors focused on their dish and conducted a mass gulp as the number appeared.

"We might have to have an equity offering to handle this," said Booker.

"We have that much sitting in investments right now," noted Barry McPhearson. "However, it is making us a nice return."

"I wanted to be certain I had your attention," said Everett. "Now that Tammi and Sam are here we will begin. Tammi?"

Tammi conducted the same demonstration she had put on for the executive committee the day before. To her surprise, she found this group to be much more familiar with both the concepts and equipment.

"We even have a database in our factories, Everett," said Luther. "Our customers can design a part we have never seen before, enter it in the system, receive a price and delivery quote within minutes, receive the order, pay for it, and I wouldn't even know it had all happened."

"That's incredible," commented Alden Foster. "I would not have believed that such a backwater business as hardware could be that up-to-date. We do what used to be called 'desktop publishing' in our offices. A story written in Paris, in French of course, shows up ready for the Brazilian edition automatically translated, with reconstructed photos, all within a few hours. One person can assemble and produce all the editions of the world, and we publish in seventeen languages."

Everett looked at Tammi. "Are we that far behind?" he asked.

"These are special cases," she replied. "The programming required for them is specific and can be fairly standard once it is set up and working. Here we are talking about a completely open system where information is fed in each day, and new judgments must be formed continually. We will be able to translate as a matter of course, and we will be able to sort and direct customer orders with little effort. However, the challenge is in pulling together information from different sources and making sense of it."

"All the sources of data we will have are generally talking about the same thing, aren't they, Tammi?" asked Courtney. "I mean, a consultant calling in his or her daily report is going to be covering much the same material, aren't they?"

"I would think there would be a lot of repeat items, Ms. Simmons," replied Tammi. "Time on different tasks would be one; client reaction to proposals, another; there will be many standard inputs. The ones I am concerned about are those we can't anticipate. But the system does get smarter as it gains experience."

To Everett's surprise a motion was quickly made and seconded to provide the capital for purchasing the necessary equipment and software. Installation and training costs would have to come out of operating funds.

"Thank you, Tammi," said the chairman. "You may want to stay for Sam's presentation in case there are any questions about interface."

He turned to the group. "If there is one other activity we cannot neglect it is education. We do a lot of training and will continue to do so. However, we also have to keep our people up-to-date and involved, and that requires education. Naturally, we pay for any educational courses they wish to take on their own time. But we also insist that they participate in company programs. Now we are finding that our delivery systems are becoming obsolete, and the content irrelevant.

"Sam wants to show us a few things that will help make the education job easier, and then we will discuss content. Sam?"

Sam took his place in the front of the room and began to pull on gloves and place a space helmet–looking apparatus on his head. "I hope you all will excuse me while I get suited up here," he said. "I would like to demonstrate a teaching aid that also provides evaluation at the same time. You will be able to see what I see by looking at your dish."

On the dishes the directors suddenly saw the inside of a factory and had the sensation of walking down the aisle between machines.

"That's my plant number six," Luther exclaimed. "There's Charlie Browels on that milling machine. He's waving at you, at us. Is this a movie? How could he see us if it was a movie?"

"No sir, it is not a movie," said Sam. "It really is your plant and we are really there right now. I thought it would be more believable if we were able to use a facility that someone knew. Your folks were kind enough to cooperate with us, Mr. Jacobson. We can go anywhere we want in this facility. Let's go over to the control desk and see how the in-process inventory is doing."

Sam's figure walked over to the supervisor's station and up to the man standing by the desk. They greeted each other.

"What percentage of our inventory is sitting on the floor or in boxes out here?" asked Sam.

The man addressed his dish and then turned to Sam.

"It's about eighteen percent right now, Sam," said the supervisor. "It is usually less than two percent, but we have some special jobs that came in, and that always puts a lot of stuff on the floor. The computer plans it all out, but we still have to have the material available, and some of it is always long lead-time stuff."

"What kind of system is this?" asked Alden. "He is here in front of us and standing there talking in that other plant at the same time. Where is that plant, Luther?"

"The plant is eighteen hundred miles away, Alden. And I haven't the faintest idea what that system is. Ask Sam," Luther replied.

Sam turned off the image and attended to the group around the table. "This system is based on something that was originally known as 'virtual reality,' developed by a computer visionary named Myron Krueger. Later work developed it more completely, and the government took it to use in nuclear and classified projects. But no one could ever figure exactly what to do with it commercially. Frankly, hardly anyone has been comfortable with the reality of this. It is possible to travel almost anywhere that has been prepared, or at least have the sensation and appearance of doing that.

"What we plan to use it for is developing consultants and other professionals. When we are hooked up it will be possible to sit in our workroom and be beside any of our field people for most of their day. We will be able to have conferences with clients that make it look, to them, as if we are sitting right in their office. It should be a great marketing tool, too. We can take potential clients to visit satisfied ones."

The group paused to take all this in.

"Can you go, or seem to go, anywhere?" asked Courtney. "Could I stand in the middle of a tennis match going on in Wimbledon, for instance? Would the players know I was there? Would I be in the way?"

"You can go anywhere the receiving equipment is available. Actually, it only requires a small and inexpensive box in order to receive. The equipment is absolutely portable but someone has to put it there. As for standing in the middle of the match, they would see you as an apparently solid person but soon realize that you had the consistency of a ghost. Once they got used to it there probably would be no problem—but tennis pros are pretty focused.''

''My experience,'' said Nathan, ''has been that new technologies do not necessarily lead to new levels of comprehension and learning by themselves. It has only been a few years since we had such high hopes about students having their own personal computers. MBA. students carry them around on their backs and continually peck at them, but they become notebooks after awhile. At one time, engineers all had yard-long slide rules hanging from their belts.

''The papers we received as a result of the computers were better formed and had more references, but overall the students didn't seem to learn more quickly. We even have interactive learning discs where a dozen people can watch the same program, answer the same questions, and all get different responses from what appears to be the same screen. Again, there was no demonstrated increase in learning speed. There did seem to be more interest in the material, however.''

''I'm glad to hear you say this stuff is useless, Nathan,'' commented Barry. ''We are being pressured to do some of this in our Scottish schools. I will be able to tell them that it is a waste of money.''

Nathan raised his hand in alarm. ''Oh it isn't a waste, Barry, far from it,'' he replied. ''What happens if you don't keep up on the technology of learning is that they fall further behind. The students of today learn a lot more than the ones of yesterday because there is a lot more to learn. They just can't handle it unless they have this information-processing equipment. It is like trying to fly to Tokyo for a meeting tomorrow on a plane that will get you there the day after tomorrow. You may not get there smarter on the right aircraft, but you will get there.''

''Could our executives use this particular equipment to audit the performance of their people?'' asked Grace. ''Is there a way that they could offer counseling to those in the field by appearing to be beside them?''

Sam nodded. ''That is another use of the equipment, and part of our educational plan is to put experienced people out there in just that fashion.''

''So this 'reality' machine would be our prime method of education?'' asked Courtney.

"It would be a part of it," answered Sam. "The main emphasis is still on classroom lectures, holographic projections, and plain, old-fashioned study. I just thought this would be an interesting demonstration for us."

"Tell us about the overall educational plan. And since you separate training from education, could you comment on that, too?" asked Grace.

"We'd also be interested in knowing about some of the subjects involved. Are you teaching Completeness? That seems to be a management concern today," said Nathan.

"Right now we are just doing basic things," replied Sam. "The education program has not progressed into Completeness and the other Centurion concepts. However, we have hired an education consulting firm to help us. They have these courses in-hand now; I can give you the content if you would like."

Sam looked at the chairman, who nodded in agreement. He spoke to the dish and instantly a chart appeared on every communication device.

"The key to our education process is Completeness. All of this begins with the management personnel, and I might note that board members will be requested to attend certain classes and study certain material. Your role in this process is vital because everything forms from here."

"I'm not sure I know what that means," said Booker. "We make policy decisions here, but I don't know that we run anything, as a board that is."

"Let me make a couple of comments on that thought," said Everett. "I think it is essential that the directors clearly understand what management's intent is. Let me do it by discussing the ideas of Completeness, which is aimed at making the customer, the employee, and the supplier successful. Several ideas are involved in the implementation.

"The first idea is 'treat the whole as one.' Now our way of operating has always been by groups or what could be called cells. A few people worked on projects and no one knew what any other cell was doing. So we have never been a 'whole' except at the very top of the organization, where everything came together. Most of what comes together here is financial. We talk very little about the people or the clients.

"The second idea is 'build a culture of consideration.' We

always were a firm with a rather high turnover rate, among professionals as well as clerical people. It was assumed that individuals burned out after awhile and went on to quiet things. However, we have been learning, through interviews and surveys, that the company is felt by its employees to have little concern for them. I found that hard to accept, but if we look at the cold light of reality it is true. After all, who should know better how the employees feel than they themselves? We have to change the policies that cause such a situation. It is very hard to find people today, as you know; it is only good business to build strong relationships with the employees.

"The third idea is to 'make everything understood.' We have been very selective along those lines. For some reason or other we keep a lot of secrets inside, and we have not done a good job of teaching people their responsibilities. This educational process will be a big help in overcoming that.

"The fourth idea of Completeness is 'be complete but not finished.' I can see several of us looking at this layout Sam has provided and thinking, 'How much is it going to cost, and how long will we have to do it?' We will have to recognize that it is a cost of doing business and that we will never be finished with it. As soon as we learn how to teach something, there will be another entity of instruction and more people to teach. Internal education will become a large user of funds. We are thinking that we can pay for most of that by beginning to teach our clients."

Everett paused and looked around the room.

"How have we done so well for so long without a significant educational process?" asked Courtney. "I would think that we would have felt the impact before this?"

"We have felt it, we just didn't recognize it," said Nathan. "Our growth rate has been slowing for some time, but we have done well because of the firm's reputation and the lack of credible competition."

"All true," commented Everett. "We don't really have any information or services that are unique; we have no magic formulas to offer our clients. We had the field much to ourselves for years, but now we have to be outstanding. The way to do that is have people who know the most, have the best attitude, and work very effectively. We need to delight our clients."

"So today," said Luther, "we are approving a database system for all hands, and an education system for all hands. Everyone is going to know everything, or at least have an opportunity to do that. Correct?''

"Correct," said Everett. "Now let's let Sam tell us about the educational process. I want to be certain that all of us understand that this is a change of policy and direction."

"The educational material begins with a standard orientation course which every employee attends. They also go to an annual update and receive regular monthly transmissions of status and events through the CEO's network.

"Executive's Course content (one week):

- Understanding the ideas and principles of Completeness
- Case histories of successful and unsuccessful clients
- The role of the senior executive in making policy
- Causing the development, documentation, and teaching of clear requirements
- Systems integrity—measuring performance in order to identify lack of conformance to requirements
- Corrective action systems to continually identify and eliminate nonconformance
- Communications with employees, suppliers, and customers

"Manager's Course content (two weeks):

- Understanding the ideas and principles of Completeness
- Case histories of application
- The Completeness implementation process
- The role of the manager in causing Completeness
- Systems integrity and measurement
- The process of identifying and eliminating nonconformance
- Communications with employees, suppliers, and customers
- Personal action plan development

"Professional's Course content (six weeks, plus one week per quarter):

- Understanding the ideas and principles of Completeness
- Content and application of the process of Completeness

- Success and failure cases
- Artificial reality workshops
- Database input and output
- Communication with clients and associates
- Presentation methods
- Systems integrity and measurement
- Identifying and eliminating nonconformance

"Knowledge Worker's Course content (two weeks):

- Database sourcing and input
- Ideas and principles of Completeness
- The development of successful customers
- Development and understanding of requirements
- Understanding my personal requirements
- Systems integrity and measurement to confirm Completeness
- Nonconformance identification
- Nonconformance elimination and prevention
- Communications with others
- Job enrichment

"Skilled and Clerical Worker's Course content (ten two-hour sessions with quarterly updates):

- Understanding the need for Completeness
- Understanding my job requirements
- Training to meet specific requirements
- Identifying and eliminating nonconformance
- Communication with others
- Systems integrity and measurement
- Continuing education

"Supplier's Course content (two-and-one-half days)

- The ideas and principles of Completeness
- The process of Completeness
- The supplier's role
- The purchaser's role
- The advantages of Completeness
- Systems integrity and measurement

"And that is a quick summary of the content," said Sam. "Most of it has been developed by our consultants or ourselves. Practice teaching will begin next week, at least according to our plans. Thank you."

Everett thanked Sam and asked the directors for their questions and comments. The response was enthusiastic and both programs were approved.

"Now," said Everett, "we need to set up a date when the directors can go to the Executive's Course. That will show everyone we are serious. Sam will give you the dates of the sessions. I would prefer that everyone make a commitment before leaving today. I'll do mine right now; I plan to attend the first one. That way Sam will worry more about it."

They all chuckled; the other agenda items were quickly discussed, and the meeting was adjourned.

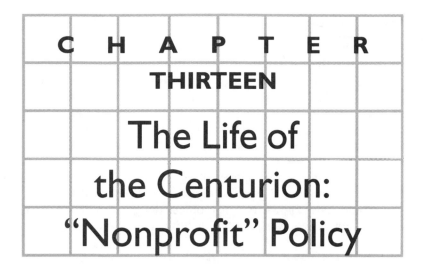

C H A P T E R
THIRTEEN
The Life of
the Centurion:
"Nonprofit" Policy

C ourtney Simmons walked beside Everett down the hall toward his office. The directors gave their full attention during the meetings but usually disappeared quickly to their other
concerns as soon as they were dismissed. However, Courtney
wanted to find out more about this Completeness business. Her
specific area of concern was the Samoline Foundation Trust and
its management culture. She had been elected as trustee two
years ago when her mother decided that she did not have the
time or the urge to participate any longer.

"You and Harvey need to take over these family things," her
mother had said. "You are up-to-date on business, and I never
really know what is going on. So you do the Foundation for a
few years, and Harvey can take over later if you don't have time.
It only meets four times a year, and it does pay a trustee fee."

Courtney had joined the board and had in turn been recommended by that body to represent them on the D-Sam board.
She bounced back and forth between helping World Autos sell
convertibles and the machinations of high finance and philan-
thropy. The Trust owned 8.5 percent of D-Sam stock and had
large investments resulting from company shares sold during the
public offering. Each year they dispersed a great deal of money
and Courtney found herself immersed in requests being sent to
the Foundation. Every worthwhile cause in the world, it seemed,
as well as many that were not so worthwhile, wanted a contribution. It was very confusing.

Seated in Everett's office, Courtney got right to the point.

"I need to ask you some questions on this Completeness business, particularly in the area of policy. And while I am at it, I want to leave this holographic film about our new 'adult sports car.' I understand that you don't have one, so I have arranged for the latest model to be delivered to your house. It should be there right now."

Everett smiled. "Very clever of you to send that car around, Courtney. However, if you had done a complete market study, you would have known that my oldest daughter is home from college. You may never see that machine again, and I may never see her."

"Never underestimate us marketeers, Chief, we track grown children the way park rangers track bears. Just have someone touch the button in the coin pocket and the sale will be registered. Funds will be deducted from your asset account and even the license plate will be mounted," she said. "I know you are busy and I don't want to waste your time, so let me state my case. The Samoline Foundation has been generous for a long time and is recognized as being well intended. However, it seems to me as if we trustees just meet, look over the recommendations the staff has made, approve the lot, and watch the checks zip out. Everyone is very pleasant, and if any member has a pet project it certainly gets consideration. I realize now that what we need is a policy that lets us approach giving in a more planned fashion, more *completely*, to pick a word. What I need to know is how does one, particularly a junior member of the organization, go about causing that?"

"A policy is the proper place to begin," mused Everett. "If it does not exist on purpose, then it will sort of happen, anyway. I suspect you are concerned because the Trust doesn't seem to be leaving any footprints?"

She nodded enthusiastically. "Exactly—'footprints,' exactly. We put out all this money, but there is nothing with our name on it—there are no diseases we have stamped out, there is no class warfare we have halted. It is hard to say what effect we have had. We have helped a lot of people, but I think Grandpa thought we would be more specific. Bless his heart, he didn't provide any direction about investment or distribution."

"He always used to shy away from that," said Everett. "He

used to cite the case of the benefactor who directed that all the funds be invested only in public electric railway stock. At the time it was a good idea, but as you know they do not exist anymore. They never did get that solved. Do you have any specific ideas of what you would want the policy to say?''

She pulled some notes from her purse.

''I was jotting while the meeting was going on. What I got in this area was that the policy of the company should be to make the customers and employees successful. I took the applicants to be the customers, and of course, grandfather. I suspect we will also require some other policies to get that message across.''

''Right,'' Everett said, nodding. ''Quality, finance, relationships—they all need specific supportive policies.''

''What I have been thinking about is an overall policy to guide donations,'' replied Courtney, continuing. ''Let me try this on you: 'Foundation gifts should be aimed at assisting the Completeness of a cause and be identified with specific projects as much as possible.' For instance, rather than providing funds to purchase food for people, we would invest in a project that would teach them to earn or raise food themselves. The old 'teach them how to fish' story. In this regard, we would deal with endowments rather than direct gifts. Endowments permit long-range actions while gifts are used up quickly. Our measurement would be the accepted success of the recipient.''

Everett smiled. ''That is an excellent beginning. I understand what you are trying to do. Let me ask you about the trustees: What kind of people are they?''

''Most of them have been around for a while. The Foundation is set up to have a majority of public members, one representing each of five disciplines: education, medicine, religion, science, and the arts. My great uncle is a family member along with one banker, one lawyer, and myself. Then there is the executive director, Arthur Wiggens. He is not a trustee, but he pretty much runs the show. We have an economist, part time, to guide investments, and a resident staff of three people who check out the applicants and do the paperwork.''

''Who does the investing?'' asked Everett.

''That's where the bank shines. Their trust departments handle most of it, and actually they do very well. The return they are getting on investment is as good as the big name firms. The lawyer does the legal work, Uncle Henry dozes, and I watch it all take place. They all are good people, serious about the work, and very proud of what has been accomplished. But as you said, 'no footprints.' "

Everett thought a moment. "I get the impression that the trustees don't have a great deal to say about where the money goes or what to. Is that right?"

Courtney hesitated and then nodded as she smiled. "I think they have sort of gotten into the habit of letting the staff do the selecting. I have been tempted to speak up but so far there has not been a good opportunity."

"I think we shouldn't assume that the staff is working around the board," said Everett. "They probably have just been placed in that position because the trustees have not insisted on being active."

"Boy, you are a real diplomat," said Courtney. "I suspect I would catch more flies with that brand of honey than the approach I was going to take. And I assume you are suggesting that I bring this up off-site before dropping it in the middle of a meeting? Like maybe I should invite the executive director to lunch?"

Everett smiled.

A week later Courtney and Arthur Wiggens met at her midtown club. She had been invited to join at the time she was promoted to head up project marketing at World Auto. Since she only had one type of car, she didn't consider her job a big deal, but apparently it was enough to get her into this old-line club her grandfather had helped found. About a third of the members were women now, so she felt quite comfortable there. Arthur arrived right on time, and they were ushered into the grill room. Courtney had arranged for a quiet corner in the back, so they could talk.

Wiggens had been with the Foundation for twenty years, first as part-time economist, and for the past twelve years as executive director. He enjoyed the work itself and also couldn't help taking pleasure in the attention he received from the charitable giving community. He was not certain what this young lady had in mind, but he was sure that it could be accommodated without much trouble. She probably wanted to arrange a special donation for some charity that had touched her.

After they had chatted for a bit, ordered their lunch, and become comfortable, Courtney decided to get on with it.

"I have been concerned, Arthur, that the Foundation is not leaving any footprints."

"Footprints?" asked Wiggens, startled.

"Footprints," she replied firmly. "I think you and the staff have done a good job investing the money, and the distribution system is certainly nothing to complain about. But I think we are not making the impact we could. In general, we just give little bits to a lot of organizations that toss it into their general funds."

"But that has always been our operating practice, Mrs. Simmons. We have never had any complaints before."

He was very nervous about this approach; it could cause a lot of problems with future plans. "Let me ask," he said, "do you want us to give more money away? I'm afraid that we can only deal with a limited amount, and there are rules, of course."

She shook her head. "Call me Courtney, please, Arthur. What we are giving is adequate and proper. My concern is that we are operating in a shotgun manner, spraying money about; I would like to see us be more of a rifle and select specific targets."

The waiter brought their salads and Courtney smiled at Arthur as she picked up her fork. "This grill room has a limited menu. For instance, it serves three salads, two soups, and three sandwiches. The main restaurant upstairs serves everything known to man. The food is much better here, and the service is without fault. This room is a rifle; upstairs is a shotgun."

Wiggens poked around in his salad. "Do you have anything specific in mind? Is there some group you would like us to include more often?"

She shook her head. "I don't have anyone in mind. My company, World Auto, has a community relations function that gives away money, among other services. They have a policy of dealing only with what they call 'real people helping real people.' So they have sponsored a dormitory for a home for troubled teenagers, and they give scholarships each year to students who otherwise wouldn't be able to go to college. Last spring one hundred and three people who graduated through that program held a luncheon for our chairman to thank the company. That's the sort of thing I had in mind."

Arthur wasn't eating. "But we get so many requests, we would have to turn down ninety percent of what comes in. As it is we deny half of them anyway. It would require a great many changes. I'm afraid we couldn't do much about it right now."

"Really," said Courtney. "What is our policy on giving? I have never seen something written down, do we have one?"

Wiggens sat back. "Policy? I don't think we have anything laid out as such. But we have developed customs over the years. No one has ever mentioned a policy before."

She fumbled in her clutch briefcase, and then offered him a folder with two sheets of paper in it.

"Here is a suggested policy and an operating procedure you might look at later. The thought is that we would seek out projects, confirm that the recipient is a real operation, and then assure ourselves that we were helping those to whom we give the money to be successful. It would cut down the number of grants we gave out, but we would have more impact than we are having now. We would be leaving more footprints."

She noticed that he was taking this personally. "You have been doing a great job with this Foundation, Arthur, and from what my mother says, I know that the trustees have not provided much direction or assistance. I just think we have the opportunity to bring it into the twenty-first century. Are you interested?"

"I need to think about it more, Courtney. But I must say that I do agree we could make more of an impact if we got specific. One of our problems is that we are required to have a majority of our trustees who represent areas of interest. We can't just divide the funds by five and distribute them equally, but it is necessary to touch all bases."

She shook her head. "I haven't picked up that these people are selfish in that way," she noted. "I suspect that they would like us to select some major items on the basis of what benefits mankind in every discipline."

"Possibly, possibly," said Arthur placing the folder in his briefcase and returning to his lunch. "Let me think about it a bit, and we can put it on the agenda for the next meeting."

"Good," said Courtney. "Now let me ask that the staff identify a couple of projects that would fit into this concept, so we could have a basis of discussion. I would bet that they have some already."

"You might win that one," said Arthur, smiling. "You know, having a written policy would make this whole thing a great deal easier to manage. I will put that on the agenda also. I don't know that it will all come about as quickly as you wish, at least not right away."

"I'm patient," said Courtney. "I'm patient."

When my mother used to tell me to come directly home from school, change clothes, and then go out to play, that was a policy. She wanted to know where I was, that I was safe, hence the come-right-home part. Boys have been known to become distracted after school and not show up for hours. Changing from school clothes to play clothes meant that I had to understand the requirements of what part of my limited wardrobe was for play and what part was for school. Most of the play clothes had at one time been school clothes.

A policy is a specific form of communication between people that is agreed to be accomplished without variation. If the real or perceived need for variation arises, then the policy needs to be discussed by those involved before any change can be made. If the teacher decided to keep me after school for some reason, good or bad, I had the obligation to call home and let them know not to expect me as soon as school was out. When I became involved in sports practice each day after school, the policy was formally changed to "come home immediately after practice." When I took up the habit of walking a young lady home after school, when there was no practice, the policy had to be changed again. My children were raised under the same system, and are doing that with theirs. Where there is no policy, there is chaos. People spend time worrying about where others are or are not. They wonder what is happening or not happening. They are concerned about the behavior of others since it may not always be predictable.

The process of Completeness requires that policies be taken seriously as constituting the foundation for developing the requirements we are going to meet every time. We just have to learn to think this way, so we can communicate with each other.

Education cannot be done properly unless it is clear what we are to learn.

When I went to college, I was met with a policy/requirement matter that brought this to my attention. At home, my parents saw to it that I got out of bed, dressed, and got off to school. Homework had to be produced for the teacher, and any lack of attendance at any planned event was immediately pounced on by the entire adult population. Coaches were specific about where one stood, what one wore, and how one did in any athletic endeavor. When I went to the Navy I found that getting up in the morning was not voluntary there either, that the uniform of the day was specified (they had play and work clothes, too), that we ate when it was time to eat, and that there were books of rules that required obeying.

However, in college if I failed to get up, go to class, turn in homework, wear the right clothes, no one cared. They just flunked me or ignored me. There were policies laid down, but no one helped me meet them. Of course, this is the initiation into the adult world. In that world the revelation strikes that we must now make our own policies. We establish that if we borrow money it must be paid back, not like it was with grandpa. We establish that if we agree to be somewhere at a certain time, it is polite and practical to meet that requirement. We establish our own policies and that makes us adults, which means we begin to use policies to communicate with those we care about. Our life is filled with these understandings, and they regulate most of what we do—from our designated highway driving speed to fidelity to our mate. Requirements stream from the policy fountain. People understand each other; people teach each other; people care for each other.

Policies are not some dead statements carved into the cave wall; they are living agreements. If they are not thought out and communicated, then Completeness can never happen. The organization will always have surprises, and big brothers will forever be sent out to search for little brothers who found something more interesting to do after school than come home.

C H A P T E R

FOURTEEN

Practicing
Completeness:
The Situation

E lston ("Ellie") Carson, the Doorkeeper of the House of
Representatives, marched importantly through the entrance
of the chamber and made the announcement he had been re-
hearsing for the past two months: "Members of the Congress,
the President of the United States." He placed the first emphasis
on the word "Members," and the second on the word "President." His wife had selected that reading from all the others he
had proposed to her. After all, there were probably three billion
people watching this program and hearing his words. He wanted
it to be just right. Apparently they all heard him because everyone in the room stood up and began clapping.

The President had been staged down the hall in the Speaker's
office, in accordance with the needs of both tradition and con-
venience. When the White House Chief of Staff signaled to Elston, he stepped into the chamber at the exact moment the
President left the Speaker's office. As the senators, representatives, cabinet, Joint Chiefs, Supreme Court justices, and visitors
rose to begin their welcome, the President entered the room.
Elston's was the first hand shaken. He had to admire the display
of timing and dignity this President put forth.

Waving to everyone, speaking special words to those she recognized, and beaming with anticipation, Elizabeth Commons
stepped up on the podium and approached the lectern for her
sixth State of the Union address. She handed the Speaker and
the Vice President copies of her remarks, and smiled in response

to their nods. The Vice President had made several significant contributions to the speech, but the concepts belonged to the President. The Speaker granted her a small smile as he accepted the package. In fact, he would be giving a "loyal opposition" commentary an hour after this address was over, and it would certainly be negative. The Speaker, at seventy, was only two years older than the President, but seemed mired in the mid-twentieth century. The Vice President at thirty-eight was trying to push everyone ahead fifty years. But they were practical men and got along well together.

The standing ovation continued, to Elizabeth's enjoyment. She knew that all of the people present were not necessarily in full agreement with her policies and practices, but on this one occasion at least they seemed to appreciate her. She had run as an independent and overwhelmed the Republican and Democratic candidates in the last two elections. They did not take her lightly. As the chamber began to quiet, the Speaker rapped his gavel one time and announced: "Members of the Congress, I have the honor to present the President of the United States." Then, as usual, the ovation began all over again. Elizabeth had noted from an examination of old films that some presidents were uncomfortable with this tradition while others enjoyed it enormously. Harry Truman, Dwight Eisenhower, Richard Nixon, Gerald Ford, and Dan Quayle, seemed to shuffle from one foot to another while it was going on. John Kennedy, Lyndon Johnson, Ronald Reagan, George Bush, Ralph Emerson, and Elizabeth Commons ate it up. They would stand there for the rest of the evening watching all these people agree on something for a while. Reagan, of course, was the master of looking humble while being appreciated.

Finally the chamber was quiet once again and Elizabeth prepared to begin her remarks. She glanced up in the balcony to make certain that her husband and the rest of the family were there. Charles had been a mountain of support during her political career, first as a senator then as President. Yet he remained absolutely separate from the affairs of state and just plain politics that swept around her. Satisfied, she smiled at the audience, and began.

"Mr. Speaker, Mr. Vice President, Members of Congress and honored guests. I am going to offer you an opportunity tonight to begin a marvelous period of accomplishment. I know all of you as colleagues and friends, having served in the Senate for ten years. All of us have worked together during my years in the executive branch, and I know that you are sincere in your beliefs. No government in the two hundred thirty-eight years since the United States was declared to be independent has been faced with the depth of challenges we now see. Even those who dealt with the great recession of the nineteen-thirties, the World War that ended sixty-nine years ago, the catastrophe of the Vietnam War, the drug and energy crises of the latter part of the century, the chaos of the Middle East, the massive invasions of boat people that caught everyone by surprise in the first years of this century, the minirecessions at the turn of the century that taught us all a new respect for debt, the environmental revolution of two thousand and six that forced long postponed actions, and caused premature elections here in our own nation—none have faced such a challenge as we do today. We are being called by our people, as are other governments throughout the world, to accelerate changing the basic way we operate, and they expect us to act, as well as listen.

"To state the situation in one paragraph: The citizens of the world are demanding that we, their governments, serve them rather than ourselves. They want to lead fulfilling lives, they want us to take care of only those things that they cannot deal with as individuals, and most urgently, they do not want us to make trouble for them. The same is true in business. The employees want management to help, not just direct. The challenge is to learn how to manage all of this completely, not just react to things or situations. The people are looking for 'Completeness'; they want no more quick fixes, they want stability, they want to live in an age of enterprise and prosperity. All this will require a new approach to management. Throughout history, governments and businesses have practiced control and containment. Now, given a willing citizenry for the first time, we have to deal with this challenge of bringing the world to a state of continual peace and prosperity.

"The thought process behind all this began twenty-five years ago when the Berlin wall fell, taking communism along with it. That event had a stronger effect on people throughout the globe than any political happening in recent history. It seemed to symbolize freedom for everyone. For the first time citizens began to realize that they did not have to be governed right down to the last detail of life. They did not need others to manage their lifestyle. They could get along much better without that. Making that point to governments required violent revolutions in China and the U.S.S.R., but since the beginning of this century the populace has been firmly in charge. Governments, including ours, were convinced to begin making less difficulty for each other and for their citizens. Economic borders began to fall, followed by the physical ones between nations. Reason began to enter worldwide diplomacy. People, as individuals, were becoming intolerant of intolerance. They were tired of being deprived of spiritual and material things because of ancient hates and customs that no longer had any meaning or relevance. In the Middle East, we have seen citizens refusing to serve in the military forces on this basis. They were seeing that other individuals were leading full lives, and they wanted to participate. Television, through satellite transmission, has shown the people each other. They have found that we are not all that different.

"When the year two thousand arrived, it brought with it a worldwide religious tidal wave, which we are all experiencing. But this has been different than any revival of the past. It is not driven by the churches, it has been spontaneous. It was and is very much constructed with the bricks of individual decision, and the mortar of personal determination. The theme, as you know, is 'God and i' with the 'little i' logo being worn on coats and banners. The churches were dragged along much as universities have been urged into the emerging worldwide quest for knowledge. Now I see the churches throwing off their own eccentricities and working together for a common fellowship throughout the world. This week, in Chicago, the heads of every religious denomination throughout the world are meeting to see if they can unify in allegiance to God. Much of the suffering people have endured over the years could have been avoided had this meeting been held successfully long ago. I will be speaking to these leaders at the end of the week and plan to encourage them in their determination.

"We, like the church leaders, have been reminded in these recent years that we govern with the consent of the governed. We are their servants, not their masters. We must learn to man-

age in an entirely new way, to help people have complete lives—
in government, business, and personal life.''

As the audience applauded this comment, two men watching
the broadcast in a New York office glanced at one another.

''She is serious about all this Completeness business; I hope
we get the chance to tell her about Pegasus.''

''I have asked Wilson to see if there is a chance to get to her
this week. He is aware of the urgency but not the reason. He
will let us know. Listen.''

The President continued. ''The invasion of Europe and North
America by hundreds of thousands of 'boat people' in two thousand and four and two thousand and five threatened to turn the
emerging positive feeling into a new world war. Governments
automatically planned drastic action against the invaders. However, the people spoke again and serious work began, which has
turned what were considered hopeless third world countries into
places where people are creating lives for themselves. They are
far from reaching their potential, but the trend is clear. Once
they saw that there was hope and caring, the invasion reversed
itself. President Emerson was properly recognized by being
awarded the Nobel Peace Prize for his work in resolving that
situation.

''When there is no political harassment, when it is possible
to earn the necessities of life and more, then people don't want
to leave their homelands. Today those areas are quiet politically
and are becoming competitive in a world sense. People are pros-
pering materially and spiritually. There is a long way to go, but
programs and agreement are in place. It is further than we have
ever been.

''We have reached a new era of technology. For several years
now we have been able to fly from Washington to Tokyo in less
than four hours on commercial aircraft. More remarkably, we
can get from downtown Washington to Dulles Airport in fifteen
minutes via the new high-speed train system. We all carry
pocket-sized communication units, our reliable PQs, that keep
us in touch with everything and everyone. I can take mine out
of my purse and call the pilot of that Tokyo-bound plane before
thirty seconds go by.

''In the field of health care, we now have true preventive
medicine through genetic applications that have extended natural

life many years. Addictive drugs are a thing of the past due to work accomplished in the same field. Abortion is no longer the divisive and destructive issue it was because of preventive measures to eliminate unwanted pregnancy. As a result of this ability to choose, our birth rate is rising for the first time in three decades. Crime is beginning to fall off throughout the world as science learns how to help people overcome destructive tendencies through chemical products and educational advances.

"We now have a common worldwide currency and stock exchange network. The business of the world seems to be business in the best sense. In every nation people are working hard to build lives and civilizations for themselves. There are those who said that such competition would destroy our nation, but we are becoming teacher, financier, and economic driver. There is virtually no unemployment, and the biggest problem executives have is finding employees. The merger of many large corporations with their counterparts in Japan and Europe has helped in this regard. They share technological development costs but retain product and service competitiveness.

"In the area of national security, we have technology and devices that would cause the destruction of any nation wanting to attack us. However, these will disappear one day along with all others like them, once we learn how to remove all the causes of potential conflict. An even more important development has been the emergence of a new personal tolerance among people. We no longer have the violent racial and ethnic difficulties that we faced for thousands of years. Everyone is busy and focused in their lives, and they do not see any benefit in putting others down or causing problems. To me this reveals that the religious revolution is genuine and real. At the same time we have retained a highly trained, fast-reaction military force that can deal with terrorism or irrationality anywhere in the world. I hope that one day the need for this group can disappear.

"Keeping everything moving in the right direction requires a government that is cooperating with its people. If they are not cooperating, they will hear about it very quickly. The members of Congress recognize clearly the message sent to us in the last election, when more than half of the Congress was replaced. People just plainly want stability. As you know, the citizens of the United Kingdom just completed a referendum in which they asked King William the Fifth to accept the role as head of government in addition to being head of state. He has veto power over any action taken by Parliament. We see the installation of 'philosopher kings' in Eastern Europe—they like the stability that the Spanish monarchy has given that nation. The people want their politicians to represent them, period. They do not want to be controlled.

"With your cooperation over the past two years, and the agreement of the states to a constitutional amendment, we have reorganized the President's cabinet and the executive branch, in order to let us deal properly with the future. The bureaucratic structure of the government is in the process of changing and shrinking to reflect this new direction. Tonight the various Secretaries are here for the first time in their new role. We have reduced the cabinet to six offices: International Relations, National Security, Finance, Human Resources, Natural Resources, and Communications. In addition, I will have a Director of Systems Integrity on my staff who will continually audit the effectiveness of these departments and provide information for corrective action. We will be conducting management seminars in the next few months so each department can provide an overview of its work and plans. These seminars will be repeated continually for the benefit of those in business, education, and other areas who wish to take advantage of the concepts and practices developed. The members of Congress have signed up for a series of their own.

"As part of this we have formed a council of recognized management consultants who have agreed to make themselves available to us as we lay out the complete approach. There will be many changes, all oriented toward government setting a good leadership example by doing jobs completely, rather than just patching up situations. This is a very complicated world in which everything seems to affect everything else. I might note that due to the need to do less governing, we have been able to reduce the number of government workers to its lowest level in forty years. Today, with a population of three hundred million people, we have fewer government employees than there were in nineteen-seventy-two. The demand for workers in the private sector has made this a less difficult task to approach. Our goal in this area is to comply with all the requirements fully and learn how to do it at a growth rate equal to half of that experienced by the population.

"On the other side of the situation, there are a great many problems that have to be dealt with and solved. As lives become longer there is more need for health care. The total solution to this problem lies in the advances of preventive medicine. There is no reason that people cannot be healthy for the entire course of their lives. In the meantime, though, health care is very expensive. Our goal is to reduce the costs five percent each year while providing each insured person with coverage that does not deteriorate their living standard. We will propose legislation on that and other challenges. As in the past, older people are the largest source of financial drain in health care.

"As part of this equation, Social Security must be completely revised; it is now the largest single item in the budget. We are taking money from the left-hand pocket and dropping it in the right. All the while, we are pretending that something is happening. Each employed person is essentially supporting a retired person. We have a specific goal in this area and will make a presentation to the Congress within a few weeks. But if we do not take the courageous actions necessary to solve this problem for good, we will be failing future generations.

"There is a great need for more research and development in order for the United States to remain the world leader in technology. Much of this funding is provided by corporations, but there are some areas that government must encourage, perhaps through tax incentives. The 'orphan diseases,' for instance, where there is no potential reward for corporate investment due to the small demand for the medicine. Also, some aspects of space exploration are still better left with the government, although private organizations are doing well with the space stations. Next year's Mars survey trip will lead to many more ventures, but the colony on the moon has become a lot more expensive than we thought. Incidentally, I received a communication from them last week asking if I was interested in helping them become a separate state. There will be a special report on their status next Tuesday at eight p.m. eastern time. After that report I will announce the specific goals developed for this program.

"Our biggest single problem is education. There is enough

money, and people want to learn, but over the years the field just has not kept up. Modern methods of learning are not being utilized, companies are still having to teach people the basics. I have asked the Secretary of Human Resources to call the nation's top educators together next week and let them know that if they do not attack this problem in a way that lets our people learn, that we will find another way to do it. Every person should be able to find the education appropriate to their capabilities and interest. People should pay their own way, but grants and loans are available to be utilized by those who need them.

"In closing, I would like to take advantage of having this worldwide audience in order to pass along some thoughts for the citizens of the world. Due to the new instant translation devices each person can hear me in his or her own language. This provides me with an opportunity that none of my predecessors have enjoyed. Let me aim this part of my address to all of you in other countries.

"At each age we can look back and remember things we did or did not do, and wish we had 'known then what we know now.' This is a normal part of life, a routine thought process. We learn from the past, if we know what is good for us. Unfortunately, it is typically necessary to absorb a great many bumps and bruises along the way.

"I have lived many more years than most of you—after all, the current average age of the world population is eighteen. Half are younger than eighteen, half of us are older. During my share of those years, like everyone else, I have bruised my body and mind in order to learn what life is all about. My life has turned out to be very satisfying, but it could have been even more so had I known a few things and known them earlier. In the personal sense, Completeness requires making the difficult long-range decisions that will affect us and those we influence throughout our lives.

"Technology has changed the world dramatically over the years. However, the basic life of the individual is not very different. We still must work and sleep, we have to eat, and we need to feel useful. We marry, raise families, and live life. The worth of our lives depends, for the most part, on the way we approach them. Unless some destructive force, such as a totalitarian government, interferes, our life is pretty much up to ourselves. As you heard during the United Nations summit conference last month, the elected leadership of the world is determined to provide everyone the right to be free within our agreed upon world structure. And for the first time in world history, there are no governments that sit without the permission of the people. We are at this moment completely without armed conflict anywhere on this globe. That has never happened before.

"We only receive one trip through life. Many people waste that journey by indulging in self-pity, wishful thinking, and so on. It is possible to grab hold of life, enjoy the trip, and leave some footprints when it is over.

"Members of the Congress and honored guests, we have a unique opportunity to leave some footprints in history that will be long remembered and long appreciated. We also have the opportunity of wasting our knowledge and energy on things that make no difference. We, like our citizens, have a choice.

"Thank you."

As the camera followed the President working her way out of the House chamber the two men watching in New York sat back in their chairs. Nick Barrows was chairman and CEO of Advance, Inc., a large and independent research organization. "Doctor Nick," as he was known at the laboratories, was the creative person's ideal leader. He never knew when to quit on a project and always assumed the best about everyone. He had never made much money personally, and Advance was usually on the brink of bankruptcy. But he was liked and well respected by both business leaders and scientists. Everyone liked Nick and admired him.

Harold Broom, on the other hand, although respected as a businessman, was liked by hardly anyone. Even his wife, Esther, felt he was rude and thoughtless, which he was. But he was also honest and very smart. Nick had decided that those two characteristics far outweighed the lack of social graces. But he kept working on his friend.

"Commons' Man," said Nick.

"What does that mean?" asked Harold.

"That is what the papers are going to say tomorrow. She has laid out the specification for us to be successful as individuals.

They will put her name on it, and she will not know exactly how to react. They will call us 'Commons' Man.' "

"Sounds like a good idea to me," replied Harold. "The way things work now, the employees run the company anyway. They might as well think they are successful even though they are very difficult. She seems like a nice lady. I wonder what her reaction will be to our information?"

"She is pretty cool and reasoned. I think she will recognize that there will be a great environmental benefit with the oil industry practically shut down. It has an enormous cash flow and influence, but it doesn't employ all that many people. The automobile industry probably affects one-third of all jobs in one way or another. Maybe more if you count commuting."

"That's what cars are for, aren't they?" asked Harold.

"She is going to remind us that oil is the world's largest industry," replied Nick.

"We'll just say it used to be the largest. Pegasus should quadruple the automobile business. I'm sure she hears that kind of thought six times a day. If I had her job I would not take comments like ours too seriously without some evidence. I would want to know for sure."

"What would you do to know for sure?" asked Nick.

"I would want a couple of people I really trusted, someone I know no one could get to, to tell me 'these guys are telling you the truth.' I'm going to suggest to our guy that he use that idea on the White House; otherwise, they aren't going to let us near her."

"And what if we don't get near her?" asked Nick.

"Then we just go ahead and she gets a surprise like everyone else. But it really is so important that we try to manage this introduction in a way that shakes up the world as little as possible."

Nick nodded.

"This is a great example of the need for the 'Completeness' she was talking about. We can't leave any empty corridors or unfinished projects on this one. No short-range solutions. She mentioned Social Security—that has been fixed a dozen times. However, it never has really been handled completely. The foundation was wrong to begin with: all they had to do was let people save money tax-free for their retirement, and then force them to do it."

Harold cocked his head.

"And just let people build up individual retirement plans? They tried that in the eighties."

"And it worked great—then the short-rangers took over to increase tax income. Not very complete thinking. Anyway, get on with your call."

Harold pulled the PQ from his shirt pocket and turned the open speaker switch, then he put the device to his lips.

"Wilson?" he asked. There was a short pause.

"Hi, Harold," replied Wilson. "What did you think of the lady's speech?"

"Great, just great," said Harold. "Where are you?"

"In my bathroom at home," replied Wilson. "There is no place to hide from you apparently."

Harold bristled.

"I better not catch you hiding when I need you," he growled.

"Take it easy," Wilson said laughing. "What can I do for you?"

"Nick is here with me. How are we doing with an appointment to see the President?"

"Not too well. They want some idea of what it is all about and since I don't know what it is all about, I can't tell them. They are willing to see Nick briefly because she is interested in research, but not you."

Harold forced himself to remain calm.

"How about telling them that we have something world-shaking to discuss and are going to need an hour with her all by herself?—wait a moment—let me finish.

"Tell the staff that she should pick out two people whose word she absolutely trusts, and we will take them away for a few hours to show them something. After they report back she can decide to see us or not. And Wilson, this has to be done within the next two days. Don't be mushy about this thing—insist!"

"It is hard to insist with the President, Hal," said Wilson.

"Remind them that Roosevelt agreed to meet with Einstein even though he wasn't told the subject. Do it, dammit."

Harold looked at the communication device and frowned.

"There is no way to slam this damn thing down," he said. "Intimidation isn't what it used to be."

Nick shook his head.

"I am afraid that it is not a practical management style these days. The new employee shareholding arrangements literally turn them into owners with the rights to decide if management is doing a proper job. I think that is a wonderful idea, but it can put quite a bit of strain on the management corps."

"I call that 'bottom-up socialism,' " said Harold. "Years ago when all those countries were trying socialism they did it from the top down. The government took over the corporations with the mission of running them for the benefit of the people, but they wound up doing it for their own enrichment. The result was a methodical lowering of living standards until the people threw the rascals out.

"Now we are doing it upside down. The people own the companies, but business is managed by professionals instead of someone appointed because of political considerations. I always felt, like Socrates, that the best person should be selected as the unquestioned leader. Since that is impractical, I guess this is a better way. You know what happened to Socrates."

"There have been a few cases of power being abused under this system—from both sides I might say. However, stock ownership might provide one answer to the Social Security problem that Madam President was talking about," noted Nick.

Harold raised an eyebrow.

"I was just thinking that if people had equity in various enterprises, then they could live on that instead of this old-fashioned Ponzi scheme we have going now. Taking from the working to pay the nonworking has never worked," said Nick.

Harold nodded and then changed the subject.

"How much advance notice do we need to take the White House people out to the proving ground site? And how much time will they need? How do we keep this all quiet until we are ready?"

"The team is ready when we get there; they would require no more than thirty minutes," said Nick. "They are very anxious to get back into the real world; none of them have been off that site for eighteen months. As for keeping it quiet, there will be no need to do that once the President knows and has the time to lay out a strategy. She will want to make a few calls. Is that my PQ ringing?"

Nick reached in his pocket, lifted out his card and said his name. The familiar voice of President Commons came to him.

"Is that you, Dr. Nick?" she asked and then proceeded anyway. "I understand you want to see me, but you want me to send out Joshua and Caleb beforehand? Is that right?"

Nick found it hard to speak. Harold reached for the PQ but Nick, fearing what this direct person might say, held it back.

"Yes Madam President, we would like to demonstrate something and thought that this might be the best way to assure you that it is worth your time."

"Where is it and how long do you need?" she asked.

"It is a thirty-minute helicopter flight from Washington and we would need about two hours. Whom would you like to send?"

"If this is as big a deal as you seem to think, I would prefer to come myself. Unfortunately, it is not possible for me to do anything in secret. We have even had to line our dressing rooms on the second floor of the White House with lead to keep out these new "Superman" cameras. The press is literally everywhere these days. So my personal participation is out of the question. Perhaps you could bring something back for me to see.

"But I will send our Director of Systems Integrity, Robert Lorenzo, and my husband, Charles. Those are two people who have absolutely no axes to grind or chickens to feed. I presume you want to do this tomorrow?"

"Yes ma'am," Nick replied. "It would be best accomplished in daylight. If they could meet us at the old National Airport helicopter pad at ten a.m.?"

"Done," she replied. "Did you hear my speech? What is your opinion?"

"I thought you were right on the mark," he said. "Harold Broom and I were just discussing the different requirements in managing people and resources today."

"I know about Broom—he is an explosive type, I understand."

Nick smiled.

"Actually, he has learned to be quite calm and reasoned. But people insist on being treated with dignity these days, and with the worldwide shortage of workers there is not much alternative, even for the most 'explosive' people. Once they try it, they find that the results are much better.''

''I would like to offer you an invitation to participate in these seminars we plan to conduct on the management challenge items,'' she said.

''I would be honored. Just have someone let me know where and when.'' Nick blushed, to Harold's amusement. Since the PQ was tuned to Nick's personal frequency, Harold could not hear what the President was saying and was trying to decipher that from Nick's expressions.

''Good,'' she said, ''I would like you to conduct the one on relationships; sign up anyone you wish to help or do it yourself. If you have any trouble getting responses, just let us know. The seminar is scheduled for forty days from now. Good talking to you, give my best to Harold and to your family.'' She signed off.

Nick paused for a moment as he began to realize that he had only forty days to pull together a national seminar on a subject he knew very little about. Harold was impatiently waiting to be filled in on the call, and Nick pulled back abruptly from his reverie.

''She is going to send her husband Charles and Robert Lorenzo. We better get the arrangements made. I'll call the site, you make the travel stuff.''

''Done,'' said Harold, then paused. ''What does the President know about business? Has she ever really worked?'' he asked. ''I know she was with some companies, but it could have been public relations or something besides meeting a payroll, as they used to say.''

Nick smiled. ''She was president and CEO of Eastland some years ago, and was appointed to the Senate, as a Republican, when O'Conner died. She served his four years and got elected on her own as an independent for another six, and by the largest margin New York ever provided. As you know, she ran for President by popular acclaim in twenty-oh-seven as an independent and won, blowing the incumbent out of the water. So she came into office not owing anybody but the people. Her reelection was a walk-away; no one even wanted to run against her. She is very feminine, but beneath that soft exterior beats a heart that can be hard as a diamond.''

"What kind of a business manager was she?" asked Harold.

"She turned Eastland from a mushy conglomerate into the toughest competitor in the industry. Chased the Japanese right out of her markets and opened up Latin America to the consumer products business. She is a powerhouse."

"Good," said Harold, "that agrees with my research. But you know she only has a couple of years left, and then we could get one of several people. Do you think she will endorse someone specific? If so, she better get started."

"My money is on Lorenzo, the Systems Integrity guy. He is Hispanic, which will help with that vote; he is Harvard cum laude, which won't hurt him; he has had a lot of tough jobs and done them well; and he speaks about a dozen languages. In this beige world that has to be an asset."

"Speaking of getting started," said Harold, motioning Nick to make his calls.

"Right," said Nick.

CHAPTER

FIFTEEN

Practicing Completeness: The Product

As Nick and Harold waited beside the rented helicopter, they began to realize that their development phase would be coming to an end, and the thought depressed them both. Life was relatively simple while something was in the cocoon. Once it emerged, nothing was the same. If their product was accepted at all, the entire project could be instantly jerked from their hands by the clients and the rest of the world. Also, the awareness that the whole effort might be a total bust had not escaped them. Suppose no one cared about it; suppose it was suppressed; suppose the situation was unmanageable.

"Actually," said Nick, "we are coming to the hard part. Managing the implementation of this product without turning world economics upside down will take a bit of doing."

"And a lot of cooperation," reminded Harold.

"A lot of first-time cooperation," noted Nick.

"Speaking of cooperation, look at this," said Harold.

Two White House cars were quickly pulling up to the pad as a Secret Service helicopter hovered just off to the side. Security people, two men and two women, poured out of the second car as the President's two representatives emerged from the first. The four men approached each other briskly.

Charles Commons shook hands with Nick and Harold, introducing Robert Lorenzo in the process. Charles, tall and slim, looked as though he could, at seventy-two, still fake his way through a good game of tennis. Robert, small and intense, had the quizzical look of the educator. He had been lured to the White House while still president of a large university, although he had done previous time in government policy positions.

"Robert is in charge of Systems Integrity, as you know," explained Charles. "He spends most of his time explaining what that is and how it is not going to do anyone any harm."

Robert smiled and nodded in agreement. "For some reason people become very concerned when anyone associated with the government becomes interested in what they are doing. I tell them that we want to make things easier for them; they tell me to go help someone else."

"Every corporate executive in the world has that problem, Robert," said Nick. "I can't think of anything more corporate than being based in the White House. Well, we really do need your help, and we are honored that you gentlemen have come. I hope you will think that this is an interesting day in your lives. The helicopter is ready. Shall we be on our way?"

The four men, crouching low even though the blades were fifteen feet in the air, entered the aircraft. The copilot seated and buckled them as he explained that the machine was capable of speeds up to 400 knots per hour, but that they would be traveling much slower, flying at an altitude of 5,000 feet. He showed them how to wear the headsets that made conversation possible during flight. The Secret Service helicopter picked up three of the agents and followed along beside them.

"I notice you didn't escape the Secret Service today, Charles," said Nick. "Are they with you continually?"

"They're relentless. But they do let me slip out now and then when they are sure I am in secure areas. They call me Prince Albert, and my code name is Adam, for 'first man.' It really is quite entertaining, but they sure do get involved in a person's life. I think they don't worry about anyone doing me harm, they are just nervous about losing me. Sometimes they are a help if crowds of people are involved. Prime Minister Thatcher's husband once offered some fatherly advice when he was asked about this problem, and I have taken it to heart. He said he was just going to relax and get used to people opening doors for him. I have organized an informal group of 'first men' with the husbands of chief executives from several nations. We sort of encourage each other. One day we may have a summit of our own."

"Well, you certainly look as if it agrees with you," said Harold.

"Actually, it does," nodded Charles. "I accompany the President to formal functions and on the longer trips, but outside of that, I have time to work on my own projects. I am very careful to make certain that none of those have anything to do with the government in any way."

"He's writing a book on General Sherman," said Robert. "He is a closet scholar who wasted his working life as a businessman. He has spent the last fifteen years trying to get Sherman's statue in New York to shed that tacky gold finish they put on it back in nineteen-eighty-nine. To no avail, I might note. So much for influence. By the way, where are we going?"

"To Quantico," said Harold. "We have an installation there."

"That was once a great Marine base," said Charles. "I remember several friends of mine going to officers candidate school there. It was shut down in twenty-oh-two when the Marines couldn't find anyone else to fight. The President was quoted as saying he wished he had them back when the boat people invasion started."

"That was an interesting determination, if I remember it correctly," said Robert. "The business of having four services that duplicate each other in many ways was always difficult. The Marines were absorbed into the Army mostly, and the Air Force was divided between the Army and Navy. We're back where we started before World War Two. My suspicion is that the Marines are slowly taking over the Army."

"When can we talk about what we are doing today?" asked Charles.

"As soon as we are on the ground and in the building, we will reveal it all to you," assured Nick. "We will be there within five minutes. Do we need to do anything about the Secret Service people?"

"They are very self-sufficient. They won't need to come into the building if that would be inconvenient."

"Good," said Nick, "that will make us more comfortable about security. It is a funny world when you have to keep the security people out of the security area."

The aircraft landed about fifty yards from a group of government-issue-looking buildings with two men standing in front of one of them. The four visitors crouched their way across the tarmac to the men.

"May I introduce Dr. Abramowitz and Dr. Kelley? They already know who you are," said Nick.

Hands were shaken all around and the scientists led the way into a conference room. Five chairs were arranged behind a table halfway down the room. A holographic VCR-3D unit was in the front area. Dr. Abramowitz waited until everyone was seated and then began.

"Some time ago, we at Advance became concerned that dependence on fossil fuel was harming the world's environment and retarding its economic growth. We thought if we could develop a small nuclear energy system, based on the cold fusion principle, it would be possible to provide automobiles, homes, businesses, and other applications with their own nearly permanent sources of power. This would also make energy available to people in underdeveloped countries who otherwise might have to wait for years. Electrical energy is being transmitted via satellite now, but it still requires a reception station, cables, plus a plug and cord at the other end.

"Nick approached the four worldwide automobile companies with this proposal, and we were delighted when they agreed to form a joint venture and fund our research. They considered it a way to eliminate pollution from automobiles and at the same time permit them to expand their marketing areas to places where fossil fuel distribution is impractical or unreliable. The venture has worked out well. They have not bothered us and have not questioned our costs, which have been modest. I am pleased to say that we have reached the point where we have a production model of our device."

He pressed a button and the VCR projected the three dimensional unit to the middle of the area. It was about the size of a basketball with two cords emerging from the top of it. The ball revolved exposing two dials built into the case.

"We call this power source Pegasus because it has power on its own. Also we couldn't think of anything else at the time. It weighs twenty-five pounds."

The figure in front changed into that of an automobile which then rolled gracefully over on its side. Pegasus inserted itself into the engine compartment which already had a slightly larger package, the new engine, in it.

"The engine we developed really is a motor. This electric unit generates several hundred horsepower. Several designs are available. There is one application, for instance, of a compressed fluid system that works like a steam engine. The present configuration of the power source will last for around four thousand hours, or more than two hundred thousand miles in a car, before needing to be energized, but there is really no limit to what can be accomplished. Our current experiments indicate that it could last for twenty years with a fuel repackaging now and then. Existing automobiles can be converted to this power source by having the combustion engine removed and this package installed. We anticipate it will cost about a thousand world dollars to accomplish that, or about ten percent of the cost of a new car. Since there are a couple hundred million automobiles in use right now, that would become quite a market in itself. Dr. Kelley will now talk about nonautomotive uses."

Kelley came to the front and signaled to the VCR.

"We see several uses for Pegasus. One is in home heating and air-conditioning. This unit, at a price of under three hundred world dollars, will provide the energy to drive the heating and air-conditioning system for a single family house over a period of twenty years. Homes that already have a centralized system will have a very small modification cost. A larger unit, or several smaller ones, will take care of buildings and even ships. Since the output is essentially electricity, it can run machines and do all the things that power coming from the utilities can accomplish. But no high-tension wires, no power stoppages, no smoke—it really is a marvelous unit."

Kelley paused, and Lorenzo took that as an invitation to ask questions.

"Let me get this straight, Doctor," he said. "Are you saying that this energy supply will replace gasoline, coal, natural gas, and all those other sources? Are you saying that the entire energy industry is going to be unnecessary?"

"It is a matter of choice, of course, Mr. Lorenzo," replied

Kelley. "But this does replace fossil fuel in every use we can think of, and it does it without contamination and at a fraction of the cost."

"And how about nuclear problems? Is there any danger that these things could be exploding or giving off radiation?"

"None whatsoever, it is completely safe. Just like bread and yeast, the action is chemical, not vital."

Charles was nodding.

"You may have something here, gentlemen. Why did you want the President to know about it? What was behind your thinking? You have a fortune here in your hands."

Nick nodded to Harold, who stood up and went over to the machine. He punched up a few numbers on the computer keyboard and then stepped back as three-dimensional charts began to form.

"These charts show the usage of fossil fuels over the years. It grows continually, the prices go up and down, economies tremble whenever some greedy group decides to turn the flow on or off. Many nations are held hostage to this supply.

"This chart displays the pollution index of the world as it has been and is going to be. As you can see, in this calculation at least, we are going to be gasping for breath all over by twenty-sixty. Los Angeles, Milan, Mexico City, and several other population centers are virtually dead at this moment. There will be no trees you could sit under in the Northern Hemisphere by twenty-ninety. The major cause of all this is the burning of fossil fuel; most other sources are under control since the environmental revolution.

"Attempts to change to methanol and other artificial sources have not been successful. Besides, they are just more of the same, burning something that then goes out in the world to be breathed.

"Nuclear power has never been accepted by the public because each plant looks like an atomic bomb to them. There is something accurate in what they feel. Hot fusion plants are virtually fail-safe now, but people still don't like them. However, we found that they are quite comfortable with cold fusion; they assume, again correctly, that it will not blow up or radiate them.

"So when we thought we had found a way to generate cold fusion in a small space, we didn't actually know what to do with it. We didn't want it to become a scientific curiosity and get bounced around from lab to lab for forty years. We wanted to put it to good use and see if we could save the planet in the process.''

"So," said Robert, "you went to the automotive people instead of the energy industry on the assumption that one would like it and one would block it. How did you contact the automotive executives?"

Harold smiled. "It was Nick's idea. I belong to a very old and incredibly exclusive famous golf club in Scotland. My great great great great grandfather was a founding member and the membership has been passed down ever since from eldest son to eldest son. It is the only place left on the planet where no women can enter the clubhouse or even step foot on the grounds. Members are reluctantly permitted to have three guests a year, but they must be cleared at least one month in advance, and their handicap cannot be more than eighteen.

"Being President of the United States won't get you in, being CEO of a two hundred billion world dollar automobile company won't do it either. They play the 'Open' there once every twenty years, under protest. One year the winner came back at the end of the day to stand and look out over the course to savor his victory one more time. They had him arrested."

Charles brightened. "So you invited the four CEOs to come play with you? And they all accepted? But how did you manage having that many guests?"

"They were like little children," said Harold. "I asked a friend to join us and use up two of his guest rights so Nick could come also. We had the four CEOs, who had not met each other socially, Dr. Kelley, Nick, myself, and my friend. Two foursomes went out and came back. Then we fed them and took them into a private room to tell them what we had in mind. They agreed beforehand never to tell anyone what we said if they decided not to become part of it."

"And their reaction was positive right away?" asked Charles.

"Immediately. They all picked it up immediately. Look at this chart. Of the six billion people in the world, almost two-thirds do not have access to an automobile, and if they did they would have a hard time finding fuel for it. The automotive executives didn't care about the environmental improvement as much as they did the thoughts of being able to produce less expensive, stand-alone vehicles all over the world. They agreed at that moment to each put up ten million dollars, to give our firm twenty percent of the joint venture, and to each take ten percent of the rights.''

''And the other forty percent?'' asked Robert, already knowing.

''For the energy companies to make them want this to succeed. But if they want no part of it, then the four parties will take it themselves. It is going to cost several billion dollars for capital investment to get these power sources and engines into production. It will take a few years before there is a complete replacement of existing vehicles, and it will take cooperation among a lot of different organizations,'' said Harold.

Nick nodded and pointed to the chart. ''This whole thing is going to have to be thought through completely, as the President has been advocating. It can serve as a model for others to follow. But to get people to sit still long enough to do that will require some public pressure. There could be a panic when all this is announced, if we do not do it right.''

Kelley gestured toward the door. ''If you are ready, gentlemen, we would like to offer you the opportunity to drive a car equipped with Pegasus. If we could all go out the way we came in?''

The group moved to the outside. Both Charles and Robert were visibly excited. Two new cars were drawn up with the hoods open. Dr. Kelley took Lorenzo while Charles was led to the other vehicle. The scientists explained the engine and power unit installation and answered questions. Robert looked in the trunk to assure himself that no auxiliary power supplies were hidden away. Then the visitors were invited to drive the cars, their hosts taking the other seat.

Twenty minutes later both cars returned. Charles leaped out of his with wonder written all over his face.

''You can't believe the authority of that power unit. I thought it would be slow to react, but it takes right off. And it is so quiet I could hear my quartz watch tick,'' he said.

''Quartz watches don't tick,'' reminded Robert.

''Exactly,'' said Charles. He excused himself and stepped

aside, taking his PQ from the shirt pocket. He spoke one word into it, listened for a few seconds, and replaced it.

"You have your meeting, gentlemen. We can fly directly to the White House lawn. If possible, we might want to bring that VCR tape along."

Landing on the lawn at the executive mansion and being escorted into the Oval Office via the side door was something that even two world travelers like Nick and Harold had never experienced. Nick glanced at the floor as they entered and heard the President say, "They replaced the floor some years ago, but the boards with Ike's cleat prints are still around. I always watch to see if people coming in that door look for the marks. The old floor was cut into small pieces so we could give them to people who cared. I will see that you receive one. Glad to see you again, Nick. This must be Harold—welcome. Please sit down."

They moved to the seating arrangement in front of the fireplace. Charles had disappeared, leaving Robert to bring the Chief Executive up-to-date. Using the VCR tape, he provided a quick review of the system.

"This will be a wonderful development for the world," said the President. "Those areas of Africa, Asia, and South America who have very little energy now can be transformed. We can eliminate the environmental problems everyone has been struggling with. I am amazed that you have been able to keep this so quiet; usually this office knows about everything. Apparently it will also come as a great surprise to everyone else, particularly those in the fossil fuel industry, which is the biggest business in the world. What do you want from me?"

Harold spoke up: "Actually, Madam President, you have put your finger on it. The effect this announcement will have on the oil industry and all that supports it is going to be dramatic, unless we manage it properly. The whole world could be thrown into a panic and even a depression. It is as you said in your speech last night, we have to learn to handle this new world we live in. What we need is your help in getting the oil and utility people interested before it all drops on their heads. We need to set up an implementation strategy and plan that will let everyone benefit from this development. Then we will have something useful that will let people live better for less expense, let corporations continue to provide jobs and make money for their investors and nations in the process. Otherwise, they could wind up fighting the whole thing.''

Nick continued: ''The utility people were not interested in being part of the joint venture; they felt it was only a dream, and the oil people have never been interested in nuclear power plants, either. They remind me of the way the railroads felt about trucks and airplanes. Our partners, the automotive companies, would very much like to make this a smooth transition with everyone involved.

''The automotive companies are going to have to spend billions of dollars on capital investments in order to produce the power unit and the engine. They do not want to get involved with home appliances and such. They would like to present this power source to a mutually formed company that would license people to produce and use the power source. They would get their research money back, along with a small, but regular royalty payment. Each of the participants would be shareholders, including Advance.''

''How about the OPEC nations?'' she asked. ''Would they be involved?''

''Over the years they have made life difficult for the oil-consuming nations, so there is little sympathy for them. However, they could be invited to participate at some specified level,'' said Harold. ''Their citizens would be some of the chief beneficiaries of this device. Perhaps they could produce it in those areas.''

''How long would it take to get the automotive people together?'' she asked.

''The four CEOs are at Quantico this afternoon having their briefing on the project status. They have no idea that we are this far along. In fact, the biggest problem we had was making sure we had enough cars so they could all drive their own company models on the test drive.''

''And how long before meaningful production on the unit would begin?'' she asked. ''How long before it would be available to be used to heat Third World homes?''

''It is not a complicated unit to build. The engine, which will only apply to automobiles, will take a couple of years before it is in production. Pegasus itself could be coming off a line within eight months. The heating and air-conditioning units for homes still have to be designed, so that would be a hang-up for another year. However, they could be converted to the units in modern housing.''

"But inside of two years it will be available, everything?"

"Yes ma'am, it will. The best way would be for units to be manufactured regionally, except for the automotive ones. But that will all work itself out," said Nick.

"I also need to be clear on what you two gentlemen and your organization will get out of this, and I need to have an idea about who would manage the entire situation. Nothing personal, I just need to know."

Harold nodded. "Actually, the organization we want to set up will just license the products and provide technical support. Advance would be the skeleton of that group, which would probably not be very large. It would be sort of like Coca Cola was in the old days, selling syrup to bottling plants. In our case, the syrup would be paper and words.

"Nick and I specifically will each receive a one-time payment and then a share of the royalty trust. We would be employed by the joint venture, at least for a while. The Advance people, who sacrificed several years of their lives, will also participate. I don't know the exact numbers, but it would be the equivalent of ten or so years' salary. Over the years there will be a great deal of money from the license agreement, which will pay salaries and expenses, but most of it will go into further research. Does that answer the question?"

"It does. I would suggest you also think about a way of diverting some of those royalties to advancing the arts worldwide. You could put theater groups in every nation to develop material and tour, for instance."

"A good idea," said Nick. "We want to do everything necessary to make this creation valuable."

The President went over to her desk, sat down, and began talking to what seemed like no one in particular. The men in the room could not hear her. When she had finished she came back over; the men stood until she was seated.

"This is the 'silent desk' system that has just been installed," she said. "I can talk to anyone anywhere just by speaking their name, and no one in the room, or anywhere else for that matter, can hear me. They wanted to put in a special desk unit, but this is the same old desk that Franklin Roosevelt and a dozen others have used (although Nixon moved it out for a while). I refused to let it go, so they had to do some fancy cabinetwork when they came up with this new device.''

She turned to Nick. ''Will your four automotive CEOs be available tomorrow morning at eleven a.m.? Could you invite them to join us here in the cabinet room? It is right next door.''

Nick and Harold nodded nervously in agreement.

''Robert will manage all this activity, but we are inviting the three oil company CEOs, the chairman of OPEC, and the Secretary of Natural Resources to come meet with you tomorrow. I will open the meeting and then leave. My office is merely serving as a catalytic agent in this case. My thought is that we have a wonderful and unique chance to save the whole world a bunch of trouble.

''After the meeting you can make your announcement in the press room down the hall. I suggest you prepare for an announcement either way, and bring all the attendees along with you so everyone can see that there is an agreed upon plan. The White House press corps is a difficult and cynical group; they haven't liked anyone since Barbara Bush.''

Robert added, ''We are going to have to prepare to ask the stock exchanges to stop trading in those companies for a period, and perhaps we should consider scheduling calls to the heads of government who will be affected.''

''Set it up, Robert,'' said the President. ''We have the capability for concurrent communication, let's use it.''

''I wonder,'' said Harold, ''if we could get the other people to go to Quantico first—that would save a lot of explaining. I am certain they will want their chief scientists to look at Pegasus—actually, I'm certain they will want to do tests in their own labs eventually.''

The President looked at Robert.

''Good idea,'' he said. ''Let's get started setting all this up. Thank you, Madam President.''

The President went out the curved door and left the three men alone in the Oval Office.

''This is a pretty classy place for a planning session,'' said

Harold. "Do you have a room somewhere with a board we can scribble on? I would feel more comfortable."

Robert stood up. "We can go to my office, it's down in the basement where Kissinger used to have his slave quarters. I took the liberty of asking the Secretary of Natural Resources to meet us there; he is not aware of any of this."

"What is his name?" asked Nick.

"Winstead, Harvey Winstead. He was president of a couple of oil companies and then left the industry to work on environmental issues. He is going to like this idea."

Winstead was waiting for them in the basement and after introductions Robert played the VCR tape for him, supplying all the information he had picked up that day.

Winstead just sat there for a few moments after the projection was complete. "I find this very hard to believe, Robert," he said finally. "Cold fusion has been shown to be ineffective in this type of application for some time. The last nuclear power conference would not even accept a paper on the subject. Are you sure that all of this is not being done with mirrors?"

Harold bristled, but Nick laid a restraining hand on the older man's arm.

"I think," said Nick, "that pretending to do what this device does would be a bigger challenge than doing it. Actually, we found that the cold fusion studies and application attempts of the past contained some basic errors. They were working on the wrong assumptions; our research just took the right course. As you know, Mr. Secretary, the scientific community is hard to convince once it has its mind made up."

"I agree with that, Nick. However, I would like to have some personal assurance on the subject. What could we arrange?"

Robert checked his watch. "We will be having a demonstration for energy company executives early tomorrow morning. Could you arrange to leave about seven a.m.?" he asked.

"No problem," the Secretary replied. "Just let me know where and when. Can I bring the Chief Scientist along? She is going to be a real pain on this if she isn't convinced."

Robert glanced at Nick, who shrugged his shoulders.

"Okay," said Robert, "be at the helicopter pad at old National Airport at oh-seven-hundred hours tomorrow, and we will get you all the evidence you need. Now let me suggest that for the purpose of this planning session, we agree that the thing works as advertised.''

The three men nodded and focused their attention on the computer unit in front of them. Each of the table areas had a work planner unit which interfaced with the National Data Bank.

''I know that you have seen these strategy machines before,'' said Robert, ''but let me give you a brief orientation, so we will all be working on the same frequency.''

He turned a switch on his unit and the wall-sized display screen became active. It introduced itself by displaying: ''THE COMPLETENESS PROGRAM IS READY—JANUARY 20 2014.''

''As we lay out the subjects,'' he said, ''the Completeness program will lead us through some of the questions that have to be answered. The object is to reach a point where everything has been taken into consideration, so that, no matter what happens, there is a strategy for it. Completeness, for this exercise anyway, is defined as 'not lacking anything.' ''

''Have you ever put something through this process and found that every single little and big thing had actually been taken into consideration?'' asked Harold. ''There are so many variations possible in a project like this and so many unknowns.''

''We have had some very good results, Harold,'' said Robert. ''I can't say that every micron has had its hair counted, but we have been able to prevent a lot of problems. You will find that the system lives in the real world. One recent project could not get past the second step because the program decided that one of the participants was not serious about it. Took us awhile to figure that out.''

''We tried to use it on our forestry evaluation and found that it was not cooperative,'' said the Secretary. ''There has been so much bad and opinionated data put in over the years that the machine was giggling, if that is possible. We were forced to go back and get real. Let's get started.''

Nick nodded and drew a sheet of paper from his jacket pocket. ''I put together a list of questions that might get us started. What do we need to do first?''

''We need a summary of this situation,'' said Robert. ''Why don't you state it as briefly and objectively as possible, and the program will take it from there.''

"Okay," replied Nick. "We have developed a consistent, inexpensive energy supply using the nuclear cold fusion concept. It will eventually replace every known reason for burning fossil fuels. It will permit many people who do not have automobiles or home energy to have it. It will let the energy-denied countries have reliable sources of energy. We need to know how to introduce this product into the world without causing economic distress, without having problems with the current energy-producing nations, and we need to know how to get cooperation from everyone involved."

He glanced at Harold and Robert. "Is that enough?" he asked.

"We'll see," replied Robert. "Ask the program to reply."

"Please reply," said Nick.

"GIVE IT AWAY" stated the screen.

"Does it always talk in capital letters?" asked Harold.

"is this better?" replied the screen. "i dont want to do anything to intimidate those who have brought their problems to me"

Everyone laughed and began to relax a little.

"It is just a little difficult to get used to having an intimate conversation with a machine, regardless of how smart it is," said Nick.

"youll get used to it" said the computer. "in the meantime you people do not have a technical problem—you have an ego problem. all these executives in the energy business are not going to appreciate being pushed out into the weeds by a bunch of inventors. everyone will know that they missed the boat—that they didn't even care about the boat for that matter. the only way to get all this resolved completely is to give the thing away. of course that won't keep you from charging a little royalty. one dollar per unit would make a comfortable nest egg."

Everyone was silent.

"I think we knew that we were going to make a joint venture and get everyone involved, but I hadn't thought about giving it away. I'm not even sure how we would do that," said Harold.

"create a charitable trust—give it to the trust—let the trust pay you some of what it gets from leasing the inventions to the automobile utility and energy companies. you all sit on the

trust board and keep everyone honest.   the trust gives money
to the arts health care education religion and science.   an independent representative of each field sits on the board along
with four others—that's an irs rule not mine.''

"We are going to have ten chief executives tomorrow morning. How can we possibly negotiate with all of them to get this
thing accomplished?'' asked Nick.

''do it first and then negotiate'' said the machine. ''each
company can have one chance to join up or it loses its opportunity forever.   you know the automobile people will hop
right in.   opec will fuss a little but be delighted that they
are going to have a source of income.   of course dont forget
that fossil fuels are a primary source of chemical and pharma-
ceuticals.   it isnt like they are going to be completely out of
business.

''the secret of completeness'' it continued, ''is to take the
reasons for conflict off the field and then permit only civilized
weapons to be utilized.''

Robert nodded. ''This approach would eliminate the up-front
positioning that makes negotiations so difficult. You would be
offering them the opportunity to manufacture and distribute this
creation.''

''and make a lot of money in the process'' the computer reminded them.

Nick smiled. ''This fee they pay will be based on their gross,
or be fixed, or on profit? How would we deal with inflation?
What do you recommend?''

''never on profit'' said the program. ''these guys are terrific
with the accounting procedures.   there will be no profit for
50 years if you give them that latitude.   i would suggest that
it be done on a per unit price based as a percentage of
gross.   that way inflation will be accommodated over the
years.   actually the real rate of inflation is about 1.5 percent
worldwide at this time but it will jump to 5 percent in 2016.''

''I have never heard anyone say that inflation was going to
rise that dramatically,'' said Robert. ''The President's advisors
are not expecting much change.''

''if you dont want to know—don't ask'' said the machine
rather testily.

''This seems like a rather uncomplicated solution,'' mused

Harold. "But it makes sense. We eliminate the product as something to fight about, and we funnel a large part of the profit from it into works that will improve the world. In the meantime, everyone in the business has a chance to stay in the business—with a stronger future potential than they have now. We and our people will receive our proper reward and recognition. Everyone should be happy."

"And," said Nick, "we won't have the problem of companies trying to stall or compromise the product because they will have the opportunity to benefit from it."

"when someone comes on the trust board give them a guaranteed income contract for life with strict rules about any other sources of funds.   their loyalty needs to be to the trust. never let them make any product decisions however—that has to be done by technical people.   they just hire people to administer the license agreement and distribute the allocated funds to the appropriate groups.   you have anything else?" asked the machine.

"I think we are through," said Robert. He looked around the group. "Any other questions?"

"I have one," said the Secretary. "What if we should decide, in the interests of national security, to hold this invention back for a few years. After all, the economic reactions around the world could bring on a depression."

The computer bristled.

"people with small minds like yours had the same ideas about the steamboat the railroad the electric light the jet plane and just about everything else.   in the world today over half of the citizens are without basic electrical power—this will let them have it.   you wouldnt agree to live 10 minutes without electricity.

"also—if you tried that the populace would tear you limb from limb.   they have had enough of government deciding what is good for them.   you were at the presidents speech the other night—didnt you listen?"

The Secretary blushed while the other men stared at the screen, which then went blank.

"I know a good lawyer," said Harold. "Perhaps he could draw us up a trust agreement before the meeting tomorrow. You and I have the authority to do that, Nick."

"Make sure it is done *completely*," Robert said, smiling. "I don't want to come back here and explain that this strategy didn't work. I'll escort you out and make certain you can get back in for the meeting tomorrow. Luck."

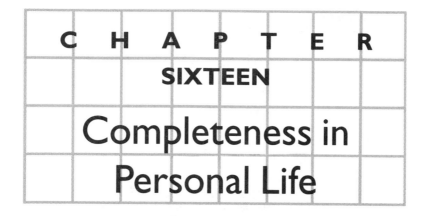

C H A P T E R
SIXTEEN
Completeness in Personal Life

W hen it comes to formally establishing policies and requirements for our personal lives, we tend to be less disciplined than we are at work. After all, we are a family, we know each other well, we all live together, and we communicate continually. It doesn't seem that we need to put something on paper and stick it in a leather-bound policy book in the hallway, for all to see. However, if we are going to have lives of quiet contentment, we really must organize and coordinate our personal ways of thinking and planning—even if only in the privacy of our own minds. Otherwise, how will we know where we are headed and why? How will we know when we get there?

Reading the autobiographies and biographies of successful people shows us that most of them had a clear vision of what they wanted their lives to be. They had determined what they considered important, a list of priorities. Even those whom we would consider unsuccessful, or those who caused a great deal of harm, had their criteria laid out. It may have been negative, or even destructive, but they knew what it was. Hitler spelled out his complete plan in a book written in prison. It was so outlandish in concept, and so poorly written, that no one took it seriously or realized that he meant exactly what he said until it was too late.

Many of us wander through life without taking this navigational matter to heart. When we are young the adults try to tell us these things, but it is difficult for us to grasp how doing something now will have a positive effect much later. Even when we have lived many years, we know very little of the complete world. Trying to keep up with what we do know is a full-time job, and even then it is impossible to adjust to everything that is "in" while avoiding everything that is "out."

Putting yourself under the management of others is one way to deal with the demands of life, but that is not so satisfying as having your own hand on the tiller of your personal destiny. You are not always going to be the boss of your professional and work life, but you can certainly take charge of your personal life.

Self-determination will become even more important in the twenty-first century because the potential for personal misadventure will be even greater. Communication and mobility alone will offer unique opportunities to place ourselves up against the wall. There will be new and original temptations. Recreational drugs, for instance, will be available to provide almost any feeling one would like: We will be witty, sexy, philosophical, religious, or just about any other human condition for as long as we want. It will be able to be turned off and on, it will all be legal, and it will be big business.

There will be a shortage of desirable workers in the business place, and those who qualify will write their own tickets. Automatic ego feeding will be available worldwide as companies court those desirables. Nothing destroys a life, and relationships, quicker than a runaway ego.

The interesting thing about egos is that they are fed by a lack of reality. People think they are what they are not; their feet are in the clouds of fantasy. I can remember learning quickly as a high school football running back that my yardage gains came from the efforts of the linemen who blocked people out of my way. Every now and then these unheralded laborers would teach their colleagues a lesson if the ego factor got too strong. All they had to do was not provide so much protection.

People who have a firm foundation do not have ego problems, do not need recreational drugs, and can have positive continuing relationships with others. They are able to establish Completeness and contentment in their lives because they can identify requirements and meet them.

There are five things you can do to provide such a foundation:

1. Love God.
2. Love your fellow creatures.

3. Keep learning.
4. Set goals.
5. Be happy.

LOVE GOD

When I was a youngster it always seemed patronizing for elders to advise: ''Make God the center of your life.'' I realize now that I didn't know what ''the center of my life'' meant, and they probably didn't either. At that time a relationship with the Almighty, as I understood it, consisted of my paying regular homage, usually at a Sunday church service, and God's leaving me alone in return.

Each summer my family moved to Bethesda, Ohio, where my grandmother ran a hotel. I did dozens of labor-oriented jobs during those times and had a wonderful social life summer after summer. Church groups came from all over Ohio for weekly sessions and recreation. The rules were very rigid: no card playing, no dancing, no late evenings, no alcohol—there was a whole list of things not to do. And Sunday was a day when absolutely nothing was permitted to happen that didn't go on in the church or the dining room. However, the rest of the week there was a lake with swimming and boating, acres of cool woods, and every week began with a whole new batch of young people showing up every Saturday, so any earlier missteps didn't count.

One Wednesday evening, while I was in my teens, I was to escort a lady friend to the Coke and jukebox place, but first she had to play the piano for Vespers. She asked me to stand by the piano and turn the pages of the music for her, which I did happily. During the service it was decided to take up a collection, and my heart came to a complete stop. The only thing I had in the whole world was a five dollar bill, my week's wages, which had just been given me by my grandmother's cook. As I stood there, in front of the congregation, with the ushers coming inexorably closer, I fought a battle within myself. I didn't want to embarrass my mother and grandmother sitting in the second row, and I didn't want the young lady to think I was cheap. But more than anything I didn't want to give up an entire week's pay—my total fortune—in one gesture.

Then it occurred to me that God would appreciate the sacrifice, and perhaps this act would seal the deal on my getting into heaven.

I had placed my hand around the money and had started to draw it out of my pocket when suddenly I received a very clear mental message: God knew I was about to make a donation for show, and out of desperation, rather than from my heart. I would get zero points toward going to heaven, and would in fact be considered vain and showy. In addition, I would have no funds to complete my obligations for the evening. I returned earnestly to my job of turning pages and ignored the outstretched plate. The moment passed. After that my mother made certain I remembered to bring an offering with me each time.

This was the first time I ever thought about God as a real force rather than some sort of misty presence in the firmament. Here was someone with a sense of humor, who was all-powerful and wanted to be my friend. How could I pass up an arrangement like that? I carried the thought in the back of my head through high school, World War II, college, the Korean War, getting married, and the beginnings of a career—all without going to church much. It was as if I knew He was just there watching. I didn't know what else to do about it; there was no relationship, just awareness.

As life proceeded and I learned about its realities—never having enough money, illness, losing parents, facing unfair evaluations, concerns both general and particular—I began to realize that I was not doing too well going it alone. People were wonderful helps, but basically we are all made of sand. I needed solid rock, and as the Bible says, the only real rock is God.

Finally, I just gave myself to Him. Ever since, I have clutched that rock, and I have never been let down. Everything doesn't work out exactly as I want it to, but I believe it works out as He wants. My life has been much more comfortable, rewarding, and exciting since I made that decision. I am also much more content.

It is just not possible for us to handle life and the world on our own. When people tell us that strength and knowledge come from within ourselves, they are not being dishonest, they are just misinformed. It is also the ultimate ego trip: People just aren't strong or consistent enough to generate all that energy.

God provides the steady support of life by always being there and always being the same. He does not change with fads or current events, He never takes time off, and He is as timely now as ever. To establish this relationship it is only necessary to accept His offer of Grace, through prayer. Even if it is not totally clear to you, don't worry about it. I don't understand how television works, but it does work. God is so much smarter than we are and knows so much more than we do. It is only sensible to invite His help. Belonging to a church can help in terms of fellowship and teaching, but I think the only real necessity is the personal relationship that comes with giving yourself to it.

All of this has a "selfish" side also. It is amazing how much a person with an unshakable foundation can accomplish and how much that person can enjoy living and serving.

LOVE YOUR FELLOW CREATURES

People are known by their enemies even more than by their friends. Many individuals I have met have sorted the world into categories of people, animals, insects, and fish alike. They use this predetermination to direct their relationships with others. If we choose bigotry, cynicism, and such we will reap that also.

These individuals will tell you with certainty that people of certain races are lazy and shiftless; others are mercenary and ambitious; some are snobbish; others are stupid; still others are sex-crazed and irresponsible. Being forced to hire and live near such people, they say, drives companies and property values down. They will tell you that teenagers do not accept the restrictions of their age; old people hoard money; politicians are all crooked; retail stores take advantage of you; nothing works right because "they" want it that way.

Animals have their own undesirable characteristics that tend to bother humans; bears, raccoons, squirrels, and other furry things should be wiped out; stray dogs, of course, should be rounded up and shot; cats should be neutered when found wandering around; deer that eat bushes on private property should be eligible for instant extermination. And fish? Some fish eat humans, for heaven's sake; some fish are bony and therefore not desirable; some are being unnecessarily protected, which stops development. Those who hate would like to drop nuclear warheads on certain insects, eliminating all of them for good. And the list of actions requested in order to improve comfort goes on. They have a clear idea of how to rearrange God's world.

All of this preconception does provide them with an eternal agenda for attitude and conversation, as well as an unassailable list of reasons that keep them from doing the things they would like to do. It focuses their life but limits it at the same time. The effort spent hating or distrusting others, or defending against them, detracts from their own resources. It cuts down the time that people can work at the positive things of life. Life, as they say, is too short for that kind of foolishness.

The happiest people are those who take other people and other creatures as they find them. They let them present themselves without prejudice. Some may be accepted, some may be rejected, but only on the basis of what they really are. Those folks I know who are firm about their preconceived definitions of the behavior and attitude problems of specific groups always turn out to have no direct experience. They have never had a conversation with the people under consideration, never been in their homes, and when questioned cannot identify anything bad done to them by these people they dislike. Now certainly there are a lot of people in the world we may not want to spend time with. There are those whose actions, concepts, or attitudes are not in line with ours; there are those with whom we disagree; there are those who do disgusting things. That is all right, we can accept them anyway, while regretting their actions, concepts, or attitudes. We may even have the opportunity one day to help these folks find a better way. They are not going to listen, however, if they can see in our eyes that we consider them inferior or inadequate.

KEEP LEARNING

The half-life of a high school or college education is about four years: After that time half of what we learned will be out-of-date. When another four years passes we will be down to a quarter. This discouraging thought applies to our personal activities as well as our work lives. Just look at the family members who cannot program a VCR and think what is going to happen to them in the age of really advanced technology. They may not even be able to open the refrigerator door one day.

Learning is not just a matter of signing up for a course and having information force-fed. (That has its own rewards and is something that should be considered—continued education can be formalized.) Real learning, however, comes from being routinely curious about the world and digging into various opportunities that arise. It requires continuous reading and questioning. Those who rely on the TV evening news or *USA Today* for their total news input are going to be shallow. There is only time for five or six stories on the TV, and while *USA Today* covers a ton of subjects, there is only room for a paragraph or two on each of them. That is the way these media components are designed and they do a good job of what they are supposed to do.

The personal Centurion has to be up-to-date. In the business world, elaborate databases are constructed in order to keep everyone informed and operating. Many people make inputs to the base; we can take advantage of it just sitting at a desk. But the world of a company is, after all, much narrower than the world of the individual. Companies want to examine volumes of financial data, they like marketing analysis, they want the figures on everything that doesn't move. But basically, business information is an uninspiring and dull bunch of material without a complete sentence in the lot.

By contrast, individuals can usually do their finances all on one sheet, and once a month is plenty. And as people we are interested in *paragraphs* of information, let alone sentences. We need to know about health, arts, entertainment, geography, automobiles, watches, literature, lives, sports, animals, dining, decorating, and a hundred other subjects. We are eclectic in our interests, swinging from antiques during one period to baseball in another. There are unending sources of material available in these fields, but we have to develop the habit of arranging to obtain it. The habit of learning is what keeps us fulfilled, surviving, and interesting.

The key to a life of quiet contentment is knowledge. Unfortunately, the acceptable minimum amount of knowledge is constantly growing, and the knowledge itself changes with the steadiness of a waterfall. What came over the top previously has nothing to do with today. It is possible to be quaint, perhaps, when outdated, but not interesting. And interesting comes from being interested.

SET GOALS

Every goal we set for ourselves should have a number in it. We can't get away with "I am going to read more," we have to be specific: "I will read two books and six magazines each week"; "I will lose sixteen pounds in the next six months, and not gain more than two pounds back over the following year"; "I will save ten percent of my gross income"; "I will practice two and a half hours each day."

When individuals learn to think routinely in terms of specific goals, they suddenly find themselves accomplishing more. They realize that they have a personal power that did not exist before: concentration. Accomplishments planned in a mushy or unmeasurable way usually do not get accomplished. I can recognize that playing a game of golf without keeping score makes for sloppy execution on my part. Not being a competitive person I find myself dropping a ball to give myself another chance. However, when I stick to the rules, playing every shot, or dealing every card, I do much better. It is the same with all of us, I think.

The central aspect of goals is that they force us to analyze a situation and take it more seriously that we might otherwise. When we are providing transportation for a group to some location, for instance, we create a whole series of goals in response to questions: How many are going? (I will drive four other people to the meeting.) What time do we have to arrive, and how long does it take to get there? (I must be on the way, with everyone in the car, by 6 P.M. in order to arrive by 7:15.) How much fuel will it take? (I will make certain there are at least five gallons of fuel in the car.)

BE HAPPY

I have always felt that we have at least one choice in life that is strictly up to the individual: We can be happy or we can be sad. The advantages are not always obvious. Sad people get a lot of attention as folks try to make them happy. Happy people are not felt to need much attention, and certainly no one deliberately tries to make them sad. Happy people are a pleasure to be near. Sad people are to be avoided.

When we wake in the morning and begin the process of presenting ourselves to the world, we can look at what is to come in a way that will make us happy, or the reverse. If we have no money, we can look at ourselves as poor, or we can just be broke. ''Poor'' is a terminal disease; it is in the bones and the soul. Once we decide that we are poor we are forever going to be faced with a struggle that cannot be won. Nobody ever fought their way out of being poor. But ''broke'' is a different story. There are always honest ways to get money; there are always ways to better manage the funds that we acquire. Work is always available for those who are enthusiastic and energetic about it, and success lies just the other side of work.

Many people think they could be happy if only they had something or other. A new car, a trip, a more sensitive mate, a great romance, a three-carat diamond—always the list is of material things. It is well known that couples with a failing marriage will sometimes build a new home or have a new baby just before parting for good. This last desperate effort to satisfy their emptiness only adds to the totality and complexity of their failure. They have looked to objects for solutions that have to be accomplished from within. It is not necessary to take an unrealistic view of life in order to be happy—quite the opposite, for most imagined problems never happen. Those who doubt this should make a list of all the things they are worrying about right now, and then look at it in a week. Very few will be left, if any.

Remember, it takes less muscle energy to smile than to frown.

These actions can help us focus ourselves during our lifetime journey. Most young people never look at life as a whole but move from incident to incident. Adults tend to be caught up in the events of living, one at a time. They do not deliberately create a pattern that could qualify as a process. They do not enjoy the future; they wallow in the past. We need to see how we want our world to be and be able to identify the towers out there on the horizon. At the same time we need to be marching toward them on a road that is built of solid material.

Someday each of us will have a memorial service of some sort. We need to think about what they are going to say and think about us at that time. Will we have left some footprints? Will we have made a difference? Will we have led a life of quiet contentment?

It is all in our hands.

REAL-LIFE PERSONAL COMPLETENESS

You are probably wondering what the effect is of planning one's life along the concepts listed; if it will put you into conflict with what customers, co-workers, and family consider to be the normal way of doing things; if it possible to be placed at a disadvantage by trying to guide your own life rather than reacting to what comes along; if it will turn people off to learn that God is taken seriously by a professional businessperson; if the thought of being happy will be misunderstood cynically.

On the contrary, the Completeness I am describing for individuals is designed to keep them from making trouble for themselves.

C H A P T E R
SEVENTEEN
The Centurion Career

The concept of life's work, as I was taught it during my childhood, was that a person should learn how to do some specific thing and then work hard at it for their lifetime. Everyone needed a trade of some sort, whether it were manufacturing or service—it provided an identity as well as a living. Girls were encouraged to be nurses or schoolteachers. "You can always get a job" was the refrain. Boys were led to skilled labor or a profession. Laying bricks or practicing law, it made no difference. You had to learn how to do something specific. Since the world changed very little in those days, this was not a bad strategy. It was indeed possible to do the same work one's entire lifetime.

In high school we were separated into college preparatory courses and trade school. While the decision swung partly on grades and intelligence, the primary distinction was the subjective determination of whether one could afford college or not. It was far easier to see the benefits of being good at woodworking or mechanical drawing than Latin and world history. It was possible for the trade school people to think clearly about salaries, expenses, and opportunities. The college prep folks had only vague assurances that they would be useful four years after the end of high school.

Today, we are in a business world where perhaps 80 percent of current jobs did not exist fifteen years ago. They probably cannot be completely learned in school and are probably not taught there—it usually takes formal education several years to catch up with reality. So the individuals have to keep going back to learning in order to retain mastery of their trade. Watching people crowd around a new computer program in the office, trying to figure out how it works, will provide a clear picture of the situation today.

So how does one get ahead when formal education and seniority are quickly losing their point value? Education is considered a given: We are supposed to be able to read and write. We are supposed to know what city is the capital of Peru, who wrote *A Streetcar Named Desire,* what was on the news last night.

Recently, an interviewer asked me something concerning my own career that I had never thought about before. She pointed out that I had begun as an inspector on an assembly line and had emerged thirteen years later as corporate vice president of ITT, then number eleven on the list of largest industrial firms. My education had been as a podiatrist, a trade I never practiced because of being recalled to the Navy during the Korean War.

"I contacted some people who knew you during those years and they confirm that you were bright, but certainly not a genius or having even an exceptionally high IQ; that you were able to provide a thoughtful, and usually original, analysis of any situation, but were absolutely nontechnical; that you were energetic and ambitious, but usually went home at quitting time. Actually," she said earnestly, "if you don't mind my saying it, you seem to be rather ordinary, except that people seem attracted to you. I didn't hear one word of criticism from anyone, even those who think your ideas are a little off base."

While I was trying to figure whether I should be indignant or honored by this profile, I ran the initial comment through my mind. Having been denied a useful education for business I became a compulsive reader, particularly of history and human behavior. I had realized that I could never know everything about technology and didn't care much about it anyway, so I concentrated on people and what they do. I became helpful to others.

"Helpful" is a trade, like being an electrician. Almost no one knows what is going on in other areas of the company, and almost no one wants to bail others out of their problems. But if one is to be known not only to solve but to prevent problems— the best of all lower level reputations—then one must be able to unveil the actual source of problems. Once unveiled, the source has to cooperate and be appreciative. An amazing amount of progress can be accomplished by anyone who does not insist on getting the credit. That statement has probably been made in every generation since Eden, but it is true. What some do not realize is that such behavior becomes known rapidly, mainly because no one else engages in it.

As a Centurion, you have two options: one is to depend on the "kindness of strangers" for promotion and success, a chancy strategy at best; the other is to arrange for them yourself by just overshadowing the competition. That does not require kissing the boss anyplace, but it does require a plan. Progress has to be anticipated, laid out, and followed with dedication. And if we find we are in a place where they are not sensitive enough to appreciate us, then it is time to move along. During the first ten years of a career it is acceptable to work for three or four companies. After that, ten years is the minimum, and one might stay forever if the atmosphere is correct.

I found that two and perhaps three levels of growth are about all that will be forthcoming from one company even if they adore you. This is because we are always remembered as being the level and age at which we joined the firm. This means it is possible to still be considered a bright young thing at the age of sixty. We have to take a cold, calculated look at what is going on, stay clear of politics, and just do an outstanding job. At the same time we have to keep up with what is happening in other areas of the business world: It may be time to change areas of interest. It is best not to be lured into a dead end. For instance, I found myself labeled as a "quality type," meaning I was limited to dealing with quality control, quality assurance, and quality management rather than the real world. Therefore I was not seriously considered when it came time to pick a chairman or president.

After founding a company, building it into a worldwide organization, taking it public, and proving its success over a dozen years, I am still looked at as lucky by many others. They do not conceive that a "quality type" could have done such a thing. Speaking of categories, being a writer does not get much respect, but being an author does. Go figure.

I do not want to put forth the thought that running around sowing happiness and joy will turn the advocate into the head of the stock exchange. Results are what count, and results are what must be accomplished. But the best way of getting them, and this will be particularly true in the new century, is by having lots of help. The more we give, the more we get. When a broad segment of the organization is helping us, because they feel we are helping them, victory is inevitable. The concepts of Completeness will help the Centurion keep aimed in the proper direction for a wonderful personal career.

When the Centurion is in charge of the organization and its people it is necessary to search out and identify those who perform in like manner. Those are the ones who should be placed close to the top. They will be loyal in every respect and will set new records of efficient operation. They will relate to the employees, the suppliers, and the customers.

As I have said a dozen times since page one, make the employees and suppliers successful, they will make the customer successful, and that will make the company (and you) shine.

Guidelines
for Browsers

Not everyone is interested in working hard, and now I see the concepts and efforts of quality management's construction being diluted through superficial programs and techniques.   xv

As a result, hardly anything the government ordered conformed to their expectations.   xvi

It wasn't until the Japanese invasion of the early 1970s that the American public awoke and began demanding to receive what they had ordered.   xvi

Now the trend is for management to turn quality back to the professionals, and all the old criteria are beginning to return.   xvii

The great mass of executives assume that if the government puts it out then it must be right.   xvii

Success will be preordained before any work is done; there will only be the usable and the discarded.   xvii

This had been dawning on me for some time, but I had put off doing anything about it.   xvii

With the memory of all that in mind, I have been laying back on the subject of Completeness.   xvii

Management will become a much more serious business in the next decade and century.   xviii

Facing what I feel will be the facts of the twenty-first century has made me finally accept what I have known for twenty years—that quality management is never going to be enough.   xviii

Completeness is involved only with management.   xviii

The persons who make up the management corps of a company are the main source of trouble for that organization, just as they are responsible for most of the good things that happen.   xviii

If the targets are sound and properly aimed in the manner of well–thought out strategies and policies, then success could be just around the corner. If they are based on fairy tales, then the organization could be eaten by the wolf.   xix

Strategies change over time, but fairy tales are with us forever.   xix

For the first several thousand years of recorded history, management was mostly a matter of dealing with people and animals as they performed low-level labor.   1

In the twenty-first century we may well be back to managing people who are coping with a technology that has a mind of its own.   1

In earlier days management held all the information, while today much of it is available to all.   1

There may be a wonderfully different social environment in the next century within which the Centurions and other people will make lives and do business.   2

People all over the world will at last obtain the opportunity for the education, health, and living conditions that will enable them to manage their own lives responsibly.   2

Governments will find themselves unwelcome in the lives of their citizens and will reluctantly restrict themselves to doing those tasks that only they can do.   2

Technology will live up to its promise of providing the means of unburdening people's working and social lives, permitting them to be more fulfilling.   2

Religious conversion in the best possible sense will come upon the earth, providing the foundation for genuine peace and understanding.   2

People are breaking free from political oppression and economic distress; they will not be so vulnerable to the siren songs of would-be dictators.   2

We have the opportunity to truly see that the worth of the individual will have the chance to shine through all over our "global village."   3

The socially unacceptable person will disappear over time. (Boring people, however, will still exist.)   3

Despots, such as Caligula, Hitler, and Stalin, could do unspeakable things to their subjects without fear of retribution.   3

If we begin back in the days of the Old Testament and track mankind's course up to the twentieth century, we see a world population that was generally unlettered, short-lived, and considered—even by themselves—to be incapable of governing or managing their own lives.   4

The king was always right, even if not correct.   4

The daily lives of ordinary people did not improve a great deal in the four thousand years between the biblical Abraham and the presidential Abraham.   4

The American and French revolutions made it clear that things had to change.   5

The First and Second World Wars were the last gasps of world government aspirations by single charismatic leaders.   5

The husband and father was master of all he surveyed all those years, at least legally.   6

In an effort to eliminate such oppression and give people their fair share of everything, political philosophers devised socialism and communism.   6

The results, nearly fifty years after the Second World War, have shown that those who chose the least amount of government interference have done the best.   6

The United States, where Congress meets continually in order to pull and tug at the social and business structure, has progressed only with difficulty.   6

Japan, where government politely calls business every day to see if there is anything they can do to help, has become a world power.   6

However, we are beginning to reach the time when what governments do or not will be of less importance.   6

Now we are dealing with people who do not want to be led around; they want to be free to do their own thing.   7

All of this will come about by what I call a "bottom-up socialism."   7

This is going to require that we personally understand how to manage our lives for survival and growth in this new world.   7

The leaders of all this will be the Centurions—those who understand how to make Completeness happen.   7

If we think about it, one hundred people represent about the limit of our personal ability to govern.   7

That could be why we get the correct impression that hardly anyone actually understands his or her executive responsibility enough to do it properly.   7

People will be able to program themselves to experience different emotions or personal patterns.   8

The Centurions will have to learn how to manage so that they can deal with whatever happens, and at the same time, anticipate what is coming. They will have to be in a permanent situation of awareness in order to tell the difference between fads and reality. They will have to be able to deal purposefully and effectively with people on all levels. They will have to be able to get results, be confident in themselves, learn how to compile and comprehend information, and in short, be complete participants.   8

The next century is not going to be the place for the compartmentalized management concepts of the twentieth, which tended to seek out magic bullets and quick answers in the search for an easy way to the Grail.   9

The Centurion is not going to have the luxury of failing as often as those in previous times.   9

There will not be rows of submanagers to pass things along and sort the burrs from the fabric.   9

The top of the organization chart is going to be dealing directly with the bottom.   9

In trying to describe what the Centurion will have to be doing, it is apparent that hard work will be a given.   9

Those who want to survive will need to concentrate on Completeness. This means that the systems making up the organization must be considered as a whole.   9

The Centurion has to establish a climate of Completeness in which the urge to cooperate is normal.   10

The dream of a "paperless" office has not been realized to date, because people just have not permitted it to happen.   11

The Centurion will be dealing with generations raised to know computers as a normal part of life.   11

When everything is in the public or private data bank, there is no need to write it down.   11

The Centurion is going to have to become skilled in the art of personal communication.   11

Hiring someone will be like picking a marriage partner.   11

Dealing with people all over the world will produce a reputation, one way or the other, about the company's ability to perform.   12

Many organizations develop a negative attitude as a normal part of doing business.   12

Much of this originates from a management whose personality is to see everything in terms of numbers or actions, not noticing the people behind them.   12

When we multiply this a few times we begin to realize what all those people are doing in the hall with papers in their hands and an earnest expression on their faces.   12

As the human body cannot function without refreshed, "up-to-date" blood cells carrying oxygen, so the company needs accurate, reliable, up-to-date, and constantly accessible communications.   13

To be complete is to have the entire jigsaw puzzle together, each piece fitting exactly as planned.   13

Business has been run on a compartmentalized basis for centuries. The marketing department doesn't talk much to the sales department, which has little to do with the production department, which could care less about the financial department, which doesn't even know where the shipping department is.   13

Having served a lot of time as the "boss," my personal experience has been that the rest of the people think I already know about things, so they don't tell me.   14

The Centurion has to deliberately build Completeness into the culture of the company so that there is a compulsion to share information.   14

The most successful ventures are those that people ache for, that they take into themselves personally and simply will to succeed.   14

The concern shown by the management for the employees and all those who touch the enterprise becomes evident.   14

Sometimes people wonder why it is necessary to have so many strings or winds in a symphony orchestra.   14

Perhaps we need to hang photographs around the office, showing a bearded man wrapped in a white sheet, standing in front of a cave, right hand raised, palm outward, saying: "Work-life is a symphony, my child."   14

People usually come equipped with poor self-images as standard issue.   15

The worklife of the Centurion will be a symphony.   15

The Centurions would expect a minimum return of 20 percent after tax on the bottom line, for instance, and would be surprised to learn that any of their employees not prohibited by a physician would miss work.   16

Managements working and thinking along the obsolete concepts of the twentieth century will never make it in the coming decades.   16

The only absolutely essential management characteristic will be to acquire the ability to run an organization that deliberately gives its customers exactly what they have been led to expect and does it with pleasant efficiency.   16

A unit with proper morale has confidence, submits readily to discipline and leadership, and is filled with hope.   17

In the business world morale involves everyone who touches the enterprise and includes suppliers, customers, and the community, in addition to employees.   17

Why some managements seem to spend their time deliberately destroying morale rather than building it is something I have never understood.   17

Everyone wants to be successful, and in that light, let us consider just what success means in an organization, whether it be profit or nonprofit oriented.   17

Success is a whole bunch of things, all of which are possible when approached properly.   18

The hollering is quieter and more discreet at the CEO level.   18

It is not possible to run any part of a business without a determination of what is supposed to be happening.   18

The people as a whole usually have greater common sense than the leaders as individuals, but there is no way to package that truth inside a corporate organization.   18

It has become very clear to me that organizations of all sizes and purposes make most of their own troubles and inefficiencies.   18

While a lot of enterprises fail after a while, most do not.   18

Good products and services can survive bad management.   18

Bad ones are going to fail eventually, no matter how marvelous and competent the management proves to be.   18

To qualify as successful in this new league, the Centurion must be able to absorb and implement the principles of Completeness.   19

Completeness as a way of business and even personal life is well within the grasp of us ordinary people.   19

The purpose of Completeness is to avoid problems and guarantee success.   19

There are three principles of Completeness: cause employees to be successful; cause suppliers to be successful; cause customers to be successful.   19

Executives are willing to work on the customers but neglect the employees.   19

Management has been conditioned to think of employees as a commodity, existing in a sort of ocean stocked with an endless supply of such fish.   19

Making the customer successful is a far cry from the vague admonishments of "satisfaction" or "providing customer service" commonly made in today's management conferences.   20

They can tell stories about how, if someone is not happy, they give them a replacement or a refund, with no questions asked. They miss the point that I didn't come to them in order to obtain that service.   21

The Oxford English Dictionary does not treat the word "succeed" with much reverence.   21

I view success along the lines of "obtaining desired ends." 21

People are not always clear about what they want, and indeed may not have the slightest idea of what it takes for someone to help them become successful. 21

Success is not always something large, heavy, or expensive. 22

If an organization is to practice Completeness as its way of doing things, the first ingredient must be to consciously construct this climate of consideration. 22

Consideration is a great deal more than just being nice to each other, but that is not a bad place to begin. 22

To make certain that I knew what was happening, I had to be involved at all levels of the process. 23

We all like to do things that make us look useful. 23

Problems can only come from a few sources. 24

Everyone in the company had coat buttoned up tight, and we in the wind factor were running around with razors trying to slice the buttons off. 24

If we could help others learn not to have problems, we could be in better shape ourselves. 25

We could even help them learn to respect each other. 25

So many things and their interfaces were involved in the operation that there was an unlimited opportunity for something to go wrong. 25

These "nonmanufacturing" people were just being brought to the conclusion that everyone as an individual is in the service business and has a product of some sort. 26

The corporate staff were characterized as being seagulls ("they fly in, eat your food, squawk a lot, crap all over you, and fly away"). 27

So I spent a great deal of time and energy teaching people

how to be helpful rather than arrogant and disrespectful. Believe me, arrogant and disrespectful are easier to teach.   27

Once they found that we did not intend to feather our nest by plucking them down to their bleached bones, they cooperated.   27

"Nice" itself has to be explained.   27

Education is such a serious business that it has to be deliberately structured and induced.   27

Colleges and universities have less of a problem; they can and do teach the same thing forever in many cases.   28

None of what happened before is going to change, although views and opinions about it certainly are areas for original thought.   28

Those who have to make a living by selling something to other people every day have to keep up and keep ahead.   28

Management has to keep a close eye on the needs of the customer to make certain that a route is not being constructed around them.   28

The half-life of education varies but is rarely more than four years.   28

So those good old reliable people in accounting will be out-of-date before long, which means that the financial management process will steadily become more expensive and less efficient.   28

Imagine what it would cost today to use the fountain pens and manual entries that used to form the foundation of accounting.   28

The way to be successful, in business as well as in personal life, is to help others be successful. Reward comes from what you give, not from what you get.   30

I just went ahead and did things without making a big deal of them. This led people to believe, I realized later, that the tasks involved and the resulting accomplishments could not have been too difficult in the first place.   32

If someone just did his job correctly it was assumed that he had been issued a minimum piece of work.   32

Success was when all the personal and business objectives you could think of were met through your efforts, and you were recognized as being able to help others achieve theirs.   32

Success consisted more of a state of mind and relationships with others than an asset count.   33

Management's job is to make the employees successful.   33

Benefits show the employees you are serious about helping them have lives, but benefits alone do not guarantee that the employees are going to work hard for you.   33

To have successful relationships, management has to generate a culture built on respect for the individual.   34

Consideration and respect cannot be purchased or programed.   34

It is easy to say that a company should have respect for its employees, for instance, but exactly how does that come about?   34

Respect is the opportunity to be successful and do it every day. It is the elimination of what keeps them from being successful in the first place.   34

We have to think about building the positive atmosphere of a "great place to work" by eliminating the negatives.   34

The biggest problems we all have in our personal as well as our business lives is in relating to others.   34

There are enough available sources of depression in the world without having to put up with it at work.   35

One of the reasons for unhappy work situations is that there are usually no rules or policies that all parties accept and use.   35

Many managements, for reasons clear only to themselves, go

out of their way to irritate their employees by establishing regulations that humiliate people.   35

If we are going to have a climate of consideration in our organization we have to make clear, through the right policies and practices, the way people are going to be treated within it.   35

There is no cut-and-dried, standard book of procedures.   35

The purpose of these policies is to lay out as clearly as pos5sible the company's position on subjects that affect the business and the people involved.   35

People can expect to be disciplined if they do not earn their way.   36

It is fatal to assume that policies such as these are going to be implemented automatically.   36

In our age, it is very expensive to find good employees; it is much better to learn how to keep and develop them.   36

When employees feel the company does not care about them or is taking advantage of them, they go somewhere else. Just like customers.   36

Management's job is to provide an environment in which people can grow without having to deal with barricades and land mines.   36

Unfortunately, a company's executives, like the shoemaker's children, are often left out.   37

If they have the knowledge, understanding, energy, and are given the opportunity—they should be able to be successful, provided no one is stacking the deck against them.   37

Yet many who have all the proper characteristics, plus all kinds of opportunities, miss the boat.   37

They have to recognize that in a very real way fellow workers are their suppliers and customers.   38

Believe it or not, there are customers who think their problems are not taken seriously.   38

Do you think what you are advocating can be taught? Isn't it a matter of personality more than anything? It could be like trying to teach romance.   39

The normal career approach people select, if they consciously select one, is more inwardly oriented.   40

To me, a customer is someone we do something for, on purpose.   44

Even if we only place our uncashed checks in safe-deposit boxes we are customers.   44

Each of our families is also a customer demanding our attention and care, and our co-workers are customers wanting us to do our part in the chain that is the organization.   44

The key to having a successful customer is in determining what that customer wants and then arranging the operation to produce that.   45

The Centurion, dealing with an economy that operates worldwide, is going to have to develop an internal system that performs constant examination of the customer's desires.   45

If there is a secret to making successful customers, it is to be able to determine what they want.   45

We need to never stop learning.   50

When people make up their list of customers, and we all have several, they often omit one who is very close to them—the boss.   53

The successful boss is one who can quietly bask in the glory generated by those who do the actual work.   53

Self-image, or the lack of it, is the largest single personal problem in the world.   53

Building self-image is hard work, tearing it down is child's play.   53

Relationships are supposed to wrap clear around like an overcoat, not just cover strategic spots like a bikini.   54

Customers cannot be let out of sight.   54

Why do companies keep on doing something their customers do not want them to do?   54

People are not all that complex; they will go to the organization that creates the least problem and the most success.   54

Put your eye where the money comes from, not in the dim mists of anticipation.   56

There is an obvious extension to making both customers and employees successful. That is the successful supplier.   57

In most cases the one who buys it will never even see it, let alone use it.   58

Business buying traditionally deals primarily with the considerations of price and delivery.   58

Where the individual may return to the same grocery store for years, the company switches suppliers regularly based on price. The result is that buyer and seller never get to know each other.   58

Constant changes reduce or eliminate the consideration of commitment.   59

We will carefully identify suppliers whose products and services fit our needs and whose practices and attitudes are compatible with ours, and we will develop long-term relations that are beneficial to both parties.   59

Those who place orders have to learn that quality comes first.   59

We need to determine what parts of our products and services we will purchase rather than provide ourselves.   59

During the twentieth century many companies utilized vertical integration to eliminate suppliers all together.   59

All supplied items must meet agreed upon requirements

every time, be cost competitive, and be delivered as committed.   60

Waiting for someone to swish through the intersection or not, randomly, would be a strain on the nerves and would lead to everything shutting down.   60

They have to come into the relationship knowing that we are going to actually use their output, whether it be hardware, software, or advice.   60

We do not want to have one drop more inventory of anything than we absolutely need for right now.   60

A formal program of education and communication will be established with suppliers, to assure that the relationship is soundly based in all concerned.   61

If an organization is to communicate with its suppliers and develop positive relationships, it is necessary to reach out and share information with them.   61

Suppliers who do a certain amount of business with us, and those with whom we have long-range agreements, would be expected to attend relationships seminars.   62

We will make long-term arrangements with those suppliers who prove themselves to be reliable and interested in our success.   62

We now know that the lowest price comes from the closest arrangement.   62

When a company has the assurance of business over a long term, it can concentrate on becoming more efficient and productive.   62

Most management people do not realize that their suppliers are as important to them as their employees.   64

Supplying companies are very different from each other. Trying to have a group of folks deal with all of them might complicate things.   65

Discussing different ways of managing becomes a bit easier when systems can be compared with each other.   67

It is hard to tell the difference in the way places work unless we know what actually goes on inside.   67

Those viewing from a private box, such as the board of directors usually occupies, often cannot tell the difference between the useful and the disastrous.   67

However, goals (even those that are not easily measured) are one thing; the way you go about achieving them is quite another.   67

Many employee "development" programs are designed to keep employees working in lower level pay-grades, while expecting higher-rating work from them.   68

Quality is the easiest of all "measurements" to rationalize, since few companies are willing to measure it financially; they much prefer subjective evaluation.   68

Dictatorships (political or corporate) crumble inevitably, for instance, if only because no number two authority figure is ever permitted to emerge in such an environment.   68

Paternal and forgiving cultures crumble just as certainly, although for different reasons.   68

Companies have climates just as geographical regions do.   68

Some of these despots wear aprons, or three-piece suits, but they all share one identifying characteristic: insisting on total power.   68

They create a difficult workplace yet continually state that they wish others would do something so they could step back from their daily toil.   69

Yesterday's priority item can today be considered a wasteful and disobedient effort with one twitch of the eyebrow.   69

Inconsistency is the only consistent thing around.   70

They learn how to act, not how to reason.   70

The leader takes quick and dramatic action to discipline those who do not show the proper adoration.   70

Destruction is inevitable as individuals are robbed of their ability to think and act on their own.   70

No one is safe who shows any signs of being a problem to the leadership.   70

Customs develop, most of which are defensive in nature.   71

Blind obedience is a good place to start.   71

One of the oldest forms of stable government is to appoint a ruler and then limit the power that can be exercised. Families do this all the time.   71

The ruler provides stability, while elected leaders come and go.   71

Often there actually is no written constitution in a ''constitutional monarchy.''   71

People are aimed at certain careers early in life whether they like it or not.   72

Life for the people sort of averages out, with hardly anyone living lavishly and very few living poorly.   72

Bosses are chosen by, and thus required to listen to, the electors, which keeps them attentive.   72

Public image establishes the perceived worth of the individual.   73

Special interests at all levels can run the system off the track.   73

Modern communication systems will let the management know and understand the will of the people.   73

Everyone keeps learning due to the availability of material and freedom of choice.   73

You might think that once we find ourselves living in one particular management style we are stuck there forever.   73

While a complete dictatorship might force us to tunnel our way out in real life, business systems can be slunk away from.   73

Most people in difficult work situations are not able to get out without a great deal of cost to pride and pocketbook.   74

Banana Republic companies are easy to identify.   77

Most of the Savings and Loan organizations that fell apart were typical BRs.   77

Knowing everything meant gathering information relentlessly and having resident experts from every field who could translate it into something we could all understand and take action on.   77

It was hard to get a lot of work done if one actually went to all the meetings required.   78

The result of managing this way was to produce an organization of people who liked each other, routinely did things right the first time, and who generated a great deal of revenue per employee.   79

''Arrogance'' is not a nice word.   80

I have been trying—so far, without success—to think of a business failure that was *not* caused by the specific arrogance of an individual or the cultural arrogance of a group.   80

When people will not listen to others, when they are in love with their own knowledge, when they abuse power, they are arrogant.   80

Often the arrogant are difficult to recognize at first because they do not exhibit this behavior to those who are important to them.   80

There are no programs, systems, or even business philosophies that will make much of a dent in these people.   81

The opportunity to make such expensive and destructive mistakes is going to be much greater in the coming century.   81

The difference in whether people enjoy their jobs or cringe

when it is time to go to work lies in the way they are treated.   81

Arrogant managers or management teams make life miserable for people without good reason.   81

Going out when everyone loves you and wants you to stay is much better than seeing the organization leave you.   82

Before long we won't have anyone working, just people doing paper things.   84

The program covers what is accepted as standard in most companies now: employee orientation, executive and managerial competence in making customers successful, training on Completeness for knowledge and skilled workers, and various special subjects.   85

You have accepted their proposal and irritated them at the same time. I would be surprised if many of them stay around to do the program.   86

Is there any particular reason that you make so much trouble for yourself?   86

Business is like football, no place for sissies—it is all hand-to-hand combat.   86

My way is to have a very effective emergency room. You get sick—we find out, we fix you.   87

They are going over each order one at a time, manually; they have shut off the computer. Everything comes in, nothing goes out.   88

The real people in our company are those out there with the customers, like Smith's people. I see very little value in other functions.   88

The Centurion will be too busy surviving and growing to tolerate the waste that comes from arrogance.   89

In the case of a public company, the board of directors has a duty, which they rarely observe, to watch for arrogance on the part of management.   89

Executives of the twenty-first century are going to have to be smarter and more thorough about dealing with the real world than their twentieth-century counterparts.   91

The Centurion will have to deal with the business jigsaw as a complete entity and will not be permitted to pound pieces in place with a hammer or purchase waivers that will authorize placing a size-ten foot into a size-nine shoe.   91

The Centurion will realize that all things must be considered and worked out before the project is launched.   91

The Centurion will realize that people are the most critical asset to success and will carefully select, encourage, and raise them.   91

The Centurion will establish a philosophy of operating that is consistent with Completeness and human dignity.   92

The Centurion will be an adult, yet will have the urge for innovation and adventure of a child.   92

This is not going to be the age of consensus, but the age of the individual leader, the Centurion.   92

Socrates, who said that democracy was not the proper system for organizations that wanted to accomplish something, will be vindicated in the business world.   92

This is a case where a company that has served many people well almost died because its management was blinded to the real world by the assurance of success.   93

We have to manage at all times as though a recession, or a competitor, is about to devour us.   93

So why do companies lurch from peak to valley to peak?   93

Most victims of crime or other violence know the perpetrator.   93

Family, friends, acquaintances, customers, and others are the ones who do most of the harm to us.   93

Shoplifting, or "shrinkage" as it is known, is mostly done by the employees.   93

All those songs about hurting the ones we love have a basis in fact.   93

On the other hand, the people who do the very best things to us are also those we love.   93

Many of the executives I have worked with as well as for spent a large amount of their time terrorizing the employees of their organization.   94

This fact makes it clear that despite all the well-developed systems and concepts of management, almost every company is operated according to the formula formed in the mind and actions of one person.   94

Certainly there are always individuals who get into those jobs who are incompetent or destructive or both.   94

The worst executive I ever knew, bar none, asked me to help him write a book about his management style, so others could copy it.   94

Either way, someone is affecting our lives in a manner we did not plan, and we will feel eternal resentment about it.   94

Bad companies have bosses that are incomplete.   94

They do not discuss, they announce.   94

Unlike the Centurion, these people snarl a lot, often use obscene language regularly, do not listen to anyone, make all the decisions (and change them rapidly).   95

They take personal advantage of the facilities, services, and funds of the company.   95

Of all those who are in charge of us, probably four out of five are inadequate as bosses, and probably only a third of those are willing to learn how to become outstanding or even adequate.   95

Out of all these folks there were about a dozen whom I consider outstanding bosses and leaders.   95

The workers would have done better if left alone with an inflated dummy in the corner office.   96

To this day I never give anyone advice unless they ask me, and I usually charge them for it. That way I am sure they will listen even if they do not act on it.   96

He thought no one understood, but his real problem was that they did indeed understand.   97

I often wondered if the executives who gave us occasional lectures on having a good attitude and treating the customers properly knew about that.   97

Everyone hated the company.   97

Protests were met with a resolution worthy of a wartime leader.   98

I have watched several executives destroy their areas of responsibility in order not to appear wrong.   98

These people got so involved with wanting to make some specific thing happen that they forgot all about the business and the people who ran it.   98

There will no longer be the automatic assumption that the leader is correct and the people are misinformed.   99

They will recognize that in the twenty-first century, information flows up the organization, not down as in the twentieth century.   99

Making a lot of unnecessary changes would seem, I noted, like building a latrine in a rose garden.   99

I always felt that the only difference between the Mafia and the executives who looted these institutions was the width of the pin stripes on their suits.   99

There are also bright, hard-working, success-oriented executives who do *not* steal from their companies but cause as much disruption and loss of worth as if they did.   100

This is the key to the incomplete boss syndrome: their belief that the only things that matter are those they want to do.   100

The Centurion will recognize the need to provide a complete concept as a reliable framework for running an organization.   100

Change will come from thoughtful action rather than impulse.   100

Vest-pocket Hitlers will not be able to intimidate their employees because the employees will have choices.   100

If the captain insists on personally selecting the menu, cleaning the heads, and steering all the while, the transit will be difficult. Mutiny is one of the least things that can happen in such a case.   100

Why are such otherwise smart people so difficult?   101

In order to show that they are in charge, they run around being in charge—driving everyone nuts in the process.   101

It costs about a half-year's average salary to replace, hire, train, and support each new employee.   106

Successful is as successful does.   106

The philosophers say that people have an absolute need for food, sex, and a sense of purpose.   106

I would think that their life is their own problem. I know I feel that way about mine.   106

The training budget gets cut every time the profit goes down.   109

It is like cutting out the fourth grade and giving kids a year off in order to save money.   109

I would define a successful customer as one who bought shoes they liked, that fit as they had imagined, and that cost what they were willing to pay.   110

Very few management decisions are made on the basis of fact.   111

We are getting worse and thinking everything is wonderful.   112

Do I detect that you are concerned about what is real and what is "politically correct" in this quality business?   113

We are doing the actions laid out in the material but nothing seems to be happening.   114

I have been reading TQM material, and I have gone to several conferences, and I still don't understand exactly what it is. Also, after listening to the speakers and walking through the exhibits, I have concluded that none of them understands, either.   115

We found that once we all agreed on how we were going to do things, we were able to do almost all of our work without confusion.   116

Once we as a group determined that people would do what they said they were going to do, it became possible to create, particularly on things that made the job easier.   116

I don't see how you can ever explain to the people that so many do not have to do things as agreed.   118

We seem to believe that management is the problem, not the people. We feel that employees get their bad habits from management's direction or lack of it.   118

What they learned in class was how to pass the test.   119

We have been treating quality as though it were something beyond management's ability to comprehend.   119

Management's job is to develop clear requirements that the employees, suppliers, and customers understand.   119

Senior management in most cases just wants some education, and some flag-waving.   120

We will deliver defect-free products and services to our customers and co-workers, on time.   121

I see no reason why an oil tanker can't turn around quickly, provided it has tugs like us pushing and pulling.   121

They had a reputation for performing effective work on behalf of their clients, and also one for being insensitive to the fate of employees and suppliers of said clients.   122

The business appeared to be changing rapidly, but no one in the company was insisting that it was time to change their ways, or offering something innovative.   126

Here we are in the year 2020—one hundred years after my grandfather was born, as a matter of fact—and we are still operating with twentieth-century data.   127

The problem of information was both that there was an enormous amount of it, and that one never knew which part was accurate and which was off-center.   129

When it came to news, getting the complete story was not easy.   130

Nor was it easy when it came to running a company.   130

Information was like running water—one could only drink so much at a time, and during the necessary pause for breath, tons of the fluid rushed by.   130

Executives would work on thinking up the questions rather than memorizing the data.   130

It has taken society a long time to realize that disasters, for instance, don't just happen in one moment. They build up over time, and the clues are there for us to see.   136

All of this comes under the concept of Completeness, which has to do with taking care of every aspect and knowing that you are doing so.   136

Running this business is like pushing a safe across the sand.   136

The board of directors meeting of this era was not the usual passive gathering known to CEOs in the past of old and carefully selected friends.   141

The directors wanted to know a great deal more about the operations than they had in the past, and that required companies to become more sophisticated in their status systems.   142

No one was really safe as long as the compensation committee was in session.   144

New firms entering the field as our competitors start up with the current technology, while older organizations such as ours have to deal with the past in order to get to the future.   145

We need to leapfrog, not fight our way out of the brush.   145

New technologies do not necessarily lead to new levels of comprehension and learning by themselves.   149

What happens if you don't keep up on the technology of learning is that they fall further behind.   149

The key to our education process is Completeness. All of this begins with the management personnel, and I might note that board members will be requested to attend certain classes and study certain material. Your role in this process is vital because everything forms from here.   150

The first idea is "treat the whole as one."   150

We have never been a "whole" except at the very top of the organization, where everything came together.   150

The second is "build a culture of consideration."   150

We have to change the policies that cause such a situation. It is very hard to find people today, as you know; it is only good business to build strong relationships with employees.   151

The third idea is to "make everything understood."   151

We keep a lot of secrets inside, and we have not done a good job of teaching people their responsibilities.   151

The fourth idea of Completeness is "be complete but not finished."   151

We had the field much to ourselves for years, but now we have to be outstanding. The way to do that is to have people who know the most, have the best attitude, and work very effectively.   151

We need to delight our clients.   151

Quality, finance, relationships—they all need specific supportive policies.   157

Foundation gifts should be aimed at assisting the Completeness of a cause and be identified with specific projects as much as possible.   157

A policy is a specific form of communication between people that is agreed to be accomplished without variation.   161

Where there is no policy, there is chaos.   161

The process of Completeness requires that policies be taken seriously as constituting the foundation for developing the requirements we are going to meet every time.   161

We establish that if we borrow money it must be paid back.   162

We establish that if we agree to be somewhere at a certain time, it is polite and practical to meet that requirement.   162

We establish our own policies and that makes us adults, which means we begin to use policies to communicate with those we care about.   162

Policies are not some dead statements carved into the wall, they are living agreements.   162

The citizens of the world are demanding that we, their governments, serve them rather than ourselves. They want to lead fulfilling lives, they want us to take only those things that they cannot deal with as individuals, and most urgently, they do not want us to make trouble for them.   165

The employees want management help, not just direction. The challenge is to learn how to manage all of this completely, not just react to things or situations.   165

The thought process behind all this began twenty-five years ago when the Berlin wall fell, taking communism along with it.   165

They were tired of being deprived of spiritual and material things because of ancient hates and customs that no longer had any meaning or relevance.   166

We, like the church leaders, have been reminded in these recent years that we govern with the consent of the governed. We are their servants, not their masters.   166

We must learn to manage in an entirely new way, to help people have complete lives—in government, in business, and personal life.   167

When there is no political harassment, when it is possible to earn the necessities of life and more, then people don't want to leave their homelands.   167

Crime is beginning to fall off throughout the world as science learns how to help people overcome destructive tendencies through chemical products and educational advances.   168

Keeping everything moving in the right direction requires a government that is cooperating with its people.   168

The people want their politicians to represent them, period. They do not want to be controlled.   169

As lives become longer there is more need for health care.   170

In the personal sense, Completeness requires making the difficult long-range decisions that will affect us and those we influence throughout our lives.   171

For the first time in world history, there are no governments that sit without the permission of the people.   172

The people own the companies, but business is managed by professionals instead of someone appointed because of political considerations.   175

If people had equity in various enterprises, then they could live on that instead of this old fashioned Ponzi scheme we have going now. Taking from the working to pay the nonworking has never worked.   175

People insist on being treated with dignity these days, and with the worldwide shortage of workers there is not much alternative, even for the most ''explosive'' people.   176

Life was relatively simple while something was in the cocoon. Once it emerged, nothing was the same.   179

We thought if we could develop a small nuclear energy system, based on the cold fusion principle, it would be possible to provide automobiles, homes, businesses, and other applications with their own nearly permanent sources of power.   182

The secret of Completeness is to take the reasons for conflict off the field, and then permit only civilized weapons to be utilized.   194

When it comes to formally establishing policies and requirements for our personal lives, we tend to be less disciplined than we are at work.   197

If we are going to have lives of quiet contentment, we really must organize and coordinate our personal ways of thinking and planning.   197

Reading the autobiographies and biographies of successful people shows us that most of them had a clear vision of what they wanted their lives to be.   197

Trying to keep up with what we do know is a full-time job, and even then it is impossible to adjust to everything that is "in" while avoiding everything that is "out."   197

Self-determination will become even more important in the twenty-first century because the potential for personal misadventure will be even greater.   198

Recreational drugs, for instance, will be available to provide almost any feeling one would like: We will be witty, sexy, philosophical, religious, or just about any other human condition for as long as we want. It will be able to be turned off and on, it will all be legal, and it will be big business.   198

Nothing destroys a life, and relationships, quicker than a runaway ego.   198

People who have a firm foundation do not have ego problems, do not need recreational drugs, and can have positive continuing relationships with others.   198

This was the first time I ever thought about God as a real person rather than some sort of misty presence in the firmament. Here was someone with a sense of humor, who was all-powerful, and wanted to be my friend.   200

People are wonderful helpers, but basically we are all made of sand.   200

It is just not possible for us to handle life and the world on our own.   200

He does not change with fads or current events.   201

God is so much smarter than we are and knows so much more than we do, it is only sensible to invite His help.   201

It is amazing how much a person with an unshakable foundation can accomplish.   201

People are known by their enemies even more than by their friends.   201

Being forced to hire and live near such people, they say, drives companies and property values down.   201

Those who hate would like to drop nuclear warheads on certain insects, eliminating all of them for good.   202

All of this preconception cuts down the time that people can work at the positive things of life.   202

The effort spent hating or distrusting others, or defending against them, detracts from their own resources.   202

The happiest people are those who take other people and other creatures as they find them.   202

Those folks I know who are firm about their preconceived definitions of the behavior and attitude problems of specific groups always turn out to have no direct experience.   202

There are those whose actions, concepts, or attitudes are not in line with ours.   202

The half-life of a high school or college education is about four years.   202

Learning is not just a matter of signing up for a course and having information force-fed.   203

Real learning comes from being routinely curious about the world and digging into various opportunities that arise.   203

The personal Centurion has to be up-to-date.   203

The world of a company is, after all, much narrower than the world of the individual.   203

Business information is an uninspiring and dull bunch of material without a complete sentence in the lot.   203

The habit of learning is what keeps us fulfilled, surviving, and interesting.   203

The key to a life of quiet contentment is knowledge.   203

It is possible to be quaint, perhaps, when outdated, but not interesting. And interesting comes from being interested.   204

Every goal we set for ourselves should have a number in it.   204

When individuals learn to think routinely in terms of specific goals, they suddenly find themselves accomplishing more.   204

Accomplishments planned in a mushy or unmeasurable way usually do not get accomplished.   204

The central aspect of measurable goals is that they force us to analyze a situation and take it more seriously than we might otherwise.   204

I have always felt that we have at least one choice in life.   205

Happy people are a pleasure to be near.   205

"Poor" is a terminal disease.   205

There are always honest ways to get money.   205

Many people think they could be happy if only they had something or other.   205

Couples with a failing marriage will sometimes build a new home or have a new baby just before parting for good. This last desperate effort to satisfy their emptiness only adds to the totality and complexity of their failure.   205

It takes less muscle energy to smile than to frown.   205

Most young people never look at life as a whole.   205

Someday each of us will have a memorial service of some sort. We need to think about what they are going to say and think about us at that time.   206

Index